Additional praise for *The Art and Craft of Novel Writing*

"Oakley Hall's *The Art and Craft of Novel Writing* is more than just a text on writing—it's a literary experience. Not only is it an invaluable aid for beginning novelists, it's inspirational reading for experienced writers who need a reminder of the magic that drew them to the novel form in the first place."

—Carolyn Doty

"Sober, precise, intelligent, and useful"

—Herbert Gold

"Oakley Hall is a brilliant novelist. In this book he shows that he is also a brilliant teacher. *The Art and Craft of Novel Writing* is far and away the best work I know on how to write fiction. It is practical, wise, dramatic—a classic! I recommend it to every student I see."

—Max Byrd

"I've often told my students that writing your first novel is the equivalent of an aspiring architect, building his first skyscraper, without an instruction manual. Now Oakley Hall has given us the basics of how you actually build a novel, along with many accessible examples. This is a book any teacher of creative writing might use and any aspiring (or even accomplished) novelist might learn from."

—Mary Morris

The Art & Craft of Novel Writing

9/30/94

Myron,

You've got more to offer the world than Crunching a few numbers. Focus on you talents and put those abilities to ~~you~~ use. It'll be a better place. Good Luck!

Robert

Dear Myron,

The world awaits the pearls of wisdom only you can offer!

Write – write!

Rosemary

The Art & Craft of Novel Writing

OAKLEY HALL

STORY PRESS
CINCINNATI, OH

The excerpt from *The Columbus Tree*, by Peter Feibleman, published in 1973 by Atheneum Publishers, is reprinted by permission of Peter Feibleman.

 Published by Story Press, an imprint of F&W Publications, Inc., 1507 Dana Avenue, Cincinnati, Ohio 45207. 1-800-289-0963. First edition. First paperback printing 1994.

98 97 96 95 94 5 4 3 2 1

Library of Congress Cataloging-in-Publication Data

Hall, Oakley M.
The art & craft of novel writing.

Bibliography: p.
Includes index.
1. Fiction—Authorship. I. Title. II. Title: Art and craft of novel writing.
PN3365.H34 1988 808.3 88-27941
ISBN 1-884910-02-5

Design by Clare Finney.

 *The Art and Craft of Novel Writing* is printed on recycled paper.

This book is dedicated to the students in my workshops at the University of California at Irvine, who have given me the greatest satisfaction in return for the advice herein.

CONTENTS

PART ONE
Fictional Reality

2
Dramatization
Historical Research and Detail 6
Detail in Motion 13
Sensory Perceptions 19

28
Point of View

42
Characterization

60
Plotting

PART TWO
Other Elements of Fiction

80
Style

94
Dialog

116
Indirection
Implication 117
Symbol and Metaphor 120
Objective Correlatives 123
Epiphanies 125

128
Information and Sex

PART THREE

The Process

140
The Germ

146
Planning

152
Beginning

156
Continuing

164
Finishing

Appendix A 170

Appendix B 190

Appendix C 202

Appendix D 207

Index 209

I began trying to write fiction as the Adjutant of an Amphibian Tank Battalion stationed on the island of Maui, preparing for the invasion of Japan. I had been reading Chandler and Hammett and trying to plot stories that might be published in *Black Mask* magazine, but with time on my hands, I got into Hemingway, and, later, Faulkner, from the post library. Horizons expanded. Ambitions changed. How did they *do* it? There were no other would-be fiction writers I knew, to talk to. I dimly understood that Hemingway left everything out but the essentials, while Faulkner jammed in so much that his novels were enormously rich. I was learning that good reading was the route to writing. But how did you even start, sitting alone in your tent with a typewriter propped up on an ammunition case?

More and more these days writers are communalized; in college writing programs, in local writing groups, in evening writing classes and summer writers' conferences. But in the end this craft and sullen art is a solitary one. The writer confronts his typewriter or word processor, stares out his window, and cudgels his brain for inspiration. This book is intended as a companion in his lonely state. When the demands of a craft he can only imperfectly comprehend overwhelm him, perhaps it will comfort and tutor him.

My first teacher was Caroline Gordon, a southern lady novelist and short story writer of considerable reputation and strong opinions, who taught at Columbia University, which I attended on the GI Bill. She had sat at the knee of Ford Madox Ford, who had been a pupil of Henry James, which gave me a rather direct line to the Master.

Miss Gordon worked from rules of writing established by James and Flaubert, but also had many of her own devising. Sentences could only properly begin with certain words (I have forgotten which these were). In making fiction "come to life" usually two sensory details were necessary, although sometimes a particularly felicitous one would be sufficiently vivid. If more than two were called for, the writer should bear down on Selection, from the Jamesian dictum of Select, Contemplate, Render. In dialog the writer should beware of employing more than two sentences per line, so that the line did not become a "speech." The names of principal characters and titles should contain long vowel sounds, with shorter vowel sounds for the names of lesser characters.

As a beginner I found it comforting to be governed by a set of rules, and I was happy under Miss Gordon's dictatorship, especially as the two novels I completed at Columbia, the first a mystery and the second a mainstream, were published. Later on, as I began to question her rules, I found that they had established themselves in my technique so strongly that it was difficult for me to flout them. I still am uncomfortable employing anything but a strict point of view, even though I have come to realize that in fiction, as in life, what works, works.

Clover Adams said of Henry James that he chawed more than he bit off. And in my readings, too, I had felt that in James there was sometimes more art than red meat. At Miss Gordon's knee I had imbibed the lessons from James and Flaubert that everything in a novel—plot, character and action, scene, setting, and narrative—should mesh together like the gears of a watch. However, my second novel, *Corpus of Joe Bailey*, which was a bestseller and received a good deal of critical attention as well, was a messy, sprawling novel of growing up, with plenty of red meat to it. Miss Gordon wrote, expressing sadness at my betrayal of her standards in going the "naturalistic" rather than the "classic" route. Her letter was, in fact, a severance of relations. I was feeling my oats by then and did not think that I had been justly rebuked.

I saw her again years later, by sheer chance, at a hacienda in Mexico where both of us happened to be guests. She was quite old. By now I had published almost as many novels as she had, but I immediately fell into my old teacher-pupil subordination. "What is your newest novel called, Oakley?" she asked me. When I replied that it was *Report from Beau Harbor*, she nodded approvingly. "That is a good title. The long vowel sounds convey to the reader the fact that it is a novel of serious intent."

Novels of serious intent are what I write, and it is to would-be authors of novels of serious intent that this book is addressed. Probably novels that are not of serious intent are constructed and written in pretty much the same way, with the same necessities to be provided for. Indeed, it may be that a novel that is not of serious intent is a contradiction in terms. The task of putting 70,000 and more words down on paper coherently, with a beginning, a middle, and an end, is such an overwhelming task that "serious" seems inadequate to describe it.

The groundwork of any novel is effective writing, what Truman Capote called *writing* as opposed to *typing*. The first sections of this book are devoted to the making of good fiction, bringing it to life, making it vivid, employing it to take a grip upon the readers' sympathies and imagination; dramatizing it. I have rather arbitrarily categorized the elements of fiction. As Henry James said, what is plot but character in action, and what is character but plot personified? I couldn't think of any way to deal with these slippery and intertwined entities except as separate headings. There is some sense in treating them so. Dialog is considerably easier to write for those who have a good ear, but those endowed with such an ear tend to depend too heavily upon dialog. Any of the elements of fiction, if employed disproportionately, will become monotonous, and it is in the use of the full range available to them that writers most effectively appeal to the reader's eye and ear, and thus to his or her responsive emotions.

The first parts of this book are designed to help you, the writer, with your writing, with plot, character, and dramatic scene, and to aid you, in your own reading, to find the brilliant bits, passages, and construction devices that you can emulate, as all the writers before you have searched out such nuggets and devices in their reading, to enhance their writing. Many of the suggestions and examples presented here pertain to the writing of short fiction as well as to novel writing, but I am primarily a novelist, and it is to the writers of novels that this book is addressed.

Novels, of course, vary tremendously in scope. A simple one may be no more than a book-length short story, with few characters and a slender thread of plot. A more complex novel may embrace a number of plots, from the two of *Anna Karenina* to the seven of *War and Peace*. An author attempting anything so ambitious needs to be a general as well as a fiction writer, marshaling research materials, plots, and characters in their multitudes, and trying to devise an ending that is inevitable, surprising, and grand enough to cap what has gone before it.

The final section of this book is concerned with the actual construction of a novel, from the first stirrings of the Idea to the delightful drudgery and happy torture of the writing. Several appendices follow: the first chapter of a published novel examined for the author's techniques and methods; the first synopsis of a published novel; a reading list of contemporary fiction of particular interest to writers, and books concerned with fictional techniques, etc.

What I have tried to assemble here is what works in fiction, and why it works, and what does not, and why it does not. In fiction everything must be specific rather than abstract, and the lessons of this book are concrete ones—examples from published fiction, with my comments. I would hope that this book will be helpful to you, sitting alone before your typewriter or word processor, praying that you will be able to find the means to set down on paper what you have in your head in such a way that the experience will mean to the reader what it has meant to you.

PART ONE

Fictional Reality

O N E

Dramatization

Storytelling is an elaborate form of lying. Both "fiction" and "story" are euphemisms for lies. It is the concern of liars to give their falsehoods the semblance of truth, and a storyteller uses every device at his command to instill in his fiction the verisimilitude that convinces the reader. Writers seek to convince in order to deceive. They also deceive in order to convince. They alter, select, and exaggerate facts in order to create truth. They distill, distort, and, above all, dramatize—for dramatization is the process by which the writer holds engaged the imagination of the reader.

The fiction writer's first task is the establishment of a fictional reality, of mimesis (the imitation of real life), and of verisimilitude (the semblance of truth). Henry James insisted that fiction be *rendered, presented, dramatized*: "That in art what is merely stated is not presented, and what is not presented is not vivid, and what is not vivid is not represented, and what is not represented is not art."

The art of fiction does not begin until the novelist thinks of his story as a matter to be shown, *to be so exhibited that it will tell itself.*
—The Craft of Fiction, *Percy Lubbock*

These terms are important to the fiction writer. Among the dictionary definitions of "render" are "To put into a state. To cause to be or become. To put into artistic or verbal form. To depict or express (never merely pointing, naming, summarizing). To give an interpretation, translation, visualization of."

In fiction what is not rendered, dramatized, is merely reported. Thus it is secondhand. It does not happen before the reader. He is only told about it after the fact. What is not shown is merely told. What is rendered will spring to life off the page and capture the reader's emotions. What is merely stated, reported, told, is inert, dead matter.

In the following passage from Chekhov's story "The Lady with the Pet Dog," the author does not *tell* us that Anna Sergeyevna is falling in love with Gurov, he *shows* it. Anna's falling in love is rendered.

> Owing to the choppy sea, the steamer was late, after sunset, and it was a long time tacking about before it put into the pier. Anna Sergeyevna peered at the steamer and the passengers

through her lorgnette as though looking for acquaintances, and whenever she turned to Gurov her eyes were shining. She talked a great deal and asked questions jerkily, forgetting the next moment what she had asked; then she lost her lorgnette in the crush.

Fictional reality rendered by implication.

Fiction is the unfolding of a tale, the events of which exist, before the writing, only in the writer's mind. His effort is to enable the reader to experience those events he has seen in his imagination. To do this he must arrange patterns of stimuli to *evoke* those events so that his audience will react to the characters and events that are not real but only ink smudges on paper. Writers of fiction have invented, borrowed, stolen, and inherited a bag of tricks to provide those evocations. The sum of these tricks is the art of literature.

If those who have studied the art of writing are in accord on one point it is on this: the surest way to arouse and hold the reader is to be specific, definite, and concrete. The greatest writers . . . are effective largely because they deal in particulars and report the details that matter.
—The Elements of Style,
Strunk and White

The following passage is from *The Odyssey,* Robert Fitzgerald's translation:

> Over chair-backs in hall they dropped their mantles and passed in to the polished tubs, where maids poured out warm baths for them, anointed them, and pulled fresh tunics, fleecy cloaks, around them. Soon they were seated at their ease in hall. A maid came by to tip a golden jug and draw a gleaming table up beside them. The larder mistress brought her tray of loaves and savories, dispensing each.
>
> In silence across the hall, beside a pillar, propped in a long chair, Telemakhos' mother spun a fine yarn.

The passage is alive, vivid, rendered, dramatized, because it is dense with specific detail. Penelope sits *beside* a pillar, *in* a long chair, and spins fine yarn.

Fictional reality requires strong specification, rendering, dramatization. The basis of all this is detail, and the best of detail is implicative, in motion, and appealing to the senses.

. . . I may therefore venture to say that the air of reality (solidity of specification) seems to me to be the supreme virtue of the novel—the merit upon which all its other merits . . . hopelessly and submissively depend. If it be not there they are all as nothing, and if these be there, they owe their effect to the success with which the author has produced the illusion of life. The cultivation of this success, the study of this exquisite process, form, to my taste, the beginning and the end of the art of the novelist. They are his inspiration, his despair, his reward, his torment, and his delight. . . .
—The Art of Fiction
Henry James

Detail

Michelangelo said that great art, "which is not a trifle, consists of trifles." In fiction these trifles are called details: realistic detail, corroborative or circumstantial detail, concrete detail, specifics. Rendering, showing, vivid dramatization, depend upon the concrete rather than the abstract.

Concrete details "prove" a scene by convincing the reader of the reality of the characters and the action. In his novel *Time and Again* Jack Finney has a complicated problem in convincing the reader. By a time device, his protagonist has penetrated the New York City of a hundred years ago. Finney is convincing his character that he has actually gone back into the past at the same time that he is convincing his readers. The burden of proof that we are really in New York of Back Then lies in the corroborative detail the author has selected:

Fictional reality: historical detail of clothing.

> There they were now, moving along the walks, crossing the streets—the people. And I looked out at them, at first with awe; at the bearded, cane-swinging men in tall shiny silk hats, fur caps like mine, high-crowned derbies like the man's across the aisle, and—the younger men—in very shallow-crowned derbies. Almost all of them wore ankle-length greatcoats or topcoats, half the men seemed to wear pince-nez glasses, and when the older men, the silk-hatted men, passed an acquaintance, each touched his hat-brim in salute with the head of his cane. The women were wearing head scarfs or hats ribbon-tied under the chin; wearing short, tight-waisted cutaway winter coats, or capes or brooch-pinned shawls; some carried muffs and some wore gloves; all wore button shoes darting out and disappearing under long skirts.
>
> There—well, there they *were*, the people of the stiff old woodcuts, only . . . these moved. The swaying coats and dresses there on the walks and crossing the streets before and behind us were of new-dyed cloth—maroon, bottle green, blue, strong brown, unfaded blacks—and I saw the shimmer of light and shadow in the appearing and disappearing long folds. And the leather and rubber they walked in pressed into and marked the slush of the street crossing; and their breaths puffed out into the winter air, momentarily visible.

Detail in motion.

Technical historical detail.

Light and shadow in motion.

Implicative detail.

Clincher detail.

Finney has done his homework well, researching detail in the stiff old woodcuts he mentions, in the Sears Roebuck catalogs and magazine advertisements of the period. His observation of the "new" dye colors is impressive, as are the gestures, and the greetings with canes. Very happily selected is the print of the rubber and leather soles in the slush of the street-crossing, but most effective, most vivid, is the actual *breath* of these people of a hundred years ago, congealing upon the winter air.

In researching the clothing and artifacts of historical time and place, it is well to remember that other writers have been there before you, searching for detail, and some details have been overused to the point of becoming cliches. In her book *Biography: The Craft and the Calling*, Catherine Drinker Bowen warns writers to beware of samovars and wolves when writing of old-time Russia, and: "Anyone who writes of the American Revolutionary period must beware of buckled shoes, quill pens and night watchmen calling the hours." These details have been dulled by overuse.

Rendering vs. Reporting

Consider the failure of the following to render, show, prove, dramatize, or do anything at all. There are no specifics, particulars, or concrete details. This is merely *typing.*

> Our trip to Disneyland was an unforgettable experience. We all got up early and had breakfast, then we packed the car and left, full of anticipation. The day was fine and we had fun on the way.

All abstractions and generalities.

> When we had bought our tickets, we rode the monorail craning our necks to see the wonderful sights. It was one of the most thrilling experiences I've ever had.

Almost a concrete detail.

> We took a boat trip down a jungle river and saw many interesting animals. It was just like Africa. Then we visited a western frontier town, which gave us valuable knowledge about American history. There were many other educational things to see.

Abstract and general.

> We were tired but happy when we piled into our car for the long ride home. On the way we enjoyed our dinner in a good restaurant.

This is instantly forgettable stuff. Everything is abstract and general: "unforgettable experience," "full of anticipation," "the day was fine," "wonderful sights," "thrilling experiences," "interesting animals," etc. Neither the reader's interest nor emotions are engaged. What would help?

Specific time. Aural sensory. Specific food.

> The alarm hassled us out of bed at 7:15; *briiiinggg!* Dad

Implication of fun.
Specific characters.

made a terrific breakfast of pancakes and peanut butter while Mom slept in. In the car the two of them sang "Roll Me Over in the Clover," while in the back the twins and I chanted, "Be there! Be there! Be there!"

Craning necks at something specific.
Implication of height of the monorail.
Action.

After Dad had shelled out money for tickets, groaning, we rode the monorail rumbling all around Disneyland—craning our necks to see the gorilla rock group jumping up and down with their guitars and the giraffes winding their necks together like twin corkscrews, while tiny people down there strolled along pegging pebbles at the lions and sticking their faces into their pink cotton candy—

Specific place. Specific food.
Specific distance.

On the way home we stopped at McDonald's for Big Macs and Pepsis. Then we got back on the stack for the long fifty-two miles home, chanting, "Be there! Be there!——"

Historical Research and Detail

Here is a paragraph from Wright Morris's *God's Country and My People*. The particulars employed might be called nostalgic detail, for their magical evocation of the past. The strong voice or point of view contributes to this:

Details. Sense-memories. Characterization. Strong voice.

> ... I was enrolled in Mrs. Partridge's class at Farnam School. In the morning we pledged allegiance to the American flag and exercised to the music of "The Clock Store." The exercises began fast, then got slower and slower as the Victrola ran down. If we all wrote on the blackboard at the same time, the chalk dust in the air gave Mrs. Partridge splitting headaches. The squeak of the chalk put her nerves on edge and she would have to lie down in the nurse's annex, a towel over her eyes. On the stairs we had to be careful not to step on the tassels of her shawl. After school Betty Zabriskie, Bryon Minter and me would clean the basket of erasers at the fire-escape window, slapping them on the bricks. The chalk dust made your fingers squeaky and whitened the bricks around the fire escape window.

A protracted example of strong specification is the Duke of Dorset's proposal to Zuleika in Max Beerbohm's *Zuleika Dobson*, where for eight pages the Duke lists his possessions and honors. He possesses 340,000 acres, seventy horses, and five Watteaus. In his great house there are five ghosts in the right wing, two in the left, and eleven in the park. The Swiss Guard in the courtyard of his mansion in the Champs Elysées stands six-feet-seven in his stocking feet . . .

These items are strongly specified and witty, but it is well to remember that it is not the quantity of details that counts, but their quality, and that mere lists can quickly become monotonous.

In William Weber Johnson's biography of the conquistador, *Cortes*, he employs lists of factual historical detail he has come upon in his researches to describe Cortes's departure from the City of Mexico to punish a defecting captain:

> There was further evidence of Cortes's grandiose notions in his preparations for his expedition against Olid. His entourage included several hundred foot soldiers, about half as many horsemen, a majordomo, two masters of the household, a butler, a chamberlain, two stewards (one of them in charge of gold and silver plate), a doctor, a surgeon, various pages, eight grooms, two falconers, five musicians, an acrobat, a magician-puppeteer, a string of mules to carry freight, a herd of swine to provide food en route and several thousand Indian porters carrying huge loads of powder, horseshoes, iron tools, tents, beads and other trade items.

Historical detail list.

The details here are specific and concrete, but they are essentially a list. Margaret Shedd, in her historical novel *Malinche and Cortes*, had access to the same sources of research, and she fictionalizes the scene, expanding upon the details, setting them into action, and employing them in characterizing her principal characters. The scene is considerably more vivid. It has been dramatized:

> They left the city in self-assurance and perfect jubilant formation, hardly a battle display because there was so much music with them in this parade along the causeway. There were Spanish military drums and carved ones which Indians beat and high-voiced flutes. Then came the banners; not those worn emblems the Spanish brought with them when they entered this city. Now they were so sumptuous one bearer could hardly manage. . . .
>
> After the banners came jugglers and a tumbler and two puppeteers who marched their comic alter egos to the rhythm. There were handsome Spanish mules recently arrived with their muleteers and falconers with their birds and a surgeon and a doctor with their insignia. Behind them three thousand Indian allies. . . .

Then came the Spaniards, armed and armored, on foot and riding. First and last, horses were the measure of Spanish power and they had many this time, one hundred and thirty. The horses dance-stepped on the causeway not built for horses. . . .

Here was Cortes, the pale, small actor's face, sensitive large nose, black beard, and his great shoulders and full chest. He was wearing a black doublet not armor like the others, with an elegant gold chain around his neck. . . . The fanfarrons of the captains clattered against their armor, but Cortes was in all ways quiet, his chain pure gold but smaller than theirs. He looked like a controlled man, truly genial yet whose smile came from a careful habit, harboring passions until he chose to launch them. . . . with great solicitude he leaned toward a city official who was seeing him on the road.

Dramatization. Historical detail. Motion. Color. Characterization.

Historical detail. Motion. Color. Sound. Characterization.

Malinche . . . was a little behind and to one side of Cortes. The only woman, she was dressed in her people's manner, *huipil* and skirt, and with her long hair down her back. She was quiet, not like Cortes's control but as if she would not know how to act otherwise, which was a measure of her skilled dissemblance; she rather than Cortes was the sublime impersonator of this pageant. Her head was bowed slightly but her back was straighter than any Spaniard's. . . .

Characterization by implication.

My own version of this departure, in the novel *The Children of the Sun*, has the advantage of a *strict point of view*, already established—that of the conquistador Andres Dorantes—so that nothing here is merely stated by the author. I have added to Shedd's use of detail, and to the action, and the camera is held closer:

Dramatization: Detail color.

. . . Cortes rode in the lead in his burnished breastplate, gold chain and black feathered cap. With him were the captains Gonzalo de Sandoval and Juan de Jaramillo, and Dona Marina, her dark face and plain clothing contrasting with the fair skin and bright silks of the ladies who floated in barges alongside the causeway, fluttering their scarves and calling out farewells. . . .

Motion. Listing.

Also with the advance party were Cortes's master-of-the-household, butler, chamberlain, doctor and surgeon, pages, grooms, musicians, and master-of-the-hounds with his pack of grayhounds. On their white horses, cloaks drawn around them, with feather crowns above their proud, dark faces, were the emperor Cuauhtemoc, his cousin the lord of Tacuba and two other Aztec princes, whom Cortes did not dare leave behind for fear a rebellion would be launched in his absence.

The Spanish cavalry was a hundred and thirty strong. In the second rank Andrés rode between Blas and Bernal Diaz. Sumptuous new banners were carried that seemed to him cheap and gaudy compared to those precious, tattered ensigns of the Conquest.

Point of view.

Behind the cavalry marched the infantry, armed and armored, vizors raised on sweating, bearded faces, metallic clatter of their tread. Drumbeats echoed unevenly across the gray water. After the infantry came three thousand Indian allies in quilted armor, the captains wearing helmets and carrying swords, each division with its own proud banner, the flying crane of the Tlaxcalans, the mysterious red figure of the Cholulans; following them, an enormous mass of native bearers, loads suspended from tumplines, last of all a herd of squealing pigs.

Sound.

So they passed off the causeway onto the mainland, leaving behind the barges filled with admiring ladies, and the canoes of fishermen and bird watchers who had paddled close to watch this grand departure.

Often the most prosaic detail, closely observed and dramatically rendered, so *true* as to be unquestionable, can bring a passage brilliantly to life. Glendon Swarthout's novel *They Came to Cordura* is set in the Pershing Punitive Expedition into Mexico in 1916. Swarthout discovered a detail in the official journals of the expedition which he was able to use to great effect in the following passage:

They rode to the base of the butte and dismounted. While the private unsaddled the horses Major Thorn built a fire with dry twigs from an *encino* tree. The wood snapped, flared, and light reached up the wall of rock. Hetherington had no grain and the officer offered to share the last of his corn so that both animals might have one more feed. Spreading a blanket he poured grain onto it and showed the trooper how to pick out the little pebbles found in native corn, for once a horse bit a stone, he would not eat.

Dramatization: Researched clincher detail.

Final Clincher Details

The first part of the following description, by Herman Melville, is couched in ponderous classic nineteenth-century American prose, until the vivid description of Billy Budd's hand leaps off the page and brings the handsome sailor to life:

Boring.

Clincher detail.

> Cast in a mould peculiar to the finest physical examples of those Englishmen in whom the Saxon strain would seem not to partake of any Norman or other admixture, he showed in face that humane look of reposeful good nature which the Greek sculptor in some instances gives his heroic strongman Hercules. But this again was subtly modified by another and pervasive quality—the ear, small and shapely, the arch of the foot, the curve of the mouth and nostril, the indurated hand dyed to the orange-yellow of a toucan's bill, a hand telling of tarbuckets and halyards . . .

Here is another paragraph of undramatic and expository writing, pulled together at the end by a brilliant detail; from Benjamin Constant's *Adolphe*:

Boring.

Boring.

Clincher detail.

> It was one of those winter days when the sun seems to light the greyish countryside with a melancholy light, as if to look pityingly on the earth which it had ceased to warm. Ellénore suggested going out. "It is cold," I said. "No matter, I would like to go for a walk with you." She took my arm; we wandered a long time in silence; she was walking with difficulty and leaning almost entirely on me. "Let us stop a moment." "No," she replied. "I like to feel I am still supported by you." We relapsed into silence. The sky was calm; but the trees were leafless; no breeze stirred the sky, no bird flew through it: everything was motionless and the only sound to be heard was that of frozen grass crunching under our feet.

Here is a description of the Texan, Buck Hipps, from William Faulkner's "Spotted Horses":

Dramatization: Detail.
Motion.

Detail.

Dialog.

> This was the second man who had arrived in the wagon. He was a stranger. He wore a heavy densely black moustache and a wide, pale hat. When he thrust himself through and turned to herd them back from the horses they saw, thrust into the pockets of his tight jeans pants, the butt of a heavy pearlhandled pistol and a florid carton such as small cakes come in. "Keep away from them, boys," he said. "They've got kind of

> skittish, they ain't been rode in so long."
>
> "Since when have they been rode?" Quick said. The stranger looked at Quick. He had a broad, quite cold, wind-gnawed face and bleak cold eyes. His belly fitted neat and smooth as a peg into the tight trousers.
>
> "I reckon that was when they were rode on the ferry to get across the Mississippi River," Varner said. The stranger looked at Varner. "My name's Varner," Jody said. "Hipps," the other said. "Call me Buck." Across the left side of his head, obliterating the top of that ear, was a savage and recent gash gummed over with a blackish substance like axle-grease. They looked at the scar. Then they watched him remove the carton from his pocket and tilt a gingersnap into his hand and put the gingersnap into his mouth, beneath the moustache.

Implicative detail.

Motion.

Faulkner supplies many descriptive details here, but they are not given all at once, separated by action and dialog. First come the moustache and the hat, then there is action as Hipps thrusts his way through the men watching the horses. Next we have the pistol and the box of gingersnaps, then some dialog. In the final paragraph we are given the most telling detail, the fresh scar, which implies the viciousness of these horses Hipps is trying to sell the Mississippi bumpkins.

The gingersnaps become a continuing detail in the ensuing passages: the action of Hipps taking the box from his pocket and slipping a cookie under his moustache serves to enliven the Texan again and again.

Again from *They Came to Cordura*, Major Thorn's glasses, described in this passage, remind us of the major's cowardice in Pancho Villa's raid on Columbus, New Mexico, in which the glasses were broken:

> The major waited before speaking. He took hold of the steering wheel with one hand. He was a man of medium height and stocky build. The skin of his rather round face was grimed with dust. He wore steel-rimmed glasses which had evidently been broken, for the left bow was taped to the rim hinge by a knot of friction tape. It impaired vision. Whoever observed him was conscious of it, as he must himself have been, the black knot constantly at the corner of his eye.

Dramatization: Detail. Implication.

This detail is "symbolic" as well as "realistic." Certainly it helps to establish the man's presence, but as a symbol of cowardice it stands at the very center of the novel. The black knot is the constant reminder of Thorn's cowardice. He is always aware of it, at the corner of his vision; so are the other soldiers observing him. Yet it is also a suspense device. Will that knot holding his glasses together fail at some crucial instance? We feel anxiety that it will as we come to care about the fate of Major Thorn. It can almost be said that one of the devices driving the reader to finish the novel is the necessity of finding out what happens to that frail black knot of friction tape.

Observation and Perception

In the preface of *Pierre et Jean* is the very famous piece of advice that de Maupassant received from his master Flaubert:

> "Talent is a long patience. It is a matter of considering long and attentively what you want to express, so that you may discover an aspect of it that has never before been noticed or reported. There is a part of everything that remains unexplored, for we have fallen into the habit of remembering, whenever we use our eyes, what people before us have thought of the thing we are looking at. Even the slightest thing contains a little that is unknown. We must find it. To describe a blazing fire or a tree in a plain, we must remain before that fire or tree until they no longer resemble for us any other tree or any other fire.
>
> "That is the way to become original."
>
> After repeating over and over again this truth, that there are not in the entire world two grains of sand, two hands or noses that are absolutely the same, Flaubert made me describe in a few sentences, a being or an object in such a way as to particularize it clearly, to distinguish it from all the other beings or all the other objects of the same race or kind.
>
> "When you pass a grocer sitting in his doorway," he used to say to me, "or a concierge smoking his pipe, or a cab-stand, *show* me that grocer and that concierge, the way they are sitting or standing, their entire physical appearance, making it by the skillfulness of your portrayal embody all their moral nature as well, so that I cannot confuse them with any other grocer or any other concierge. And make me see, by means of a single word, wherein one cab-horse does *not* resemble the fifty others ahead of it or behind it."

Henry James said that a writer must be one upon whom nothing is lost. What writers must not lose are, at the heart of it, vivid and revealing details. A writer must be an observer, and what he observes, and collects, are the details that *show*, that reveal, that imply, that specify, that build character and forward the story. He finds details in the life around him—a scene observed in the Safeway or the laundromat, a conversation overheard on the bus, for example, as well as in the books he reads. Someone said that a novelist's mind is a garbage pit of odd information. It is also a storehouse of detail. Contemplating a scene that he must bring to life in fiction, he *selects* the details that will best serve his purpose, he *contemplates* the best means by which to employ them, and he *renders* the details by the use of action, by the employment of sensory impressions, and by means of point of view.

Detail in Motion

Here from *Madame Bovary*, Charles has come to call upon Emma Rouault. The scene is presented in terms of detail in *motion*:

> One day he got there about three o'clock. Everybody was in the fields. He went into the kitchen, but did not at once catch sight of Emma; the outside shutters were closed. Through the chinks of the wood the sun sent across the flooring long, fine rays that were broken at the corners of the furniture and trembled along the ceiling. Some flies on the table were crawling up the glasses that had been used, and buzzing as they drowned themselves in the dregs of the cider. The daylight that came in by the chimney made velvet of the soot at the back of the fireplace, and touched with blue the cold cinders. Between the window and the hearth Emma was sewing; she wore no fichu; he could see small drops of perspiration on her bare shoulders.

Motion.

Motion.

Figurative motion.

Motion.

William Weber Johnson's description of Cortes's expedition departing from the City of Mexico is meticulously specific. In her fictionalization of the same scene, Margaret Shedd puts the Spaniards, their horses, and their allies, the tumblers, surgeons, falconers and grooms, into *motion*. I added the fluttering scarves of the goodbye-ladies and the fishermen paddling. When Jack Finney shows us those New Yorkers of a hundred years ago, they are, unlike the stiff old woodcuts, in *motion*, walking, tipping hats, saluting with canes—even the folds of their clothing are in motion.

Then marvel not, thou great and complete man,
That all the Greeks begin to worship Ajax;
Since things in motion sooner catch the eye
Than what not stirs.
—The History of Troilus and Cressida, *Shakespeare*

A character introduced merely in terms of static detail may

catch the reader's eye if the detail is dramatic enough, implicative enough, but it is motion that convinces the reader that the character is *alive*. Here is the mercenary soldier, Wolfie, introduced, in Peter Matthiessen's *At Play in the Fields of the Lord*:

Dramatization: Detail. Motion/Action. More detail.

> Wolfie wore habitually, even at night, a black beret, outsize dark glasses, the green fatigues of one or more foreign armies, and a gold earring in his left ear. He had been talking loudly when he lost his footing in the slime and fell, and because he was drunk he continued talking in mid-air and while still on his hands and knees, as if nothing were amiss. He was still speaking as he rose. He was a broad squat powerful man, with big loose hands and a big shaggy beard, a chest like a nail keg, and small feet, and he was tightly sprung; one had the impression that Wolfie, fitted out with rubber soles, could bound five feet straight up into the air from a standing position.

Here is another military man, General Quait, from Paul Horgan's *A Distant Trumpet*, presented in action:

Dramatization: Detail.

Action. Gesture.

> He was well over six feet tall, and bone thin. He wore his white hair trimmed close to his skull, and yet his moustache and beard were allowed to grow as long as those of a Chinese sage. His beard was brushed apart into two long forks that came halfway to his gold bullion belt with its starred buckle. His eyes were black and piercing. From years of squinting in the sun and at the pages of books, he had developed deep sets of wrinkles that ran from his eyes down the hollows of his cheeks until engulfed by his whiskers. His mouth could not be seen under his moustaches. The skin of his face and hands was tanned a walnut brown. If his thinness suggested a skeleton, his movements even further underlined the impression. He almost clattered when he talked or gestured. His gestures were free-flung. He often hung his right hand by its bony claw in his beard while he talked or speculated—and he was often lost in speculation even while gazing at someone with whom he was supposed to be conversing. He had a wet, thin cough which wracked his angular frame frequently. When this happened, he would fix his interrupted remarks in the air with a lifted finger, and smile brilliantly through his cough to excuse the nuisance.

The detail here has been laid on with a shovel. It is a catalog. The beard, the moustaches, the cropped hair, the brown skin, the manner of conversing, are vivid enough as details, but become lost in their own numbers. Two or three carefully chosen ones would have done the job.

The most effective detail, and the one that Horgan leads up to, is the cough and the raised finger. Here we have the motion that best catches the reader's eye. It is interesting to consider how the Faulkner of "Spotted Horses" might have constructed this scene; some detail, then some action, more detail—not so much detail crammed into the first half of the paragraph. Even the action would be more effective if presented directly—happening before our eyes. Here the action is merely reported habit: "he *would* fix his interrupted remarks in the air," etc. This technique undercuts the effectiveness of the action by moving it from the present into the habitual.

In the following passage from the beginning of Henry James's *The Portrait of a Lady*, we are shown first the *shadows* of the characters we are to be introduced to, and the shadows are in motion, or dramatically not-in-motion. The motion of those shadows helps to convince us of the reality of the characters who cast them in the same manner as the heel prints in the slush and the fogging of breaths convinced us of Jack Finney's old-time New Yorkers.

> The shadows on the perfect lawn were straight and angular; they were the shadows of an old man sitting in a deep wicker-chair near the low table on which the tea had been served, and of two younger men strolling to and fro, in desultory talk, in front of him. The old man had his cup in his hand; it was an unusually large cup, of a different pattern from the rest of the set and painted in brilliant colours. He disposed of its contents with much circumspection, holding it for a long time close to his chin, with his face turned to the house. His companions had either finished their tea or were indifferent to the privilege; they smoked cigarettes as they continued to stroll. One of them, from time to time, as he passed, looked with a certain attention at the elderly man, who, unconscious of observation, rested his eyes upon the rich red front of the building. The house that rose beyond the lawn was a structure to repay such consideration and was the most characteristic object in the peculiarly English picture I have attempted to sketch.

Dramatization: Shadows in motion (implication of actual action).

Detail.

Description in fiction often deals with things rather than with persons, and things are static and so are difficult to introduce in motion. Here, with a brilliant piece of invention, F. Scott Fitzgerald dramatizes an essentially static scene at the beginning of *Tender Is the Night*. He activates the scene by showing the surrounding landscape reflected in the ripples of the sea, and then brings in a bather to grunt and flounder in the shallow water.

Dramatization: (Static nature presented in action).

Detail.

Individual in action.

> The hotel and its bright tan prayer rug of a beach were one. In the early morning the distant image of Cannes, the pink and cream of old fortifications, the purple Alps that bounded Italy, were cast across the water and lay quavering in the ripples and rings sent up by sea-plants through the clear shallows. Before eight a man came down to the beach in a blue bathrobe and with much preliminary application of his person to the chilly water, and much grunting and loud breathing, floundered a minute in the sea. . . .

Here is another example by Fitzgerald, this from *The Great Gatsby*. An essentially static scene is provided with action:

Dramatization: Nature in action.

Detail in action.

Visual and aural detail.

Motion

Implication.

> He walked through a high hallway into a bright, rosy-colored space, fragily bound into the house by French windows at either end. The windows were ajar and gleaming white against the fresh grass outside, that seemed to grow a little way into the house. A breeze blew through the room, blew curtains in at one end and out the other like pale flags, twisting them up toward the frosted wedding cake of the ceiling, and then rippled over the wine-colored rug, making a shadow on it as the wind does on the sea.
>
> The only completely stationary object in the room was an enormous couch on which two young women were buoyed up as though upon an anchored balloon. They were both in white, and their dresses were rippling and fluttering as if they had just been blown back after a short flight around the house. I must have stood for a few moments listening to the whip and snap of the curtains, the groan of a picture on the wall. Then there was a boom as Tom Buchanan shut the rear windows and the caught wind died out about the room, and the curtains and the rugs and the two young women ballooned slowly to the floor.

Fitzgerald has used the breeze to great effect. The curtains are blowing, the rug is rippling, even the couch upon which the two young women recline seems to Nick Carraway's imagination a kind of magic carpet. The airy scene is punctuated by the dramatic slam of the window, Tom Buchanan bringing everything back to earth, which will be his function also in the novel as a whole.

> None of them knew the color of the sky. Their eyes glanced level and were fastened upon the waves that swept toward them. These waves were of the hue of slate, save for the tops, which were foaming white, and all the men knew the color of the sea.
>
> The horizon narrowed and widened and dipped and rose, and at all times its edge was jagged with waves that seemed to thrust up in points.
>
> Many a man ought to have a bathtub larger than the boat which here rode upon the sea. The waves were most wrongfully and barbarously abrupt and tall, and each frothtop was a problem in small boat navigation.
>
> The cook squatted in the bottom and looked with both eyes at the six inches of gunwale that separated him from the ocean. His sleeves were rolled over his fat forearms, and the two flaps of his unbuttoned vest dangled as he bent to bail out the boat. Often he said, "Gawd, that was a narrow clip."
>
> The oiler, steering with one of the two oars in the boat, sometimes raised himself suddenly to keep clear of the water that swirled in over the stern.

Dramatization: Detail. Motion. Implication. Point of view.

Rhythm. Specifics.

Specifics.

Pattern in motion.

The famous beginning of Stephen Crane's story "The Open Boat" is crammed with specifics and action. The action verbs in the first paragraphs are potent: "glanced," "fastened," "narrowed and widened and dipped and rose." These last four, connected by *and*, give the actual rhythm of the pitching boat. The cook looks at a specific "six inches of gunwale," not the more abstract "narrow strip." His rolled sleeves and the points of his vest make a pattern of circles and triangles in motion as he bails. In the last paragraph it is not merely stated that waves sometimes swirl in over the stern; rather, the action is rendered by showing the oiler raise himself to keep out of the water.

Marcel Proust, in *The Remembrance of Things Past*, uses the same device of a moving pattern in his description of the Baron de Charlus:

> The tuft of his gray hair, his twinkling eye, the brow of which

Dramatization: Detail.

Pattern. Motion.

> was raised by his monocle, the red flower in his buttonhole, formed as it were three mobile apexes of a convulsive and striking triangle.

Another famous beginning is that of Joseph Conrad's *The Nigger of the Narcissus*. The passage is dramatized by the play of light and shadow, the chiaroscuro functioning as action:

Dramatization: Light and shadow in action. Detail.

Aural detail.

> The main deck was dark aft, but halfway from forward, through the open doors of the forecastle, two streaks of brilliant light cut the shadow. . . . A hum of voices was heard there, while port and starboard, in the illuminated doorways, silhouettes of moving men appeared for a moment, very black, without relief, like figures cut from tin. . . . The two forecastle lamps were turned up high, and shed an intense hard glare; shoregoing round hats were pushed far on the backs of heads, or rolled about on the deck among the chain-cables; white collars, undone, stuck out on each side of red faces; big arms in white sleeves gesticulated.

In *A Flag for Sunrise*, Robert Stone uses pure light—the beam of the searchlight in action—to limn individual scenes in its glare, which combine to produce upon the page this dreary little Central American port town:

Dramatization: Aural detail.
Light and shadow in motion.
Implication.

> At the stroke of darkness, the band broke into a reedy *paso doble* and the great searchlight sent forth an overpowering light. The light broke up the foremost ranks of the crowd, sending the people there reeling back, forcing them to turn away, hands to their eyes. Then it swept through the square, ascending until the beam was pointed straight upward, a pillar of white fire heavenward. A great gasp of joy broke from the crowd.
>
> Spinning again, the column of light descended on the plaza, catching each second a dozen transfixed faces, dazzled the old men in their wicker chairs in the Syrian's shop and the lounging Guardia, electrified the posters of *Death Wish* in front of the cinema. It made the whores' beads sparkle, shone on the balloons and patent-leather shoes of the better-off children and on the slick flesh of the banana plants. As it whirled, the crowd screamed and applauded.

Elizabeth Bowen said of modern fiction, "We want the naturalistic surface, but with a kind of internal burning." Stone has provided the naturalistic surface here by cleverly illuminating with the searchlight different aspects of the town in a dramatized fashion; but there is an internal burning also, in the theological implications of the pillar of white fire aimed heavenward with the attendant gasp of joy, and in the mortal implications of the name of the movie playing at the cinema, *Death Wish*.

Details are rendered when they are presented in action. Static detail may reveal or imply, but details in action will bring a scene to life.

Sensory Perceptions

In the passage from *The Great Gatsby*, the details were mainly visual, but there were aural ones also, which served to heighten the dramatic presentation: "the whip and snap of the curtains, the groan of a picture on the wall," and most dramatic, the climactic boom when Tom Buchanan shuts the window.

Sensuous Prose

Other senses besides the visual are dramatically important—hearing, smell, taste, and touch. Prose that employs more of these than merely sight can be called *sensuous*, meaning appealing to the senses. Sensuous prose reaches the "secret springs of responsive emotion," of which Joseph Conrad speaks, below:

> All art, therefore, appeals primarily to the senses, and the artistic aim when expressing itself in written words must also make its appeal to the senses, if its high desire is to reach the secret springs of responsive emotion.
>
> Preface to *The Nigger of the Narcissus*, Conrad

Here is a sensuous passage from Flaubert's story "A Simple Heart":

> On days when it was too hot they did not leave their room. From the dazzling brilliance outside, the light fell in streaks between the laths of the blinds. There were no sounds in the village; and on the pavement below no sound. The silence around them deepened the quietness of things. In the distance where men were caulking, there was the tap of hammers as they plugged hulls, and a slight breeze wafted up the smell of tar.

Dramatization: Light in action.

Sense impressions: Sight. Sound. Smell. Touch (heat).

With the heat, the light, the near silence and far-off tapping of hammers, and the smell of tar, Flaubert has brought four senses into play. He does it again in this scene from *Madame Bovary*, with the twisting of paper around the flowers bringing in the tactile sense, and the flowers listed selected for their strong smell:

Dramatization: Light in action.

Sense impressions: Sight, sound, smell, touch.

> Silver gleamed in the jewelers' windows, and the sunlight slanting onto the cathedral flashed on the cut surface of the gray stone. The square, echoing with cries, smelled of the flowers that edged its pavement—roses, jasmine, carnations, narcissus and tuberoses interspersed with well-watered plants of catnip and chickweed. The fountain gurgled in the center. Bareheaded flowerwomen were twisting paper around bunches of violets.

The beginning of human knowledge is through the senses, and the fiction writer begins where human perception begins. He appeals through the senses, and you cannot appeal through the senses with abstractions.
—Mysteries and Manners, *Flannery O'Connor.*

A convincing sensory detail brings to life this scene from Hemingway's *A Farewell to Arms*:

Clincher sensory detail.

> I went to the window and looked out. The gravel paths were moist and the grass was wet with dew. The battery fired twice and the air came each time like a blow and shook the window and made the front of my pajamas flap.

The shock of air that shakes the window and makes the front of the narrator's pajamas flap is something that might not have occurred to most readers, but, considered, it seems exactly right and true. The reader experiences it even though she has never leaned out a window while a battery was firing from the next garden.

Not dramatized: Weak specification.

No vivid details. No sensories.

One specific.

> They turned left at the harbor, and drove swiftly past the shipping companies, the warehouses and docks. At the outskirts of the harbor were sagging buildings, and abandoned wharves with rotten pilings.
>
> There was a stone jetty with a paved road over it. They turned onto the jetty. At the end was the Johnson City sewage plant, its two tall smokestacks outlined against the sky.

This passage is inert. There is no detail, except for the two tall smokestacks outlined against the sky, no specific except the name of the sewage plant. Where are the smells one would expect around abandoned wharves with their rotten pilings, not to speak of the sewage plant? Where are the gulls? How could the drive out onto the jetty be rendered? Squealing tires and the rattle of gravel under the fenders would dramatize the turn. Smoke rising from the stacks, to be blown away in a breeze would give some motion. The late sun might turn the rotting piles to velvet.

Here follow two descriptions of Pancho Villa, the first in purely visual terms, the second employing another sense impression to great effect:

1) Villa, whose hat was off, had a round, full face, and a rather dusky complexion. His small brown eyes were good-natured; his dark somewhat curly hair was close-cropped, and he wore a big, black moustache. He was dressed in a baggy, gray worsted civilian suit with a vest. His feet were quite small for such a heavy-set man and his legs were covered with leather puttees. A tie around his neck contained a stickpin, and a large chain and fob dangled across the front of his waistcoat. Under the sides of his coat, on either hip, bulged a large six-shooter, and the lower half of the large nickel buckle of his cartridge belt showed at the bottom of his vest.

Detail: Static.

Listing.

The above paragraph is from a novel called *Other Gods*, by Lew Holston. The author has given us a great deal of detail of Villa's appearance, but it is presented as a list without the care Faulkner took to break up description with action and dialog. Moreover, none of the details are inherently dramatic, except for the six-shooters on either hip. Nothing is presented in motion, and all the details are visual. Compare this description with that of Villa by Martin Luis Guzman in *The Eagle and the Serpent:*

2) There was Pancho Villa.

He was lying on a cot, covered to the waist with a blanket. He had raised himself up a little to receive us, one arm acting as a column of support between his body and the bed. His right arm hung by his side; it was unbelievably long. But Villa was not alone. At the head of the bed two other revolutionists were sitting on turned-up boxes, with their backs to the light. They seemed to have cut short an important conversation. Neither of them moved as I came in, or showed more than a vague curiosity, indicated by the way they turned their heads, half hidden in their enormous hats, toward the door.

Amador's words of introduction were flowery as they were long. Villa listened to them unblinkingly. His mouth was a

Specific detail.

Menacing detail of posture.

Light and shadow.

Menacing detail.

> little open and there were traces on his face of the mechanical smile that seemed to start at the edges of his teeth. . . . At the general's invitation I had seated myself on the edge of the cot, a few inches from him. *The warmth of the bed penetrated through my clothes to my flesh.*

Menacing detail.

Clincher detail.

This description contains many fewer details than does Holston's, but the menace of Villa's long arm and mechanical smile and of the half-hidden faces, rivets our attention, while the heat of the bed brings Villa, and the scene, vividly to life.

Probably the most effective sense-evocations for conveying images to the reader, especially when used in combination, are the visual—something in motion, dramatically *not*-in-motion, or of very striking appearance or implication; sound, or the dramatic absence of it; the other senses—smell, texture, taste. Least effective are visual images *not* in motion and *not* inherently dramatic—outline, form, grouping, etc.

Dos Passos' sensitivity to smells was his compensation, perhaps, for his myopia. Throughout his life people observed him sniffing. Whether indoors or out, Dos Passos caught the waft of fragrances or other odors unnoticed by most people and catalogued them mentally for recall later.

—Dos Passos, *Virginia Spencer Carr*

Smell may be the most evocative of the senses. Odor memory is simpler, more primitive than the visual, noncognitive, and there is evidence that it is more lasting than visual recall: consider the salt air, mildew, damp swimtrunks, and furniture polish smells of old beach houses, or the cigarette smoke, urine, and orange peel redolence of wartime Greyhound Bus stations.

Cheever warned his writing students not to forget the smells. Norman Mailer uses smells effectively. So does Hemingway; here is Robert Jordan, in *For Whom the Bell Tolls*, sniffing:

> Robert Jordan pushed aside the saddle blanket that hung over the mouth of the cave and, stepping out, took a deep breath of the cold night air. The mist had cleared away and the stars were out. There was no wind, and, outside now of the warm air of the cave, heavy with smoke of both tobacco and charcoal, with the odor of cooked rice and meat, saffron, pimentos, and oil, the tarry, wine-spilled smell of the big skin hung beside the door . . . wine that spilled a little onto the earth of the floor, settling the dust smell; out now from the odors of different herbs whose names he did not know that hung in branches from the ceiling, with long ropes of garlic, away now from the copper-penny, red wine and garlic, horse sweat and man sweat dried in the clothing (acrid and gray the man sweat, sweet and sickly the dried brushed-off lather of horse sweat), of the men at the table, Robert Jordan breathed deeply of the clear night air of the mountains that smelled

> of the pines and of dew on the grass in the meadow by the stream.

At first thought there seems a lack of English vocabulary in regard to smells, and they are often implied or suggested, or likened in simile to some other sense. But a number of words can be used: *aroma, bouquet, effluvium, fragrance, fume, odor, perfume, redolence, reek, savor, smell, sniff, stench, stink, vapor*; or, more delicately and peripherally: *aura, hint, reminder, suggestion, tinge.*

In *The Hotel New Hampshire*, John Irving gives us the smell of the tame old bear called State of Maine, or Earl:

> We were, all of us, really too young to have *known* Earl, but the bear's presence—the stiff feel of his fur, the heat of his fruity and mud-like breath, the dead-geranium smell of him. . . .

The narrator's sister, Franny, has been taking baths three times a day since having been raped:

> I was aware of Franny's smell—a smell I hadn't known for awhile: a rich but never rank smell, a little salty, a little sweet, strong but never syrupy. And in the darkness I knew that Franny had been cured of taking baths.

In the narrator's sexual initiation, Ronda Ray's smell is then likened to Franny's:

> Her morning breath was slightly sour—but it smelled nice to me, and *she* smelled nice to me, although I would think, later, that her smell was simply Franny's smell taken several stages too far.

Toward the end of Faulkner's novella, *The Bear*, Ike McCaslin encounters the rattlesnake. The snake is established *not* by the conventional buzzing—for the snake has been surprised and has not had time to activate his rattle yet. The absence of sound is more dramatic than buzzing would have been. The snake is shown in motion—one loop cast sideways—and then rendered by his smell:

> . . . It had not coiled yet and the buzzer had not sounded either, only one thick rapid contraction, one loop cast side-

> ways as though merely for purchase from which the raised head might start slightly backward . . . the head raised higher than his knee and less than his knee's length away, and old, the once-bright markings of its youth dulled now to a monotone concordant too with the wilderness it crawled and lurked: the old one, the ancient and accursed about the earth, fatal and solitary and he could smell it now: *the thin sick smell of rotting cucumbers* and something else which had no name, evocation of all knowledge and an old weariness and of pariah-hood and death.

Clincher sensory detail.

Faulkner's authority is such that we accept his comparison of rattlesnake stench to that of rotting cucumbers, even though we may have less sense-memory of that smell than of John Irving's dead geraniums. We are more comfortable when our senses can sniff and nod as when John Dos Passos, in *USA*, likens the smell of red wine to that of damp sawdust.

An effective combination of sense-impression occurs in Wright Morris's *God's Country and My People*, in a scene with the barber, Cahow: the smell of his talcum, the feel of nails and coins in a pocket, the taste of a matchstick, the sound of the buzzing of the flies in the bulge of the screen, and, most potent, the *feel* of the express blasting through town, sending shivers up Cahow's legs from the shaken earth:

> The customer (scented with Cahow's talcum) might admit to a complaint about the weather while he sorted the nails from the coins in his pocket: Cahow might inquire about the health of the missus or the illness of a horse. While he gossiped, chewing on a match, he might adjust his old hat to his new-size head. If there were flies trapped in the bulge of the screen he might shoo them out. If he heard the whistle blowing ahead of the train, he might stand as he did in the pew on Sunday, eyes half-lidded, waiting for the sound of the hymn books to close. As the express blasted through, vibrating the windows, rattling the bottles of tonic water, the tremor of the earth would pass like a shiver up and down his legs.

Clincher sensory detail.

How poignant in the following scene with Charley Citrine and his mistress, Renata, is the heat of the heat-lamps under the marquee of the Plaza Hotel on his balding head. His baldness, and so his age, is contrasted by the implication of this sensation, with the youth, vigor, and sexuality of Renata as she precedes him into the hotel, like a galleon under sail: from Saul Bellow's *Humboldt's Gift*:

> . . . The doorman helped her out at the Plaza and, in her high boots, she strode under the heated marquee with its glowing orange rods. Over her mini-skirt she wore a long suede Polish coat lined with lambskin. I had bought it for her at Cepelia. Her beautifully pliant velvet hat inspired by seventeenth century Dutch portrait painters was pushed off her forehead. Her face, evenly and purely white, broadened toward the base. This gourdlike fullness was her only defect. Her throat was ever so slightly ringed or rippled by some enriching feminine deposit. This slight swell appeared also on her hips and the inside of her thighs. The first joint of her fingers revealed the same signs of sensual superabundance. Following her, admiring, thinking, I walked in the checked coat. Cantabile and Stronson had agreed that it gave me the cut of a killer. But I couldn't have looked less killer-like than I now did. My hair was blown out of position so that I felt the radiant heat of the marquee on my bald spot.

Clincher sensory detail.

This sensation of heat engages the reader's empathy for Citrine.

Consider Your Reader

The effectiveness of accurate detail and sense impressions cannot be stressed too strongly. In the following excerpt, the beginning of a chapter of *Farewell, My Lovely*, Raymond Chandler is preparing the reader for a rather long passage of Philip Marlowe's reflecting on the case in which he is currently involved. To prepare the reader for these essentially undramatic pages, Chandler here lays a very strong groundwork of dramatically rendered sense perceptions:

> I lay on my back on a bed in a waterfront hotel and waited for it to get dark. It was a small front room with a hard bed and a mattress slightly thicker than the cotton blanket that covered it. A spring underneath me was broken and stuck into the left side of my back. I lay there and let it prod me.
>
> The reflection of a red neon light glared on the ceiling. When it made the whole room red it would be dark enough to go out. Outside cars honked along the alley they called the Speedway. Feet slithered on the sidewalks below my window. There was a murmur and mutter of coming and going in the

Touch.

Visual: Light reflection.

Sounds.

Smell.

Sounds.

> air. The air that seeped in through the rusted screens smelled of stale frying fat. Far off a voice of the kind that could be heard far off was shouting "Get hungry, folks. Get hungry. Nice doggies here. Get hungry."

The way all this seems to work is that the author fictionalizes his idea, out of memory and experience by means of corroborative detail and sense impressions, through the medium of words on the page. The reader translates these, by means of the verisimilitude of the details and impressions as they check with his own sense-memories and imagination, into a satisfying image in his mind of the author's fiction.

T W O

Point of View

The house of fiction has in short not one window, but a million—a number of possible windows not to be reckoned, rather; every one of which has been pierced, or is still pierceable, in its vast front, by the need of the individual vision and by the pressure of the individual will. These apertures, of dissimilar shape and size, hang so, all together, over the human scene that we might have expected of them a greater sameness of report than we find. They are but windows at best, mere holes in a dead wall, disconnected, perched aloft; they are not hinged doors opening straight upon life. But they have this mark of their own that at each of them stands a figure with a pair of eyes, or at least with a field glass, which forms again and again, for observation, a unique instrument, insuring to the person making use of it an impression distinct from any other. He and his neighbors are watching the same show, but one seeing more where the other sees less, one seeing black where the other sees white, one seeing big where the other sees small, one seeing coarse where the other sees fine. . . .

—The Art of the Novel,
Henry James

Often the most important decision a writer will have to make in a piece of fiction is how the point of view is to be handled. The imprint of a point of view contributes enormously to the process of dramatization, and the way detail is viewed contributes in turn to the characterization of the viewpoint character. The number of options in point of view may seem overwhelming to the beginner: first person, third person, omniscient, roving, revolving, detached narrator, untrustworthy narrator, close third, remote third, second person, even first-person plural. On the other hand, the choice may be blessedly automatic, a given that was established along with the plot and the cast.

Point of view is central to dramatization. It is also central to the whole concept and structure of the novel.

The matter of establishing a central authority or central intelligence was a problem that did not exist for Thackeray, who told his story as though relating it to his children at bedtime, with himself as the Olympian *I*, the super-narrator and exterior authority. But readers are no longer children, they are increasingly sophisticated, and there are no more Thackerays either. After Henry James's innovations, authors began to tell their story in a different way, through the minds and eyes of characters while the author himself kept offstage, "paring his fingernails" as James Joyce put it.

The reader wants to believe the fiction before her. She will provide *willing suspension of disbelief*, accept the covers of the book as the proscenium arch for the drama within, but she expects the author to provide a climate of believability that will allow her to experience the fiction. Since James, the chief means to believability has been the establishment of a *central authority* within the fiction. Frederick Henry in *A Farewell To Arms*, Nick Carraway in *The Great Gatsby*, Huck Finn in *The Adventures of Huckleberry Finn*, as first-person narrators, are automatically the central authorities. Yossarian in *Catch-22* and Pruitt in *From Here to Eternity* are third-person point of view protagonists, and the central authorities in those novels. In novels with a shifting point of view, such as *The Sound and the Fury* and *The Alexandra Quar-*

tet, it is more difficult for the author to conceal himself as the ultimate manipulator, but still he contrives to keep hidden as best he can.

One of the most ancient devices in the art of literature is to pass the buck for the source of the story: "Here is a story somebody told me, which I will relate to you." It is presumed that if the actual author is caught "making it up," authority and believability are lost. *Clarissa Harlowe* purports to be the letters of a girl holding out against her seducer, and *Robinson Crusoe*, to be the actual narrative of a castaway. In *The Rime of the Ancient Mariner*, the wedding guest is detained to hear the terrible story, and the reader is an eavesdropper.

In *The Adventures of Huckleberry Finn*, Huck as narrator congratulates Mr. Twain on the general truthfulness of *The Adventures of Tom Sawyer*, and, in so doing, establishes his own authority within the novel that bears his name:

> You don't know about me without you have read a book by the name of *The Adventures of Tom Sawyer*; but that ain't no matter. That book was by Mr. Mark Twain, and he told the truth, mainly. There were things which he stretched, but mainly he told the truth. . . .

In a few sentences here, the narrative *voice* establishes an authority the reader will follow a long way. It is interesting to contrast this voice with the authorial voice in *The Adventures of Tom Sawyer*. *Huckleberry Finn* is a novel for adults, *Tom Sawyer*, one for boys, with the author's voice patronizing and condescending, the vision of boyhood sentimentalized:

> . . . he saw a new girl in the garden – a lovely little blue-eyed creature with yellow hair plaited into two long tails, white summer frock and embroidered pantalettes. The fresh-crowned hero fell without firing a shot. A certain Amy Lawrence vanished out of his heart and left not even a memory of herself behind. . . .

> He worshipped this new angel with a furtive eye, till he saw that she had discovered him. Then he pretended he did not know she was present, and began to "show off" in all sorts of absurd, boyish ways, in order to win her admiration. He kept up this grotesque foolishness for some time. . . .

Choosing a Point of View

A great deal of technical nomenclature has accumulated for the discussion of point of view. The *I* of the first-person point of view is called the *narrator*, and there are *reliable, unreliable,* and *multiple* versions, as well as *letter* and/or *journal* narration. Third-person point of view can be *close, distant, detached*, or *multiple.* Fiction is also written in *Omniscient, Authorial,* and *Olympian*—the method of Thackeray, which has been rather rigorously repressed in modern fiction, though the *Omniscient Author*, almost as a character, still turns up from time to time. The Latin Americans often use the *second-person*, the *you* form, which, however, is no more than first-person narration with a concealed *I*.

Consider the choice to be made in a fictionalization of the great journey of Cabeza de Vaca. He was a member of a Spanish expedition shipwrecked upon the Texas coast in 1528. Fearful of savage Indian tribes to the south, Cabeza de Vaca and three companions decided against the shortest route that would reunite them with their countrymen and headed west; their chosen route roughly paralleled the U.S.-Mexican border for some thousand miles to Spanish-occupied Sinaloa on the west coast of Mexico. Their successful progress was attributed to the fact that Cabeza de Vaca became a healer, and it was clear that Divine Grace traveled with him.

Cabeza de Vaca said of his companions that they were "a fearful man" (Castillo), a "reasonable man" (Dorantes), and a "sensual man" (the Moorish slave Esteban). Who should be chosen to narrate the story of their journey, or to experience it as a third-person point of view protagonist—the fearful man, the reasonable man, the sensual man, or the God-invested one? Should multiple shifts of point of view or narrators be attempted?

Another hypothetical situation might concern a normal American family on an upper-middle-class street in San Jose, California: Dad, Mom, seventeen-year-old daughter Milly, and seven-year-old Billy. Next door lives an observant neighbor, retired Major Jones.

Mom and Dad fight continually. Milly is in full rebellion and in love with her high school's bad boy. Billy is troubled by parental strife. The major, appalled, watches impending tragedy. Each of these characters has a different slant on the events he is experiencing.

Mom's attitude is that of an unappreciated, wronged, and injured person. She has sacrificed career and talent (as a prize-winning art student) to her husband. Now that she is middle-aged, is no longer beautiful, and has gained a few pounds, he would like nothing better than to get rid of her. She is well aware that there is a young woman in San Francisco he would marry in a moment if she were out of the way, but he will never divorce her. Under California law he would have to give her half of his factory, which would mean selling out and starting over—she would see to that!

Dad is tough, self-centered, and his main absorption is his business, although it drives him crazy to think that Helen, in San Francisco, may be slipping away from him, indeed that she may have another, secret—and younger!—lover. It seems to him that he has done everything right in the American way, worked hard, succeeded, but the rewards are withheld from him because of a fat, nagging wife, who is turning his son into a sissy before his eyes. His daughter also drives him crazy. He admits that he has a bit of a "thing" for her, and is sometimes too lax, sometimes too strict. But her latest boyfriend, Max, is too much, contemptuous of everything American and decent, with his blue hair teased up into spikes like a rooster's comb.

Mom's and Dad's consciousnesses may be too coarse, their biases too heavy, to be used as the *center of consciousness* of a novel. Milly's would be better, a young woman coming to terms with her own sexuality, seeing the middle-class "good" life in all its selfishness through Max's eyes, and yet loving her parents also. She may be coming to maturity by beginning to understand her father's dissatisfactions, and may undertake the responsibility of saving her little brother from being torn apart by parental dissensions. Billy is also a possibility: a child's point of view has many advantages. The "innocent eye" can possess great charm, and the author can contrast the self-deceptions of the adults with the honesty of a child-observer. Moreover, the author will find dramatic possibilities in showing through the child's eye much more than the child's mind can grasp. On the other hand, for the very reasons given above, there is a danger that Billy's point of view throughout will become monotonous and turn the story into a cliche.

Then there is the major next door. He is an educated man,

endowed with a facility for understanding human nature. Perhaps he has been retired prematurely with a wound that is in part psychic. He observes the cruelties and absurdities in the lives of the Smiths next door, and he may be slightly in love with pretty, plump little Mrs. Smith. He can also sympathize with Milly in her determination to get out of this kind of life, and he loves the child Billy, who creeps through the hole in the hedge to be comforted after the terrible fights at home, and who loves to listen to the major's stories of Lee's campaigns in Northern Virginia, on which the major plans a book.

An immediate possibility is a revolving point of view—Mom, Dad, Billy, Milly, the major, even Max, the boyfriend. Still one consciousness usually needs to be central, or the novel focused upon one character, who need not carry the point of view at all. For instance, the point of view might be held to Billy as he watches his sister, as the protagonist, break free of the life that is smothering her.

Another possibility is the point of view of a detached observer, perhaps the police lieutenant who comes as a result of an eruption of violence and tragedy. A kindly, crippled, retired major has gone berserk, slaughtering his neighbor with a service revolver. Or he is bringing the daughter of the house home from a chaos of car theft and bank robbery, which she has been forced into by her punker boyfriend.

Each of the participants in the situation and its progression, like the characters in *Rashomon*, has a different slant on what happened and why, and that slant becomes an influential component of the story that would result from the use of his or her point of view, as well as aiding the dramatization; also, all the slants taken together, might give an impression of the multiplicity of truth.

First-Person Narration

A version of the hypothetical novel above might be related from his prison cell, by Major Jones, who has murdered his next-door neighbor because the brute was battering his wife. But despite the major's insistence on that story, the reader begins to see more; actually Smith has discovered that his wife was crawling through the hole in the hedge to trysts with the major, who has been threatening exposure or blackmail. Or else the true motive is that Jones has been unable to bear seeing what the boy's father is doing to Billy, turning the boy into a coward, just as his own father turned him into the yellow dog publicly shamed by General

Patton for his failure in the Battle of the Bulge. . . . The Major's voice would be striking, southern, and military, with a sense of honor, but a paranoia also. . . .

First-person narration has the immediate advantage of a strong "voice," a vividness, an automatic authority. But note the following caveats:

Henry James called the first-person singular "that accurst autobiographic form which puts a premium on the loose, the improvised, the cheap, and the easy." All too often, also, a strong narrative voice is used to cover inadequacies in characterization and plotting.

Advising Scott Fitzgerald on his first novel, *This Side of Paradise*, the great Scribners editor Maxwell Perkins suggested that the novel be rewritten in third person rather than first, in order to give the author more distance from the material. The clamp of actual events on the imagination can be particularly crippling in first-person narration. If the *I* is the author's alter ego and the events of the novel were actual happenings, the author will have great difficulty breaking out of what *did* happen into what *should* happen.

Moreover, a narrator is of necessity *relating* events that have already happened. The action is already complete, finished; examined after the fact. Thus, dangers to the narrator do not concern us as much as they might. When the narrator of James Dickey's *Deliverance*, who is trying to kill the mad sniper before he murders all the river party, leaps blindly from the cliff he is scaling hoping for another handhold, we are not as anxious as we might be. He has lived to tell the tale.

Because the narrator's brain is presumably open to us, it is difficult to maintain believability while concealing information from the reader. It is impossible to employ a first-person narrator as the murderer in detective fiction, for instance, without dubious devices of madness or self-deception.

These limitations of the narrator's perceptions, however, may also be employed to great effect by a clever writer. The character may not understand what is going on, while the reader does. Will Dora realize in time that the dear old blind man, so sympathetic to her problems, is actually the Shopping Mall Strangler?

In the following passage from *The Manticore*, by Robertson Davies, the narrator is having dinner with his father, whom he blindly worships, and his father's mistress. He fails to perceive that his father is not only a jerk, but an uneducated one: the reader understands more than he does:

> . . . I had tasted whiskey, but this was a very different thing. Father showed me how to roll it around in the mouth and get it on the sides of the tongue where the tastebuds are, and I rolled and tasted in adoring imitation of him.
>
> How wonderfully good food and drink lull the spirit and bring out one's hidden qualities! I thought something better than just warm agreement with everything that was said was expected of me, and I raked around in my mind for a comment worthy of the occasion. I found it.
>
> *"And much as Wine has played the Infidel,*
> *And robbed me of my Robe of Honour—Well,*
> *I wonder often what the Vintners buy*
> *One half so precious as the stuff they sell,"*
>
> said I, looking reflectively at the candles through my glass of brandy. . . . Father seemed nonplussed, though I knew that was an absurd idea. Father? Nonplussed? Never!
>
> "Is that your own, Davey?" he said.
>
> I roared with laughter. What a wit Father was! I said I wished it was. . . .

In Joyce Cary's *Herself Surprised*, the action is considerably enhanced by the reader's realization that the narrator does not understand the meaning of the adventures she is confessing. She considers them discreditable to herself, when actually they reveal her as a kind of saint.

In the contemporary American classic *One Flew Over the Cuckoo's Nest*, as the author, Ken Kesey, himself says, the story is a stock one, and the protagonist, McMurphy, stock as well. What makes the novel remarkable is the narrative voice, the crazed, perceptive vision of the paranoid-schizophrenic Indian, Chief Broom.

First-person narration contains two time frames. In the past, as we have seen, the action is complete by the time we hear of it from the narrator. In the present, which usually frames the past, the narrator is looking back from his present situation and knowledge to that past action. Moving back and forth between these two times, the time of the event, and the time in which it is being related, can create a fine tension—and a suspense of knowing that something momentous has happened while awaiting the disclosure of the details. These withholdings and revelations can be enormously effective, as in *The Great Gatsby*. The interval between past and present can also possess great importance; during the time between, the narrator has had leisure to reflect upon the meaning of the past action from a more mature point of view.

All this, however, from much usage, has become formulaic. The narrator, in the present, faces some crisis in his life. He turns to the past, where the bulk of the story is remembered. The climax, and the lesson of the past, bear upon the present, and determine the narrator's present decision. As in all fiction, it is necessary to find a new slant amongst hoary situations and devices.

It may be easier for an author to put a third-person protagonist through extremes of experience than a semi-autobiographical *I*. It may also be difficult to make the *I* ridiculous, boastful, sordid, deceitful, stupid or callous. For these reasons, perhaps, too many *I*s in fiction are moderate, equable, thoughtful, and too often colorless.

The greatest problem of the first-person narrator is the manipulation required always to have him present to witness the necessary events. Nevertheless, certain fictions can be fulfilled only by the use of first person. The reader's sympathies and identification are quickly given to a narrator with an authentic voice. First person gives an immediate impression of directness, candor, and honesty. The "innocent eye" is a staple of American fiction: Shane observed by a hero-worshipping boy is more effective than Shane as a third-person protagonist.

The first-person narration of a long novel can become monotonous, and novelists resort to many different devices to bring in varying points of view. In John Updike's *The Coup*, the black Marxist dictator of Kush employs both first- and third-person narration in his "memoirs," with this explanation:

> A soldier's disciplined self-effacement, my Cartesian schooling, and the African's traditional abjuration of ego all constrain this account to keep to the third person. There are two selves: the one who acts, and the "I" who experiences. The latter is passive even in a whirlwind of the former's making, passive and guileless and astonished. . . .

J. P. Donleavy often switches from third person to first and back; the objective action is given in third and the character's thoughts in first.

Third-Person Point of View

John Fowles says, "The great majority of modern third-person narration is 'I' narration very thinly disguised." Indeed, except for the pronouns, the difference can be slight. In third person the voice is less strong, but it still operates in that the character's thoughts are given, if not precisely in his own words, at least in a suggestion of his own personality. More detachment is possible in third person. The price may be less intensity, but the rewards are much greater flexibility and variety. The camera-eye can be manipulated, to rise above and behind the character, including him in its field of vision if wanted, or to be fixed behind his own eyes to see *merely* what he sees.

In *The Red Badge of Courage*, Stephen Crane remains consistently with the point of view of Henry Fleming, "the youth." We see what the youth sees, experience what he experiences, learn and grow to manhood as he does. In the following passage, Crane needs to remind us with only a little tap from time to time, that all these impressions come to us through "the youth":

> The skirmishers in advance fascinated him. Their shots into thickets and at distant and prominent trees spoke to him of tragedies—hidden, mysterious, solemn.
>
> Once the line encountered the body of a dead soldier. He lay upon his back, staring at the sky. He was dressed in an awkward suit of yellowish brown. The youth could see that the soles of his shoes had been worn to the thinness of writing paper, and from a great rent in one the dead foot projected piteously. . . .
>
> The ranks opened covertly to avoid the corpse. The invulnerable dead man forced a way for himself. The youth looked keenly at the ashen face. The wind raised the tawny beard. It moved as if a hand were stroking it.

A novelist can shift view-point if it comes off. . . Indeed, this power to expand and contract perception (of which the shifting view-point is a symptom), this right to intermittent knowledge—I find one of the great advantages of the novel-form. . . . this intermittence lends in the long run variety and colour to the experiences we receive.

—Aspects of the Novel, *E. M. Forster*

A single point of view can be a powerful unifying factor in a piece of fiction. Changing point of view, especially in a short story, takes the risk of unraveling authority as well as unity, although contemporary writers are very clever in using point-of-view shifts to dramatic purpose. In the scene of the fight between the brothers in *Sometimes a Great Notion*, Ken Kesey manipulates point of view as a tour de force, using lower case, capitals and brackets to give us Lee's, Hank's, and Viv's views of the proceedings.

A rule of thumb might be that the gains of changing a point of view ought to outweigh the losses.

In the following description of Gerda bathing, in Alan Sharp's

A Green Tree in Gedde, it is too bad that the author put Cuffee to sleep:

> Cuffee was asleep, and Gerda bathed, standing in the bath and sluicing herself all over, her hair caught up on her head and her shoulders and breasts confected with the soap sheen of lather. As the water flowed over her, the flesh seemed to shimmer and melt and her nipples made little spigots that caught bubbles and dripped soapy drops. Her eyes were closed, and as she put her head back a pulse fluttered in her throat. Satined with water, she stood, the full body pendulous with pleasure.

This fine, closely observed sensuous and sensual detail would have had much more dramatic effect as Cuffee's perception rather than the author's.

In his grand, Olympian omniscient style, Tolstoy still observed a careful point of view. When the Russian generals are having their conference after the battle of Borodino, he established the point of view in the child Malasha, who peeps out on the scene from behind the stove, dramatizing the scene for the reader's sake.

Scenes skewed by some device have an especial dramatic quality, as a pair of lovers viewed through a telescope, where the viewer's motives are suspect, or a face made pig-featured and menacing by its reflection in a chromium hubcap, or a figure glimpsed in the mirror of a store window. In the following passages, the author is dramatizing a scene by means of a specific point of view, and by a particular framing or distortion of reality that rivets the reader's eye:

> 1) She was wearing a hat that had once belonged to her mother. It was shaped like a box and it was black felt with a half-circle lace veil that covered the eyes. She liked the way it divided everything into hexagons, like looking through chicken wire.

> 2) Through the flawed windowglass he watched the three of them, halted tightly grouped in their black clothing, their faces seeming swollen out of proportion with swollen teeth protruding from their mouths and eyes recessed into slits, their whole black, concave threat seeming to expand and contract, like waterweeds in a current, in the beating of his blood

behind his eyes.

The matter of changing point of view is a continuing problem and challenge to the novelist. Maintaining a single point of view in a long novel may be limiting, but a too-casual switching from consciousness to consciousness will make the reader aware of the author as manipulator and thus detract from the reality of the fiction. An inept or careless switching of point of view similarly reveals the author's hand. A common solution is to change point of view by chapters, perhaps labeled with the name of the character carrying the point of view within. Changing point of view by paragraphs can be a much trickier business, unless the penalties of a casual approach are simply ignored.

It is interesting to observe the process that Flaubert employs in changing point of view in *Madame Bovary*, carefully preparing the reader for each shift so as not to jar him out of his capsule of belief. In the following scene, Rodolphe has written a letter to Emma ending their adulterous relationship. Notice how the point of view is passed from Rodolphe, via Girard, to Madame Bovary:

> He re-read his letter. He considered it very good.
>
> "Poor little woman!" he thought with emotion. "She'll think me harder than a rock. There ought to have been some tears on this: but I can't cry; it isn't my fault." Then, having emptied some water into a glass, Rodolphe dipped his finger into it, and let a big drop fall on the paper, that made a pale stain on the ink. Then looking for a seal, he came upon the one *"Amor nel cor."*
>
> "That doesn't at all fit in with the circumstances. Pshaw! never mind!"
>
> After which he smoked three pipes and went to bed.
>
> The next day when he was up (at about two o'clock—he had slept late), Rodolphe had a basket of apricots picked. He put his letter at the bottom under some vine leaves, and at once ordered Girard, his ploughman, to take it with care to Madame Bovary. He made use of this means for corresponding with her, sending according to the season fruits or game.
>
> "If she asks after me," he said, "you will tell her that I have gone on a journey. You must give the basket to her herself, into her own hands. Get along and take care!"
>
> Girard put on his new blouse, knotted his handkerchief round the apricots, and walking with great heavy steps in his thick iron-bound galoshes, made his way to Yonville.

> Madame Bovary, when he got to her house, was arranging a bundle of linen on the kitchen-table with Félicité.
> "Here," said the ploughboy, "is something for you from the master."
> She was seized with apprehension, and as she sought in her pocket for some coppers, she looked at the peasant with haggard eyes, while he himself looked at her with amazement, not understanding how such a present could so move anyone. At last he went out. Félicité remained. She could bear it no longer; she ran into the sitting room as if to take the apricots there, overturned the basket, tore away the leaves, found the letter, opened it, and, as if some fearful fire were behind her, Emma flew to her room terrified.
> Charles was there; she saw him; he spoke to her; she heard nothing, and she went on quickly up the stairs, breathless, distraught, dumb, and ever holding this horrible piece of paper, that crackled between her fingers like a plate of sheet iron.

From Rodolphe the letter accompanies the basket of fruit, and Girard with his great heavy steps, to be passed to Emma, between whose fingers it crackles like a plate of sheet iron. The point of view has moved smoothly to Madame Bovary.

Floating Point of View

The omniscient author oversees his novel from a height, describing matters from Up Thcrc, and diving down into the consciousness of one of his characters when he finds it necessary or helpful. He is unconcerned with the fact that his audience is aware of him within the novel, manipulating his characters like marionettes and turning up their thoughts for the reader's edification. Since Henry James, point of view has been considered a major item of literary technique. Big commercial novels pay little attention to these niceties. Here is the opening scene from Arthur Hailey's *The Moneychangers*:

> It was on Tuesday of that week that old Ben Rosselli, president of First Mercantile American Bank and grandson of the bank's founder . . . telephoned a few of his senior executives early in the morning, catching some at home at breakfast, others soon after their arrival at work. . . .
> To each, the message was the same: Please be in the Headquarters Tower boardroom at 11 A.M.

Now all except Ben were assembled in the boardroom, twenty or so, talking quietly in groups, waiting. All were standing; no one chose to be first to pull a chair back from the gleaming directors' table, longer than a squash court, which seated forty.

A voice cut sharply across the talk. "Who authorized that?"

Heads turned. Roscoe Heyward, executive vice-president and comptroller, had addressed a white-coated waiter from the senior officers' dining room. The man had come in with decanters of sherry which he was pouring into glasses.

Heyward, austere, Olympian in FMA, was a zealous teetotaler. He glanced pointedly at his watch in a gesture which said clearly: Not only drinking, but this *early*. Several who had been reaching out for the sherry withdrew their hands.

"Mr. Rosselli's instructions, sir," the waiter stated. "And he especially ordered the best sherry."

A stocky figure, fashionably dressed in light gray, turned and said easily, "Whatever time it is, no sense passing up the best."

Alex Vandervoort, blue-eyed and fair-haired with a touch of gray at the temples, was also an executive vice-president. Genial and informal, his easygoing, "with-it" ways belied the tough decisiveness beneath. The two men—Heyward and Vandervoort—represented the second management echelon immediately below the presidency and, while each was seasoned and capable of co-operation, they were, in many ways, rivals. Their rivalry, and differing viewpoints, permeated the bank, giving each a retinue of supporters at lower levels.

Now Alex took two glasses of sherry, passing one to Edwina D'Orsey, brunette and statuesque, FMA's ranking woman executive.

Edwina saw Heyward glance toward her, disapproving. Well, it made little difference, she thought. Roscoe knew she was a loyalist in the Vandervoort camp.

"Thank you, Alex," she said, and took the glass.

The above scene is almost totally authorial, with a very brief fling into Edwina's point of view: "Well, it made little difference, she thought." Characterization is by exposition; *telling*. We are *told* what Heyward and Vandervoort are like. The scene moves along swiftly, establishing what needs to be established in the most economical manner; the author, as it were, stands before us and lectures, indicating this character or that with his pointer. He dips briefly into Edwina's thoughts, and he will dip into others' as suits his purpose.

His deployment of point of view is very much a part of a particular writer's style. Marked as a young writer by exposure to Faulkner's *As I Lay Dying*, and Dos Passos's *USA*—I have often used a revolving point of view, changing viewpoint characters by chapters or sections. A beginning writer may feel that a first person point of view comes most naturally, but all things considered, a more workable choice might be a close third person with the viewpoint in the head and behind the eyes of the character. This technique has the close-camera advantage of first person, but the action is happening before the viewpoint character's, and the reader's, eyes, and so is not being narrated after the fact. Also, the author is not stuck in the narrator's voice, but can use her voice or not, and shift into an authorial one when necessary, being careful however to keep herself concealed. As she gains expertise, the writer can shift this point of view camera from behind the viewpoint character's eyes, to over his shoulder, to a spot at some distance away and including the character within the viewed scene, moving in and out; these options give third person so much more flexibility than first.

THREE

Characterization

We care what happens to people only in proportion as we know what people are.
—Henry James

It is not sufficient to assemble a character by adding characteristics as grilles and fenders might be added on an assembly line: a big nose, duck-like walk, houndstooth check jacket, taste for Beethoven and the Red Sox, and a foolish fidelity to a faithless wife.

The character must be produced on the page, whole and alive, his breath congealing on the air. It is not necessary that we know instantly what he *is*, for it is the process of learning about him that interests us. As in the representation of any physical reality in fiction, characterization is rooted in detail. It is the trifles and what they imply or reveal that create the living entity.

Richard Price has written that his novels take two years to write, of which the first is spent living with his characters. Their development is an evolutionary process in which he comes to know them so well he could take a battery of MMPI or Wonderlic personality tests on any one of them, answering hundreds of intimate questions with as full knowledge as if the character himself were taking the tests.

Where does a writer find his characters? Somerset Maugham said that he never created a character, they were all taken literally from life. Ray Bradbury goes further: " . . . the character you choose, like it or not, will be yourself anyway." And Milan Kundera, in *The Unbearable Lightness of Being*:

> . . . characters are not born like people, of woman; they are born of a situation, a sentence, a metaphor containing in a nutshell a basic human possibility that the author thinks no one else has discovered or said something essential about.
>
> But isn't it true that an author can write only about himself?
>
> Staring impotently across a courtyard, at a loss for what to do; hearing the pertinacious rumbling of one's own stomach during a moment of love; betraying, yet lacking the will to abandon the glamorous path of betrayal; raising one's fist with the crowds in the Grand March; displaying one's wit before hidden microphones—I have known all these situations, I have experienced them myself, yet none of them has given

> rise to the person my curriculum vitae and I represent. The characters in my novels are my own unrealized possibilities. . . . Each one has crossed a border I myself have circumvented. . . . beyond that border begins the secret the novel asks about. . . .

Certainly it is what the writer has experienced, actually or imaginatively, that enables him to create fiction. But the novel is least likely to be alive if he makes himself the protagonist. So although in a way he is each one of his characters ("Mme. Bovary, c'est moi," said Flaubert), no one of them should be exactly like him. Elizabeth Bowen said, "The novelist's perceptions of his characters take place in the course of the actual writing of the novel." Characters congeal as the fiction progresses; this detail from a friend, that gesture or mannerism from someone observed, something borrowed, something blue, all assembled upon an armature of what the writer himself might have become in different circumstances.

E. M. Forster makes a distinction between flat and round characters in *Aspects of the Novel:*

> The test of a round character is whether it is capable of surprising in a convincing way. If it never surprises it is flat. Flat characters . . . in their purest form . . . are constructed round a single idea or quality; when there is more than one factor to them, we get the beginning of the curve toward the round. The really flat character can be expressed in one sentence such as, "I will never desert Mr. Micawber." There is Mrs. Micawber—she says she won't desert Mr. Micawber; she doesn't, and there she is. . . .

Heroes and heroines in popular fiction are usually incapable of surprising the reader. They are strong, willful, violent, and strongly sexed, fulfilling the injunction that the hero initiates action, he is not the victim of it. No anti-heroes or Hamlets, kept from action by the pale cast of thought, need apply.

Exposition
The author explains the character to the reader, listing his attributes, *telling* the reader about him. The following is from Niven Busch's *Duel in the Sun*:

> Gilman was a clerk. He lived by rote. In spite of his outdoor body and his carbine in its slot under his stirrup-strap he was the kind of man who, if he had lived in a city, would have climbed on a high stool every day and put figures in a ledger. There was no distinction of any kind about him, not in the way he rode or roped or ate or laughed or anything he did. Yet there was a superiority he had over most tied down clerkly men: under pressure he would be adequate to whatever was necessary. . . .

We are being told the above, but the detail of the carbine in its slot under the oilman's stirrup-strap is a fine one, as is the implication that it will be put to use and that a challenge will present itself to which Gilman will prove adequate. A lot of ground has been covered in a few lines. Exposition is the most economical method of characterizing, and it can be made vivid if a few sharp details glow out of the reportage.

In the following description of Chook, from John D. MacDonald's *Bright Orange for a Shroud*, an advantage is that these perceptions are offered, not by the author, but by the narrator of the novel, Travis McGee. Also, the specifics are very precise:

> Five ten, maybe 136 pounds, maybe 39-25-39, and every inch glossy, firm, pneumatic—intensely alive, perfectly conditioned as are only the dedicated professional dancers, circus flyers, tumblers, and combat rangers. Close up you can hear their motors humming. Heart beat in repose in the fifties. Lung capacity extraordinary. Whites of the eyes a blue-white.

Description
Following exposition, description is the next most economical, and the next least effective. These descriptions are from Louisa May Alcott's *Little Women*:

> As young readers like to know "how people look," we will take this moment to give them a little sketch of the four sisters, who sat knitting away in the twilight, while the December snow fell quietly without, and the fire crackled cheerfully

> within. It was a comfortable old room, though the carpet was faded and the furniture very plain; for a good picture or two hung on the walls, books filled the recesses, chrysanthemums and Christmas roses bloomed in the windows, and a pleasant atmosphere of home peace pervaded it.
>
> Margaret, the eldest of the four, was sixteen, and very pretty, being plump and fair, with large eyes, plenty of soft, brown hair, a sweet mouth, and white hands, of which she was rather vain. Fifteen-year-old Jo was very tall, thin, and brown, and reminded one of a colt; for she never seemed to know what to do with her long limbs, which were very much in her way. She had a decided mouth, a comical nose, and sharp, gray eyes, which appeared to see everything, and were by turns fierce, funny, or thoughtful. Her long, thick hair was her one beauty; but it was usually bundled into a net, to be out of her way. Round shoulders had Jo, big hands and feet, a flyaway look to her clothes, and the uncomfortable appearance of a girl who was rapidly shooting up into a woman, and didn't like it. Elizabeth—or Beth, as everyone called her—was a rosy, smooth-haired, bright-eyed girl of thirteen, with a shy manner, a timid voice, and a peaceful expression, which was seldom disturbed. Her father called her "Little Tranquillity," and the name suited her excellently; for she seemed to live in a happy world of her own, only venturing out to meet the few whom she trusted and loved. Amy, though the youngest, was a most important person—in her own opinion at least. A regular snow-maiden, with blue eyes, and yellow hair curling on her shoulders, pale and slender, and always carrying herself like a young lady mindful of her manners.

Louisa Alcott claims that readers like to know "how people look," but there is some evidence to the contrary. Readers may pay little attention to physical description, preferring to fill in the physical details of the characters in whom they are interested out of their own imagination and tastes. A reader who dislikes red-haired women may resolutely refuse to register the fact that a heroine is redheaded, and will envision her as having coloration he likes better. In this the reader is actually using his own imagination to help create character, and this function can be useful to the writer.

The following description of Jack Durbeyfield, from Thomas Hardy's *Tess of The D'Urbervilles*, has a motif that helps to characterize by description:

> ... The pair of legs that carried him were rickety, and there was a bias in his gait which inclined him somewhat to the left of a straight line. He occasionally gave a smart nod, as if in confirmation of some opinion, though he was not thinking of anything in particular. An empty egg-basket was slung upon his arm, the nap of his hat was ruffled, a patch being quite worn away where his thumb came in taking it off.

This description is given us in terms of asymmetry, discontinuity and emptiness, but the abstractions are all rooted in specifics and presented in action: the rickety legs, the smart nod of empty-headedness, the empty basket, the worn patch on his hat with its implication of excessive servility. Legs, head, arm, hat, and thumb do not form a linear progression, but a discontinuous one, in a diminishing spiral that seems to result from his unstable and constantly biased gait. All this implies a great deal about the character of Jack Durbeyfield.

Another motif description is that of Popeye, in William Faulkner's *Sanctuary*. The motif of slants pulls this description together:

> He saw, facing him across the spring, a man of under size, his hands in his pockets, a cigarette slanted from his chin. His suit was black, with a tight, high-waisted coat. His trousers were rolled once, and caked with mud above mud-caked shoes. His face had a clear, bloodless color, as though seen by electric light; against the sunny silence, in his slanted straw hat and his slightly akimbo arms, he had that vicious, depthless quality of stamped tin.

Although the author is telling us by exposition, in the final simile, that Popeye is dangerous, the violence already exudes from Popeye's slantedness and from the motionlessness of his stance across the spring.

Action

Action is the most effective way to demonstrate character, although it is not the most economical. Action catches the eye. It shows instead of telling. It demonstrates traits. It interests while it informs, and the image, and so the demonstration, remains fresh in the reader's mind's eye as exposition or static description will not. It proves impossible to remember the characterizations of the sisters from *Little Women* from their descriptions; they become vivid only after they have been glimpsed in action.

Ray Midge, in Charles Portis's *The Dog of the South*, is characterized:

> I ordered a glass of beer and arranged my coins before me on the bar in columns according to value. When the beer came, I dipped a finger in it and wet down each corner of the paper napkin to anchor it, so it would not come up with the mug each time and make me appear ridiculous. I drank from the side of the mug that a left-handed person would use, in the belief that fewer mouths had been on that side.

Ray Midge is looking for his wife, who has left him, and we obtain a pretty good idea in his actions with the mug of beer, just why she left him. The author keeps the scene in action, and each sentence, while containing an important item related to characterization, also moves the scene along.

In the following passage from *The Ship Killer*, Justin Scott is showing by indirection, in action, that Donner, beneath a suave and pleasant exterior—in contrast to his companion here, Grandig—is utterly ruthless in the pursuit of his quarry:

> They ordered dinner at the bar. Then the waiter led them towards the dining room, stopping at the fish tank to let Donner choose his trout. Donner inspected the dozen fish swimming in clear water.
>
> "That one."
>
> The waiter dipped his net. The fish scattered to the corners of the tank, but he had already trapped the fat trout Donner had chosen.
>
> "Well done."
>
> The young man lifted the net from the water. The trout struggled frantically, slapping the water with his tail, standing almost perpendicular in thc clinging mesh.
>
> "Hold him," chuckled Grandig.
>
> With powerful thrusts of its glistening body, the fish thrashed out of the net and fell back into the water. The waiter scooped after it instantly.
>
> "No," said Grandig. "Let him go. He deserves life a little longer."
>
> "Which, sir?" asked the young man, withdrawing his net.
>
> "He's mine," said Donner with a gentle smile.
>
> "The same fish, sir?"

> Donner watched the trout circle the tank with agitated flicks of his tail. "The same," he answered. "Get him."

Two characters are revealed, contrastingly, by their actions in a difficult traverse of a beach, in James Houston's *Gig*:

> At that moment a small wave broke, swashed in, licked the rocks and pulled back to reveal a narrow strip of dark sand. Bo started running. He took four strides before the next wave reached him, calf-deep, splashing off the rocks. I could see the decision in his back and neck muscles as he turned, kicking high, and plunged in up to his waist, flailing his arms till the water reached his chest, and he was swimming around the point, thrashing out there, then wading ashore beyond the rocks, soaking wet.
>
> I started climbing over boulders, well back from the high waterline, and joined Bo in a couple of minutes.

Bo is the chance-taker, "I" the cautious one; they are also typically, the hero of a novel and the narrator who observes the hero in action, the man of action and the man of observation.

Shading

Tolstoy employed a method of characterization that he called *shading*, building a character out of contradictions. A cold, dry character will be presented first in a state of emotion, because the actuality would show an extra dimension, which would surprise the reader and eventually bring him to a better understanding of the character. For instance, when we first meet General Kutosov, in *War and Peace*, he speaks calmly of the destruction of a detachment of his soldiers, which Prince Andrey considers justified because of the general's great responsibility. But in time we learn of Kutosov's overwhelming compassion for his men, with a dramatic enlargement of our understanding.

Gestures and Mannerisms

These are a subdivision of action perhaps, establishing a character's physical presence, and his nature as well, by their repetition; an example is Faulkner's Texan, Hipps, who from time to time pops a gingersnap into his mouth beneath his moustache.

A story is told of a bit of stage business devised by the director George Abbott. The lover is helping the girl on with her coat, and Abbott instructed the actress to stand perfectly still waiting for the lover to free her shoulder-length hair from her coat collar. This characteristic demand on the part of the girl tells us a great deal about the relationship.

Here follows a repeated "stage business" from Dicken's *Great Expectations*. The finger of the lawyer, Mr. Jaggers, dramatizes his impatient and domineering nature:

> Then, and not sooner, I became aware of a strange gentleman leaning over the back of the settle opposite me, looking on. There was an expression of contempt on his face, and he bit the side of a great forefinger as he watched the group of faces.
>
> "Come!" said the stranger, biting his forefinger at him. "Don't evade the question. Either you know it or you don't know it. Which is it to be?"
>
> He stood with his head to one side, and himself on one side, in a bullying interrogative manner, and he threw his forefinger at Mr. Wopsle—as it were to mark him out—before biting it again.
>
> Mr. Jagger's own highbacked chair was of deadly black horsehair, with rows of brass nails round it, like a coffin, and I fancied I could see how he leaned back in it, and bit his forefinger at his clients.

This scene is from Don Asher's *The Electric Cotillion*:

> Now a galvanic, less voluntary movement, seized her, a seemingly spastic bit of business which I'd noticed before: her left fist, as if jerked by a miraculous string, abruptly jamming under her jaw.
>
> "Why did you do that?"
>
> "What?"
>
> "With your fist."
>
> "I have a malocclusion. If I don't block the yawn my jaw's liable to dislocate. . . ."

The mannerism is vivid and dramatic in itself; it catches the eye and continues to do so as it recurs, establishing this girl's physical presence. The fact that the novel concerns an affair of the girl with an older man provides an added intensity to the yawns.

Setting, Tastes, Interests, Etc.

> With little or no wherewithal for being left alone in a room, Mary Jane stood up and walked over to the window. She drew aside the curtain and leaned her wrist on one of the cross-pieces between the panes, but, feeling grit, removed it, rubbed it clean with her other hand, and stood up more erectly. Outside, the filthy slush was visibly turning to ice. Mary Jane let go the curtain and wandered back to the blue chair, passing two heavily stocked bookcases without glancing at any of the titles.

In this passage from the J. D. Salinger story "Uncle Wiggly in Connecticut," what is dramatic and character-revealing—especially to a writer, who *always*, when left alone in a strange room, examines the titles of the books on hand for clues to the character of the occupant of the place—is that Mary Jane ignores the books.

Here is Widmerpool, from Anthony Powell's *A Question of Upbringing,* characterized in terms of his legendary overcoat:

> . . . I cannot remember precisely what sort of an overcoat Widmerpool was said to have worn in the first instance. Stories about it had grown into legend; so much so that even five or six years later you might still occasionally hear an obtrusive or inappropriate garment referred to as "a Widmerpool"; and Templer, for example, would sometimes say: "I am afraid I'm wearing rather Widmerpool socks today," or "I've bought a wonderfully Widmerpool tie. . . ."

The following passage, from the *San Francisco Examiner*, February 7, 1988, furnishes details that raise intriguing questions in the reader's mind about the occupant of this room:

> . . . Heavy red drapes block the light as the air conditioner whirs 24 hours a day. The deep carpets are red and black: the walls black and padded. There are three 16-inch color-TV sets: two embedded in the ceiling above the custom-made king-size bed, the third at its foot.
>
> On bedside tables sit three phones next to a well-worn Bible and a statue of the Virgin Mary. There are books about martial arts, another titled "I Believe in Miracles." In the drawer sits a loaded pistol.
>
> This is Elvis Presley's private bedroom at Graceland in

Memphis, Tenn. . . .

Profiles in *The New Yorker* always pay considerable attention to the subject's home or apartment, the books, artifacts, view, working area, etc. Here, in *Hotel*, Arthur Hailey is characterizing Christine by the interior of her apartment. The point of view is Peter's:

> . . . He measured three ounces of rye whiskey, dividing it two ways, then reached for Angostura and Peychaud's bitters. "Sometime I'll tell you about it." As an afterthought he increased the proportion of rye, using a handkerchief to mop some extra drops which had fallen on the Wedgwood-blue rug.
>
> Straightening up, he cast a glance around the living room, with its comfortable mixture of furnishings and color—a French provincial sofa with a leaf-design tapestry print in white, blue, and green; a pair of Hepplewhite chairs near a marble-topped chest, and the inlaid mahogany sideboard on which he was mixing drinks. The walls held some Louisiana French prints and a modern impressionist oil. The effect was of warmth and cheerfulness, much like Christine herself, he thought. Only a cumbrous mantel clock on the sideboard beside him provided an incongruous note. The clock, ticking softly, was unmistakably Victorian, with brass curlicues and a moisture-stained, timeworn face. Peter looked at it curiously.
>
> When he took the drinks to the kitchen, Christine was emptying beaten eggs from a mixing dish into a softly sizzling pan.
>
> "Three minutes more," she said, "that's all."
>
> He gave her the drink and they clinked glasses.
>
> "Keep your mind on my omelet," Christine said. "It's ready now."
>
> It proved to be everything she had promised—light, fluffy, and seasoned with herbs. "The way omelets should be," he assured her, "but seldom are."
>
> "I can boil eggs too."
>
> He waved a hand airily. "Some other breakfast."
>
> Afterward they returned to the living room and Peter mixed a second drink. It was almost two A.M.
>
> Sitting beside her on the sofa he pointed to the odd-appearing clock. "I get the feeling that thing is peering at me—announcing the time in a disapproving tone."

> "Perhaps it is," Christine answered. "It was my father's. It used to be in his office where patients could see it. It's the only thing I saved."
>
> There was a silence between them. Once before Christine had told him, matter-of-factly, about the airplane accident in Wisconsin.

Central to the contents of the apartment, and pointed up as important, is the clock on the mantel. The Victorian clock symbolizes Christine's Victorian morality. Peter is very conscious of its glare, and goes home at a respectable hour because of it:

> Peter rose from the sofa, stretching his big body. "That clock of yours is staring again. I guess I'd better go."

In *The Portrait of a Lady*, Mme. Merle lectures Isabel on the importance of things:

> When you've lived as long as I you'll see that every human has his shell and that you must take the shell into account. By the shell I mean the whole envelope of circumstances. There's no such thing as an isolated man or woman; we're each of us made up of some cluster of appurtenances. What shall we call our "self"? Where does it begin? Where does it end? It overflows into everything that belongs to us—and then it flows back again. I know a large part of myself is in the clothes I choose to wear. I've a great respect for *things*! One's self—for other people—is one's expression of one's self; and one's house, one's furniture, one's garments, the books one reads, the company one keeps—these things are expressive.

The Opinion of Others:
This method of characterization is double-edged, for it says something both of the holder of the opinion and the object of it. In the above passage, Mme. Merle's opinions on *things* tells us a great deal about her. In that same novel, Isabel Archer appears to the reader at first as a little too cool, rather snippy and opinionated; but because Ralph Touchett finds her fascinating, and we have already come to trust Ralph Touchett, we trust his opinion of Isabel.

Travis McGee, in John D. MacDonald's *Bright Orange for a Shroud*, explains how he has sized up Wilma Ferner as a "scorpion," and not to be messed with:

> "And what have you got? Radar?"
> "Alarm systems. Bachelor devices to detect poisonous types. One good way is to watch how the other women react. You and the others, when Wilma Ferner was around, all your mouths got a little tight, and you were very polite to her. And you made no girl talk at all with her. No clothes talk. No date talk. No guided trips to the biff. No girl secrets. Just the way, honey, a woman should be damned wary of a man other men have no use for."

Dialog
Clearly one of the most effective methods of revealing character is through the character's presenting himself in his own words. Ford Madox Ford speaks to the subject:

> If the author says: "Mr. X was a violent reactionary," you would know little about him. But if Mr. X's first words after his introduction were, "God damn it, I say put all the filthy liberals up against a wall and shoot their filthy livers out. Are you with me or against me?" That gentleman will make an impression that many following pages will hardly efface. You may converse with a lady for ten minutes about the fineness of the day or the number of lumps of sugar she likes in her tea and you will know nothing about her. But let her hazard any personal opinion as to the major topics of life, and you will soon have her labeled and docketed.

The following passage of dialog is from Anne Tyler's novel *The Accidental Tourist*; Macon and his son Ethan are at the movies:

> "I got the tickets," he heard Ethan say. "And they're opening the door in five minutes."
> "All right," Macon told him, "let's plan our strategy."
> "Strategy?"
> "Where we're going to sit."
> "Why would we need strategy for that?"
> "It's you who asked to see this movie, Ethan. I would think you'd take an interest in where you're sitting. Now, here's my plan. You go around to that line on the left. Count the little kids. I'll count the line on the right."
> "Aw, Dad—"
> "Do you want to sit next to some noisy little kid?"
> "Well, no."

"And which do you prefer: an aisle seat?"
"I don't care."
"Aisle, Ethan? Or middle of the row? You must have some opinion."
"Not really."
"Middle of the row?"
"It doesn't make any difference."
"Ethan. It makes a great deal of difference. Aisle, you can get out quicker. So if you plan to buy a snack or go to the restroom, you'll want to sit on the aisle. On the other hand, everyone'll be squeezing past you there. So if you don't think you'll be leaving your seat, then I suggest—"
"Aw, Dad, for Christ's sake!" Ethan said.
"Well," Macon said. "If that's the tone you're going to take, we'll just sit any damn place we happen to end up."

We have been shown Macon's fussiness and tendency to overthink the simplest actions, which has caused his estrangement from his wife and his son's impatience with him.

The following dialog shows us something of the girl's character and her relationship with her companion:

"Don't you want a beer?" he asked.
"You know I don't like it warm, Jim. I'd rather've had some wine, like last time."
"I thought you said at the store that beer was fine."
"Oh, all right." She took the beer and jerked on the snap top. "Now I've cut my finger!"

In *The Portrait of a Lady*, Gilbert Osmond is a watercolorist who collects small objects in exquisite taste. Here he is with his daughter, Pansy, looking at a small watercolor he has just completed:

He had a light, lean, rather languid-looking figure, and was apparently neither tall nor short. He was dressed as a man dresses who takes little trouble about it other than to have no vulgar things.

"Well, my dear, what do you think of it?" he asked of the young girl. He used the Italian tongue, and used it with perfect ease; but this would not have convinced you he was Italian.

The child turned her head earnestly to one side and the

> other. "It's very pretty, Papa. Did you make it yourself?"
> "Certainly I made it. Don't you think I'm clever?"
> "Yes, Papa, very clever; I also have learned to make pictures." And she turned round and showed a small fair face painted with a fixed and intensely sweet smile.
> "You should have brought me a specimen of your powers."
> "I've brought a great many; they're in my trunk."
> "She draws very—carefully," the elder of the nuns remarked, speaking in French.

We learn that Osmond prides himself on his cleverness, and that his daughter is very careful, anxious to please, more than a little frightened of her father. These are keys to their characters. "No vulgar things" may be weak specification by James's term, but it allows the reader to use her own imagination to dress Osmond.

Thoughts
In the poker game at the beginning of *The Naked and the Dead*, Norman Mailer uses a combination of thoughts, action, dialog, and description to characterize his soldiers. Here we are shown the thoughts of Wilson and Gallagher:

> For once Wilson's hand was poor, and after staying a round because he was the heavy winner, he dropped out. When the campaign was over, he told himself, he was going to drum up some way of making liquor. There was a mess sergeant over in Charley Company who had made two thousand of them pounds the way he sold a quart for five pounds. All a man needed was sugar and yeast and some of them cans of peaches or apricots. In anticipation, he felt a warm mellow glow in his chest. Why, you could even make it with less. Cousin Ed, he remembered, had used molasses and raisins, and his stuff had been passing decent. . . .
> Gallagher had folded early in the hand too, and was looking at Wilson with resentment. It took somebody like that dumb cracker to win all the big pots. Gallagher's conscience was bothering him. He had lost thirty pounds at least, and, while most of it was money he had won earlier on the trip, this did not excuse him. He thought of his wife, Mary, now seven months pregnant. . . .

And so on through Sergeant Croft, who is a third important

character in the novel.

Narrative Voice
The tone and diction of the narrator spring from his character, and through his "voice" we come to know him, as we immediately know Jason Compson in Faulkner's *The Sound and the Fury:*

> Once a bitch always a bitch, what I say. I say you're lucky if her playing out of school is all that worries you. I say she ought to be down in that kitchen right now, instead of up there in her room, gobbing paint on her face and waiting for six niggers that can't even stand up out of a chair unless they've got a pan full of bread and meat to balance them, to fix breakfast for her. . . .

A Welsh boy has grown thirty years older, and is looking back on his boyhood in Wales, in Richard Llewellyn's *How Green Was My Valley*:

> It is strange that the Mind will forget so much, and yet hold a picture of flowers that have been dead for thirty years and more.
>
> I remember the flowers that were on our window-sill while my mother was talking that morning, and I can see the water dripping from a crack in the red pot on the end, for Bronwen was standing there, with her face in deep, dull gold from the sun on the drawn blind.
>
> Thirty years ago, but as fresh, and as near as Now.
>
> No bitterness is in me, to think of my time like this: Huw Morgan, I am, and happy inside myself, but sorry for what is outside, for there I have failed to leave my mark, though not alone, indeed.

In the above passage, his recollection is moving Huw Morgan from the present to the past, and into the Welsh vernacular that will be the diction of the novel and that here suggests Huw's then youth and innocence.

The beginning of Camus's *The Stranger* presents the dislocated, disturbing voice that characterizes Meusault:

> Mother died today. Or, maybe, yesterday, I can't be sure. The telegram from the Home says: YOUR MOTHER PASSED AWAY. FUNERAL TOMORROW. DEEP SYM-

> PATHY. Which leaves the matter doubtful; it could have been yesterday. . . .

William Goyen's *Arcadio* begins:

> "My name is Arcadio and I will do you no harm. Come under the shade of this old rayroad trestle if you wan to. Train's gone. Set down please. . . ."

The reader immediately feels at ease with this invitation, for although there are some phonetic spellings, the voice does not offend the reader by coming at him in a kind of full-court press that Goyen, in an interview, warned against: " . . . in some writers what one gets is diction more than voice. That is *thick speech* rather than voice."

Here is Raymond Chandler, in *The Long Goodbye*, working with the narrative voice of the novel. Philip Marlowe is a private eye, hard-boiled and cynical, but at the same time idealistic, romantic, and bound by a strict code of honor. In this scene Terry Lennox is leaving Marlowe's office and his life, and the emotional clout of the scene is the friendship that has existed between the two men. Here is Chandler's first-draft version:

> He turned away and went out. I watched the door close and listened to his steps going away. After a little while, I couldn't hear them but I kept on listening. Don't ask me why. I couldn't tell you.

The first version falls flat. Here is a rewrite:

> He turned and went out. I watched the door close and listened to his steps going away. Then I couldn't hear them, but I kept on listening anyway. As if he might come back and talk me out of it, as if I hoped he would.
>
> But he didn't.

The final line here spoils the passage in its insistence. Marlowe's emotions must be underplayed. Here's the final version:

> He turned and walked across the floor and out. I watched the door close. I listened to his steps going away down the imitation marble corridor. After awhile they got faint, then they got silent. I kept on listening, anyway. What for? Did I want him to stop suddenly and turn and come back and talk

me out of the way I felt? Well, he didn't. That was the last I saw of him.

Here Chandler has found Marlowe's authentic tone. The bleak last line is charged with underplayed emotion, the detail of the imitation marble corridor gives us a note of cynicism, and Marlowe's question to himself is effectively ambiguous.

Note: the first draft and revision above are from Frank MacShane's *The Life of Raymond Chandler.*

These characterization techniques again:

1. Exposition
2. Description
3. Action
4. Gestures and mannerisms
5. Setting, tastes, interests, etc.
6. Dialog
7. Thoughts
8. Narrative voice

Most effectively, of course, these will be used in various combinations.

FOUR

Plotting

There are nine-and-sixty ways of constructing tribal lays, And every single one of them is right.

—Kipling

Plot is an arrangement of events, an ordering of raw life. It is what distinguishes fiction from a mere chronicle of events, from a news story. It is the dynamic element of fiction; a progressive development toward some significant and satisfying end; a system of compulsions toward the end, along with the negative structure of anti-storytelling techniques; the partial disclosure, temporary blockage, the further mysteries, which create the tensions of suspense, leading to the final breakthrough, when meaning is revealed and emotion felt.

Life furnishes plenty of *stories*, series of events recorded in their chronological order, but few *plots*, which must make sense emotionally and/or intellectually. A *plot* is a story plus causal relationships in a meaningful sequence.

> Let us define plot. We have defined a story as a narrative of events arranged in their time-sequence. A plot is also a narrative of events, the emphasis falling on causality. "The king died and then the queen died" is a story. "The king died and then the queen died of grief" is a plot. The time-sequence is preserved, but the sense of causality overshadows it. Or again: "The queen died, no one knew why, until it was discovered that it was through grief at the death of the king." This is a plot with a mystery in it, a form capable of high development. It suspends the time-sequence, it moves as far away from the story as its limitations will allow. Consider the death of the queen. If it is in a story we say "and then?" If it is in a plot we ask "why?" *Aspects of the Novel,* E. M. Forster

Character gives us qualities, but it is in actions—what we do—that we are happy or the reverse. . . . All human happiness and misery take the form of action.

—The Poetics, *Aristotle*

Aristotle called plot preeminent in dramatic art, and Henry James said that it is "the prime and precious thing," but it has also had its detractors. In this century we have become suspicious of plots, of their stricture and contrivance, their artifice, their arbitrary relation to time and chance. Forster complained that "all that is prearranged is false," and Gertrude Stein, of the "spurious structure of eventfulness." The argument is made that fiction, if it is to possess truth as art, cannot follow an imposed scheme, but must take character and the search for psychological truths as its subject matter.

Those who derogate plot establish character as the alternative, but a spectrum of contemporary fiction, bounded on the far right by the rigid plots and feeble characters of mass-market paperbacks, would not show literature on the far left, but instead the self-indulgent stream-of-consciousnesses published by small presses, or, for the most part, not published at all. The fine novels we remember are furnished with strong plots founded on strong characters.

The Relationship of Character to Plot

If it is plot that gives a story significance, it is character that gives literature its radiance, but Henry James rejected the distinction between the novel of character and the novel of plot: "What is character but the determination of incident? What is incident but the illustration of character?" Indeed, the best plots contrive to delineate the character brilliantly, and enable the novelist to make his characters show their paces.

Isabel Archer, of Henry James's *The Portrait of a Lady*, is introduced to her cousin, Ralph Touchett, in a characterizing action that also foreshadows the plot:

> . . . a person . . . had just made her appearance in the ample doorway some moments before he perceived her. His attention was called to her by the conduct of his dog, who had suddenly darted forward with a little volley of shrill barks in which the note of welcome, however, was more sensible than that of defiance. The person in question was a young lady, who seemed immediately to interpret the greeting of the small beast. He advanced with great rapidity and stood at her feet, looking up and barking hard; whereupon, without hesitation, she stooped and caught him in her hands, holding him face to face while he continued his quick chatter. . . .

Isabel's action in picking up the yapping dog and holding him face to face tells us that she is courageous but perhaps foolhardy, that she is eager for what life holds for her but overly trusting of the motives of others. It is these character traits that are to interest Ralph Touchett, and the reader, in following Isabel's European career, with its richness of experience and its tragedies, that will make her the lady of consequence of the title; and it is these traits that will determine the course of her career and the plot of the novel.

And here is Emma Rouault courted by Charles Bovary in Flaubert's *Madame Bovary*:

> After the fashion of country folk she asked him to have something to drink. He said no; she insisted, and at last laughingly offered to have a glass of liqueur with him. So she went to fetch a bottle of curacao from the cupboard, reached down two small glasses, filled one to the brim, poured scarcely anything into the other, and, having clinked glasses, carried hers to her mouth. As it was almost empty she bent back to drink, her head thrown back, her lips pouting, her neck straining. She laughed at getting none of it, while with the tip of her tongue passing between her small teeth she licked drop by drop the bottom of the glass.

What is shown us here is Emma's character and how it will fuel the plot. She is forward for a country girl, daring in challenging Charles to drink with her, and she goes to sensual and even unattractive lengths to drain her glass, which, by extension, can be seen as her life. Not so much is to be found in her glass as there is in Isabel's, but what is there Emma will lick drop by drop. Nor will she go on laughing at getting none of it, as the contents of the glass turn into the poison that ends her life.

There are three necessary elements in a story—exposition, development, and drama. Exposition we may illustrate as "John Fortescue was a solicitor in the little town of X"; development as "One day Mrs. Fortescue told him she was about to leave him for another man"; and drama as "You will do nothing of the kind," he said.
—The Lonely Voice
Frank O'Connor

Internal and External Plots

Nineteenth-century reading audiences began to turn away from the highly contrived plots of the British novelists, plots that promised more than they could deliver, and that preached or moralized, as in much of Dickens. The Russians, with their character-oriented plots, became popular—Tolstoy and Dostoyevsky, and Chekhov in the short story. George Eliot is considered a major revisionist of the then-existing English novel because of her *internalization* of the action. Henry James identified the center of the novel as the unfolding of a consciousness, and thus the conventional story of external events became subordinate to the psychological, internal one.

Contemporary fiction places much of the action inside characters' minds, and often there will be two plots, an external one of action and an internal one of understanding. Modern plotting thus searches for revelation as well as resolution, and for secular epiphanies—moments of illumination like lightning flashes that reveal character and meaning. An effective form of the inside-and-outside plot is that of a man of action viewed by a narrator who is a contemplative man, as in *The Great Gatsby* or *All the King's Men*, in which the plot of action follows the career of Jay Gatsby or Willie Stark, but the plot of inner understanding bears upon Nick Carraway or Jack Burden.

Ray Bradbury says of characterization, "Give him a compulsion and turn him loose!" Ambition, as the force that drives the protagonist and the plot, provides a typical novelistic theme. The ambitious heroes of nineteenth-century novels, such as those of Balzac, have been called "desiring machines." Their female counterparts, from Richardson's Clarissa to Virginia Woolf's, possess the inner drive to assert their selfhood in resistance to the domination of the male world.

A strongly motivated need or desire sets in motion actions and revelations that return to dramatically affect a character, resulting in the final cry from Henry James's *The Wings of the Dove*: "We will never again be as we were!" The plot has worked from disorder to order, from an unstable situation to one of at least temporary rest, to success or renunciation.

The best fiction has a line of compulsion as strong as a hawser running through it. The reader is compelled because the characters are compelled, each equipped with a *through-line*, an actor's term for what he *wants* overall; what he *wants* in a particular scene. These through-lines are the strands of the hawser, but, complicating the figure, they run at cross-purposes with each other and with circumstances, creating conflict and oppositions. To extend Forster's royal example of story and plot, the ghost of the dead king charges his son, the prince, with avenging murder most foul. This sets a compulsion and puts the prince into conflict with his mother and his uncle. In *The Wizard of Oz*, Dorothy wants to return to Kansas, the Tin Woodsman wants a heart, and the Scarecrow, a brain. In opposition, the Wicked Witch wants the ruby slippers Dorothy acquired when her descending house mashed the colleague of the Wicked Witch, and which are Dorothy's ticket home.

Plot Diagrams

The plot opens with a situation; the characters' relationships, as well as their compulsions and the oppositions, are established; and the author sets the *closure*, the limitation of the arena and the relationships. Most literally this is the Grand Hotel that houses the characters, or the English Country House that the murder suspects are visiting; as Henry James puts it: "Really, universally, relations stop nowhere, and the exquisite problem of the artist is eternally but to draw, by a geometry of his own, the circle within which they shall happily *appear* to do so."

The characters are in conflict with each other or with some outside force. The conflicts heighten and intensify in what is called the *complication* or *rising action* to a point of overload or *crisis*. Out of the crisis springs the *showdown action*, and out of the showdown, the *resolution*, where old relationships and patterns are broken and new ones revealed.

A figure known as the Freitag Pyramid, a plot diagram devised by Gustav Freitag, a student of the five-act German dramas of his day, purports to be universal. It takes the form of an isoceles triangle, rising from Exposition through Complication to Crisis, and then descending through Falling Action to Resolution. Its neat triangular shape suggests that the Crisis comes at the precise center of the action.

A more accurate depiction might be as follows·

CLIMAX
Revelation
Recognition
(Crisis)

COMPLICATION
Deepening of oppositions
Heightening of conflicts
Intensification of tension
(The plot thickens)

DENOUEMENT
Reappraisal
Showdown

SITUATION
Relationships
Compulsions
Oppositions
Conflict
(Instability)

RESOLUTION
(Stability
with change)

The Three-Act Structure of the Plot

Beginning, middle, and end, or situation, complication, and resolution, can then be thought of as a three-act structure. In Hemingway's *The Sun Also Rises*, for instance, the text is actually divided into three Books like Acts. Book One sets up the situation and the relationships, and ends with Brett, who is to marry Mike, telling her old lover, Jake, that she will never see him again. Book Two takes the cast of characters to the fiesta at Pamplona, where their lives are intertwined and complicated, and ends with Brett running away with the young bullfighter, Romero, after his triumph in the bull ring. Book Three has Jake rescuing Brett from a hotel in Madrid. She has sent the young Romero away, proud of herself for not being "that kind of bitch," and asserting that she and Jake could have been happy together if it had not been for his war wound. To which he replies, "Isn't it pretty to think so."

In the three-act structure, the first and second act curtains mark the major reversal/recognitions of the plot. The first-act curtain denotes the end of the movement that establishes the characters and the situation, galvanizing or reversing it. The second-act curtain performs the same function at the climax of the movement of complication and confrontation, in preparation for the final-act movement of resolution. In opera, the second-act climax is often an *avalanche curtain*, which thunders down on the sustained high C of the tenor's great aria at the opera's most dramatic moment.

At the first-act curtain of *The Sun Also Rises*, Brett decides to change the destructive course of her life. The second-act curtain is a reversal of this, for she is endangering the career of the young matador by eloping with him.

Maguffin is a term employed by the film director Alfred Hitchcock for the sought-after object that is often central to suspense films and novels. The *maguffin* is something precious or potentially dangerous, for the possession of which forces are contending, for instance the black bird in *The Maltese Falcon*. The term comes from an English joke. Two men are traveling on a train in Scotland. One asks the other what the oddly-shaped package on the luggage rack might be. "That's a MacGuffin," the other said. "What's a MacGuffin?" the first asked. "It's a device for trapping lions in the Scottish Highlands," the second said. "But there aren't any lions in the Highlands," the first said. "Well, then," the second said, "I guess that's no MacGuffin."

A reversal would be the *maguffin*'s being snatched away from

Tragedy is an imitation of an action that is complete, and whole, and of a certain magnitude. . . . A whole is that which has a beginning, a middle, and an end. A beginning is that which does not follow anything by causal necessity, but after which something naturally is or comes to be. An end, on the contrary, is that which itself naturally follows some other thing, either by necessity, or as a rule, but has nothing following it. A middle is that which follows something as some other thing follows it. A well-constructed plot, therefore, must neither begin nor end at haphazard, but conform to these principles.

Plots are either Simple or Complex, for the actions in real life, of which plots are an imitation, obviously show a similar distinction. An action which is one and continuous in the sense above defined, I call Simple, when the change in fortune takes place without Reversal of the Situation and without Recognition.

A Complex action is one in which the change is accompanied by such Reversal, or Recognition, or by both. These last should arise from the internal structure of the plot, so that what follows should be the necessary or probable result of the preceding action. . . . Reversal of the Situation is a change by which the action veers round to its opposite, subject always to the rules of probability and necessity.

Thus in the Oedipus, *the messenger comes to cheer Oedipus and free him from his alarms about his mother, but by revealing who he is, he produces the opposite effect. Again in the* Lynceus, *Lynceus is being led away to his death, and Danaus goes with him, meaning to slay him; but the outcome of the action is that Danaus is killed and Lynceus saved. Recognition, as the name indicates, is a change from ignorance to knowledge, producing love or hate between the persons destined by the poet for good or bad fortune. The best form of recognition is the Reversal of the Situation, as in the* Oedipus. *There are indeed other forms. Even inanimate things of the most trivial kind may sometimes be the objects of recognition.*

—The Poetics, *Aristotle*

the possessive force by the other, and a recognition the revelation that the black bird is not made of gold and jewels, as advertised, but of lead.

Instead of the expected job offer, the mailman delivers a summons from the draft board. The concert that had been counted upon to launch the career of a young pianist, instead is such a debacle that he is ruined. The relief column approaching with a skirl of bagpipes and a flick of kilts is revealed to be not the Black Watch but mutineers who have appropriated the arms, pipes, and uniforms of the slaughtered Scots.

A three-act structure built upon two reversals can be very useful in plotting a film script or a short novel, and can certainly be extended. Fitzgerald, for instance, devised a five-act structure for his plan of *The Last Tycoon*. The format does not work so well in outlining a sprawling, episodic novel, where the author plots by the seat of his pants, as it does for a more classical structure.

Plot Progression

Plot progresses in a series of reversals and recognitions, breakthroughs and catastrophes, an inch gained here and the rug pulled out there. In a long novel, the rising line of tension is jagged with peaks and valleys in a rhythm that is the more effective because it is organic and not mechanical. Strands of tension hold the long line taut, the longest strands those of what-will-happen overall, short and intermediate strands of what-will-happen in Book I or II, Chapter 3 or 4, and in particular scenes. Chapters are hooked together so that the reader is compelled to discover the what-will-happen in the next one. If a child is lost in chapter 3, which ends with the line, "That night they dragged the river," the reader is bound to delve into Chapter 4 in order to discover what was found in the river, and if Chapter 4 ends with the arrest of the grammar school janitor, we will read on to Chapter 5.

The reader must be kept compelled. The long lines, the "long-term promises" are foreshadowings, promises made and kept, incompletions that imply a later completion, questions that will be eventually answered, dangers proceeding to safety or disaster, guns revealed with the implication that they will later be put to use, the looming empty place at the table that must be finally filled. They are series of parallels, contrasts, and revelations like running gags which imply a continuing pattern; the hows, whats, and whys continually posed and continually satisfied.

Suspense and Time

Time, of course, is an unfailingly effective means of creating suspense, and is a staple of suspense films and mystery novels, in which the time-duration of the piece is relatively short. Even so arbitrary a device as heading each chapter with a notation of the day, hour, and minute can create a spurious tension. Any stricture on the amount of time available to a given task, with a penalty for failure to meet the deadline, can set up the equation. If George does not succeed in climbing the mountain before nightfall, the Nazis will burn his wife at the stake. If Maggie-the-Cat in *Cat on a Hot Tin Roof* does not produce an heir before Big Daddy dies of cancer, the No-neck Monsters will inherit the plantation. There are longer-line and more subtle time crunches as well. Novels concerned with young people on summer vacations are limited by the beginning of the next school term, as are novels about academics on sabbaticals in Europe.

(a) A predominance of long-term promises, combined with a lack of well-developed "minor forms," will cause a reader to skip. Its effect is to make him impatient to discover "how things come out."

(b) A predominance of shorter promises and "minor forms" coupled with an insufficiency of long lines, will cause the reader to focus too much interest on the immediate scene. This is a characteristic fault of short-story writers who invade the novel. Its effects may be seen in the kind of book the reader does not finish.

—Primer of the Novel, *Vincent McHugh*

Creating Tension: Making Promises to the Reader

A tension line of the plot can be spoken of as a "gun on the wall," from Chekhov's dictum that a gun shown hanging on the wall in Act I must be discharged in Act III, for that expectation has been established. The gun, of course, can be many things other than a firearm. The messenger sent for news in *Oedipus Rex* will return with news, all right, but not the news that has been anticipated. Guns may be hung on the wall even before Act I, in retrospective action. Many of Ross MacDonald's plots are *Oedipal*, a term that refers not to a Freudian or sexual aspect, but to the messenger out of the past whose news causes a reversal and agonizing reappraisal—the sins of the parents visited upon their children, in MacDonald's use of it.

Fiction is a process of change, and the heart of interior change is discovery or recognition, the revelation of something not comprehended before. The long-lost father is recognized by his scarred foot, the dead woman identified by the concentration-camp number tattooed inside her wrist. Such a moment can be an epiphany: For instance, in *The Portrait of a Lady*, Isabel Archer's realization of the past relationship between her husband and Mme. Merle upon seeing them together in an informal posture; or, in *The Ambassadors*, Lambert Strether's revelation when he observes Chad and Mme. de Vionnet boating on the river. Such epiphanies, recognitions, and reappraisals continue on a rising line of tension to the final crisis, where the ultimate understanding and transformation—or the implication of it—takes place.

Something memorable has happened. Something worth changing has changed.

The Two-Shoe Contract

Fiction is always promising something, and suspense is created by promises made and kept, which make up the lowest common denominator of a readable book, "a page-turner," "a good read," "I couldn't put it down." In the best fiction, the promises are subtly made, for anything that the reader understands is interestingly incomplete will suggest a contract.

Another way of looking at these authorial promises may be called the "Two-shoe Contract." If one shoe drops from the man disrobing for the night in the upstairs bedroom, the second must follow. The listener experiences suspense waiting for that second shoe to drop. The first shoe is the foreshadowing, the second, the climax. The earthquake that destroys Los Angeles in the last chapter of the novel must have been presaged by warning tremors, by prophecies or publicized cycles, or by the hysterical behavior of the neighborhood cats. If the event occurs without foreshadowing, the plotting is inadequate in that it will seem to turn at the author's convenience rather than by some less arbitrary law.

Therefore, for every climactic second shoe that falls, its fellow must have been heard to drop earlier. And every first shoe that falls is a promise by the author of a second still to come.

Promises and suspense are generated in this first view of Jean Templer in Anthony Powell's *A Question of Upbringing*. A shoe has dropped:

> —a girl of about sixteen or seventeen, evidently Peter's unmarried sister, Jean, was closing the sliding doors. Fair, not strikingly pretty, with long legs and short, untidy hair, she remained without moving, intently watching us, as Peter shut off the engine and we got out of the car. Like her legs, her face was thin and attenuated, the whole appearance giving the effect of a much simplified—and somewhat self-conscious—arrangement of lines and planes, such as might be found in an Old Master drawing, Flemish or German perhaps, depicting some young and virginal saint; the racquet, held awkwardly at an angle to her body, suggesting at the same time an obscure implement associated with martyrdom. The expression of her face, although sad and a trifle ironical, was not altogether in keeping with this air of belonging to another

> and better world. I felt suddenly uneasy, and also interested: a desire to be with her, and at the same time, an almost paralyzing disquiet in her presence.

Promised here is an involvement of Nick Jenkins with this girl, with her implication of virginity and martyrdom. Or perhaps this first sense of her is mistaken, and she will prove to be just the opposite. Thus the author's intentions for Jean Templer, and Nick's connection with her, become a line of suspense.

Jane Austen's *Emma* begins:

> Emma Woodhouse, handsome, clever and rich, with a comfortable home and happy disposition, seemed to unite some of the best blessings of existence: and had lived nearly twenty-one years in the world with very little to distress or vex her—

The word *seemed* here makes a promise that sets up the whole book and will take four hundred pages to resolve. We can be assured of events coming that will distress and vex Emma Woodhouse.

Thomas Keneally's "faction" novel *Schindler's List* begins:

> In Poland's deepest autumn, a tall young man in an expensive overcoat, double-breasted dinner jacket beneath it and—in the lapel of the dinner jacket—a large ornamental gold-on-black-enamel *Hakenkreuz* (swastika) emerged from a fashionable apartment building in Straszewskiego Street, on the edge of the ancient center of Cracow, and saw his chauffeur waiting with fuming breath by the open door of an immense and, even in this blackened world, lustrous Adler limousine.
>
> "Watch the pavement, Herr Schindler," said the chauffeur. "It's as icy as a widow's heart."

In this brief scene we are given the setting, Cracow during the German occupation, and are introduced to a wealthy and influential young man who is a member of the Nazi party. He is making his way across very treacherous, thin ice. This is in fact the story in a nutshell, for Oskar Schindler, who is a party member and a factory operator, is dedicated to saving the lives of the Jews in his employ, and the part he plays is an exceedingly dangerous one.

In a mystery novel, the contracts will have to do with the revelation of facts, but in more serious fiction, the focus is upon character and motivation. In *The Ambassadors*, Lambert Strether observes Chad's apartment in Paris, with its fine, continuous balcony, "high, broad, clear . . . admirably built . . . ornament as positive as it was discreet . . . the complexion of the stone, a cold, fair gray, warmed and polished a little by life. . . ." The contract here is that what has been observed of Chad's home will reflect Chad himself, in likeness or contrast, and suspense is engendered as to the character, and the actions in Paris, of the occupant of the apartment, who is the subject of Strether's mission to Paris, and whom the reader has not yet been permitted to meet.

The protagonist of a projected novel, Zack, has just graduated from Berkeley and arrived at his parents' house to bid them good-bye before heading for New York. There he will spend some time trying to find himself while residing with a young woman, Helen, and her husband, friends of his father. At home his father demands the traditional bout of arm-wrestling, at which he regularly proves his superiority. Zack thinks he might win this time, but his father overpowers him as usual. The next day Zack begins his drive to New York, picking up a girl hitchhiker with whom he has an affair. They part in New York when he moves in with Helen and her husband. It is clear that he lusts for Helen.

The above outline of the action so far is more story than plot. There is no motivation, and the action is episodic. Because Zack has no compulsion, the trip east lacks tension. However, if the traditional arm-wrestle has aroused more competitiveness in Zack than usual, and he loses only because he is not prepared for the consequences of defeating his father; the situation takes on some torque. The father senses a near defeat, and as a consequence gets drunk and brags of his sexual conquests. Zack is stunned to learn that Helen was at one time his father's mistress. Zack has had some sexual successes of his own, and decides that here at last is a game at which he can beat his father. He sets out for New York with the compulsion to seduce Helen. Thus his lust is moved up earlier in the novel and reinforced with a stronger motivation. Now he is *compelled* to New York, where, in his obsession with a victory over his father, he loses sight of the fact that Eve, the hitchhiker, is someone who loves *him*, etc. The arm-wrestling has foreshadowed another combat still to come. A contract has been set up.

Foreshadowing and Suspense

Ideally in fiction, every episode prefigures something still to come. In Borges's words: "every detail is an omen and a cause."

Suspense is created by foreshadowing. The palmist blanches

when she examines the lifeline of the hero. It is revealed that the snakebite kit is missing from the glove compartment of the truck in which the boys are setting out on a rattlesnake hunt. More subtly, an early death is foretold in the famous first paragraph of Hemingway's *A Farewell to Arms*: "The leaves fell early that year."

Suspense is maintained by the principle of withholding the revelation, doling out bits of information, gradual unraveling. Who is the mysterious figure with the scarred face that on dark nights gazes from the shadows of the street at Mary's upstairs window? It is revealed that Mary never married, later that she never married because the one man she ever loved left her; later that the lover was killed in the war, later still that he is assumed to have died in the fire that consumed his airplane; later still that. . . .

Surprise and Suspense

Good fiction depends more upon suspense than surprise, but suspense and surprise may work in a complementary way, as in the beginning of *Great Expectations*. The opening surprise has Pip seized in the graveyard by the convict Magwitch. He is threatened (suspense) if he does not produce a file and food. He steals the Christmas pie. The suspense-contract with Magwitch is satisfied (although not the long-term contract that, if Magwitch has appeared once, he will reappear), but now there is the suspense that Pip's theft of the pie will be revealed. Pip flees this revelation, only to be surprised at the door by the squad of soldiers, etc.

Oppositions must be concrete and specific. A Jean Valjean in flight in *Les Misérables* requires a flesh-and-blood Javert in pursuit, not merely a vague force of societal disapproval or the police in general. The conflict of right and wrong, white hats against black hats, may be too simplistic to be compelling. Right against right generates more power. One antagonist may be more right than the other, but the other's imperatives should have some validity.

Tragedy is an imitation not only of a complete action, but of events inspiring fear and pity. Such an effect is best produced when the events come on us by surprise; and the effect is heightened when, at the same time, they follow as cause and effect. The tragic wonder will then be greater than if they happened of themselves or by accident; for even coincidences are most striking when they have an air of design."

—The Poetics, *Aristotle*

Listening to the Characters

Very often the novelist will plot with a "given" ending in mind, the ending itself having been the germ. Indeed, often plotting is done backwards from the ending, reknitting the circumstances that must have led to that ending, back to the situation before it, and the one before that, etc. But the plotter should also listen to the demands of his characters, who, as they begin to come to life, may insist upon a different fate than the givens seem to require. For through the characters the "unexpected inevitable," the resolution that is at the same time exactly right and surprising, may be discovered.

Truth Over Facts

If the novel stems from actual events, the writer tries not to be bound by the circumstances of those events. Truth is more important than facts, and fiction deals with what *should* have happened rather than what *did* happen. The novelist will take the haphazard and disconnected items of real life and organize them into an orderly sequence to produce a significant whole. Plot reassures the reader of order in a chaotic world. If the inner connections are missing in life, and they usually are, art must supply them.

Any novelist who has based work upon historical material knows the difficulty of finding motivations for the "real" characters. In real life, motivations are not demanded. A reader of history might accept the notion that Napoleon lost the Battle of Waterloo because of an attack of hemorrhoids, but a reader of fiction would not. Nevertheless, the *facts*, what really happened, have an iron rigidity from which it is often difficult for the writer to break away.

The motivations of his characters will take precedence over the actualities, as does the necessity of constructing a meaningful whole. Historical truths are suspect anyway, for as the same Corsican said: "What is history but fiction agreed upon?"

Beginning the Plot

Where to begin? A rule of thumb is to start as close to the climax as will allow for bringing in all the pertinent information. A long novel, such as one of James Michener's, may begin with the tectonic forces that formed the state of Colorado, in which the action will take place; another with the omens and lightning storms accompanying the birth of the hero-to-be. Many novels begin with journeys, with the action to start at the conclusion of the travel; often westerns begin with a strange gunman riding into a frontier town. Something is bound to happen upon his arrival. A beginning is often the moment when an unstable situation receives the last straw that will make it intolerable, or when some freighted occurrence disturbs a seemingly stable balance. Two questions must be answered: why is this happening at all (general motivation) and why is this happening *now* (specific motivation)?

A beginning scene is often repeated at the ending, but with a changed element or elements. The plot thus reminds us of what has been changed. My novel *Apaches* opens with Lt. Cutler and his Apache scouts in pursuit of hostiles who have escaped from a reservation, encountering a pair of prospectors who become insane with fear, thinking that they are in the hands of Apache murderers. At the end of the novel, the scene is repeated, the frame and figures in the photograph are the same, but implications altered. The hostile band has been slaughtered, and Cutler is bidding farewell to his scouts on a point of land overlooking the new railroad pushing west. A pair of railroad workers wave a greeting as they pass on a handcar. Time and circumstances have changed.

The Double Plot

In the *double plot*, a structure often used in Elizabethan drama, the main plot features noble characters meant to be the objects of the audience's sympathies and identification, and the subplot, usually comic, involves characters of a lower social order. The two plots illustrate different aspects of the same theme. John Fowles used this structural device in *The French Lieutenant's Woman*. Raymond Chandler used a different form of it, modeled on many of Dicken's plots, and the BBC miniseries *Upstairs, Downstairs* also used it. A high-life plot is alternated with a low-life plot, and a part of the suspense is the consciousness that these two must come together in a revelation of connection at the end.

In *Wuthering Heights*, the main plot, that of Heathcliff, Catherine, and Edgar is tragic, while that of the second generation's Cathy, Linton, and Hareton is a happy one. In *War and Peace*, the peace plot of Pierre, Natasha, and Andrey is alternated with the war plot of historical figures and events. This is the method of most historical novels, the historical story carried along by historical personages, and the plot of fictional characters laid against that backdrop.

The Hourglass Plot

The hourglass is also the design of the plot of Henry James's *The Ambassadors*, in which Strether's and Chad's stories converge, cross, and separate in the same pattern as those of Paphnuce and Thais.

The Episodic Plot

Of all plots, the episodic is the worst, says Aristotle. If events do not arise from the central action of the plot, there is no unity of action, and the plot is episodic. The causal relationship is lost. Picaresque novels such as *Don Quixote, Anthony Adverse,* and

Thais, *by Anatole France, is in the shape of an hour glass. There are two chief characters, Paphnuce the ascetic, Thais the courtesan.*

Paphnuce lives in the desert, he is saved and happy when the book starts. Thais lives a life of sin in Alexandria, and it is his duty to save her. In the central scene of the book they approach, he succeeds; she goes into a monastery and gains salvation, because she has met him, but he, because he has met her, is damned. The two characters converge, cross, and recede with mathematical precision, and part of the pleasure we get from the book is due to this. . . .

—Aspects of the Novel, *E. M. Forster*

*We can well remember how keenly we wondered, while its (*Middlemarch*'s) early chapters unfolded themselves, what turn of form the story would take—that of an organized, molded, balanced composition, gratifying the reader with a sense of design and construction, or a mere chain of episodes broken into accidental lengths and unconscious of the influence of a plan. We expected the actual result, but—we hoped for the other. If it had come we should have had the pleasure of reading what certainly would have seemed to be . . . the first of English novels. But that pleasure has still to hover between prospect and retrospect.* Middlemarch *is a treasure-house of detail, but it is an indifferent work.*

—On Middlemarch, *Henry James*

The Adventures of Augie March are the sequential adventures of a central character and are usually comic in tone. They are episodic in that each adventure tends to be complete in itself. Many great novels are partially episodic—*War and Peace, Sons and Lovers, The Catcher in the Rye*—unified by character and theme; those episodes that are not bound into the central action are useful in elucidating the characters; providing variety, interest, and humor; and implementing suspense by delaying the culmination of actions.

Harold Weston in his *Form in Literature* ventures to give Rules for the Picaresque:

1. The Hero has a *General Intention* which is capable of expansion or contraction, to admit every kind of experience, or to admit one kind of experience only.
2. Whether the *General Intention* (or *Hope*) is contracted or expanded, the adventures must be bound by it, and no adventure should be admitted which does not lead to the achievement of this *General Intention*.
3. The adventures are not necessarily bound, the one to the other, by a chain of causation.
4. The unit of the Picaresque form is the adventure, and not a separate unit in the adventure.
5. The units may be either positive or negative.

If, according to Kipling, there are nine and sixty ways of constructing tribal lays, there may be more ways than that of writing a novel. Some years ago The Viking Press received a plotless mass of manuscript by a writer of such promise, that, acting in the role of Maxwell Perkins with Thomas Wolfe, the editors dredged out of the manuscript a search-for-the-father, Telemachus and Ulysses plot, and appliqued it into the story of a cross-country car trip. Jack Kerouac's *On the Road* became a minor American classic. A similar operation was performed upon Peter Benchley's *Jaws*, which became a major American bestseller.

Plot and Myth

Myth is often employed as the framework of plot, as in James Joyce's *Ulysses*, John Barth's *Giles Goat-Boy*, MacDonald Harris's *Bull Fire*, Frank Herbert's *Dune* and its sequels, Tolkein's *The Lord of the Rings*, and my own *The Coming of the Kid*. Harry Brown's *The Stars in Their Courses* employs *The Iliad* as the structure of a Western, his characters' names beginning with the same letter as those of their mythological counterparts. In Nikos Kazantzakis's *The Greek Passion*, the characters of a passion play are forced by circumstance into playing their actual roles in Christ's Passion. What Joseph Campbell calls the "monomyth"—a word out of *Finnegan's Wake*—and John Barth the "Master Plan," is employed by writers who may be unaware that they have built their plots upon elements of the Oedipus myth, or of Little Red Riding Hood and her wolf, on Goldilocks, Cinderella, Orpheus, or Daedalus and Icarus.

The long journey of trials and confrontations with monsters, nymphs, and giants, that finally circles back to self-discovery, is the route of Ulysses, but also of James Joyce's Leopold Bloom, Hesse's Siddhartha, and Maugham's Larry Darrell, of *The Razor's Edge*.

My novel *Warlock* is based upon events that took place in the actual Arizona town of Tombstone in the 1880s, and its master gunman, Blaisedell, closely resembles Marshal Wyatt Earp of that place. In endeavoring to endow Blaisedell with Heroic proportions, I turned to Lord Raglan's famous treatise, *The Hero*. Lord Raglan's prescription for a hero follows:

1. The hero's mother is a royal virgin;
2. His father is a king and
3. Often a near relative of his mother, but
4. The circumstances of his conception are unusual, and
5. He is also reputed to be the son of a god.
6. At birth an attempt is made on his life, usually by his father or his maternal grandfather, but
7. He is spirited away, and
8. Reared by foster parents in a far country.
9. We are told nothing of his childhood, but
10. On reaching manhood he returns or goes to his future kingdom.
11. After a victory over the king and/or a giant, dragon, or wild beast,
12. He marries a princess, often the daughter of his predecessor, and (at about age thirty-four or thirty-five)
13. Becomes king.
14. For a time he reigns uneventfully, and
15. Prescribes laws, but
16. He later loses favor with the gods and/or his subjects and
17. Is driven from the throne or city, after which
18. He meets with a mysterious death,

19. Often at the top of a hill.
20. His children, if any, do not succeed him.
21. His body is not buried, but nevertheless
22. He has one or more holy tombs.

When you add up scores from this list, Oedipus of course does best, with twenty-one out of twenty-two. Others, however, do surprisingly well: Jesus, David, King Arthur, Robin Hood, Billy the Kid, Butch Cassidy.

Joseph Campbell, in *The Hero with a Thousand Faces*, identifies the mythological journey of a Hero as a rite of passage: Separation—Initiation—Return. This constitutes what he calls the Monomyth. Campbell explains, as follows:

> The mythological hero, setting forth from his commonday hut or castle, is lured, carried away, or else voluntarily proceeds, to the threshold of adventure. There he encounters a shadow presence that guards the passage. The hero may defeat or conciliate this power and go alive into the kingdom of the dark (brother-battle, dragon-battle; offering, charm), or be slain by the opponent and descend in death (dismemberment, crucifixion). Beyond the threshold, then, the hero journeys through a world of unfamiliar yet strangely intimate forces, some of which severely threaten him (tests), some of which give magical aid (helpers). When he arrives at the nadir of the mythological round, he undergoes a supreme ordeal and gains his reward. The triumph may be represented as the hero's sexual union with the goddess-mother of the world (sacred marriage), his recognition by the father-creator (father atonement), his own divinization (apotheosis), or again—if the powers have remained unfriendly to him—his theft of the boon he came to gain (bride-theft, fire-theft); intrinsically it is an expansion of consciousness and therewith of being (illumination, transfiguration, freedom). The final work is that of the return. If the powers have blessed the hero, he now sets forth under their protection (emissary); if not, he flees and is pursued (transformation flight, obstacle flight). At the return threshold the transcendental powers must remain behind; the hero re-emerges from the kingdom of dread (return, resurrection). The boon that he brings restores the world (elixir).

Often essential to the Hero's triumph are his helpers, each of whom may be adept at one specific power which the Hero can call upon at the appropriate moment. Thus Lancelot is a more powerful fighter than King Arthur himself, and each of Robin Hood's band has his individual specialties. So do Doc Savage's assistants, and the Scarecrow, the Tin Woodsman, and the Cowardly Lion of Dorothy's adventure in Oz, and Luke Skywalker's helpers in George Lucas's *Star Wars.*

Lucas has in fact acknowledged his debt to Joseph Campbell's monomyth in plotting the trilogy. *Star Wars* also abounds in Jungian archetypes. Han Solo is Luke's shadow-figure, and princess Leia is a classic anima. Indeed, Luke's first glimpse of her is as a shimmering dream-figure. Obi-Wan-Kenobi is at least semi-divine, whose wisdom comes from "The Force." By his departure, not into death, but apotheosis, Luke acquires the light-sword, confronts and comes to terms with the archetypes, and triumphs through his faith in The Force.

The literature of mythology can be very exciting to the novelist. As Campbell says, " . . . the symbols of mythology . . . are spontaneous productions of the psyche, and each bears within it, undamaged, the germ power of its source."

Jung's *Man and His Symbols,* Otto Rank's *Myth of the Birth of the Hero,* Erich Neumann's *The Great Mother,* Jessie L. Weston's *From Ritual to Romance,* and Robert Graves's *The White Goddess* can be tonic to the writer's imagination.

What Works

All editors and teachers of writing are familiar with beginner novels that start out bravely and even brilliantly, only to peter out in disappointment because the plot was too frail, the armature insufficient to support book-length. On the other hand, fiction can be cheapened by the heaping-on of plot. A novel may possess more verisimilitude if it contains some disorder, and it may be better to sacrifice formal niceties of structure in order to gain the quality of lifelikeness we look for in serious fiction.

Many fine novels have found the means to succeed despite inadequacies in plotting, through strengths of vitality, vivid writing, fresh perceptions, vivid settings, original characters and fascinating relationships, the I-couldn't-put-it-downness achieved by sheer authorial brilliance rather than craftsmanlike mechanics. The maker-of-rules for fiction must fall back on the global disclaimer, that what works, works.

Questions to Address in Plotting

1. What are the compulsions?
2. What are the obstacles?
3. Is the protagonist active? That is, does he make things happen, or is he one to whom things happen?
4. Is there a time-crunch?
5. Is there a need for a maguffin?
6. Is the ending inevitable and surprising?

PART TWO

Other Elements of Fiction

ONE

Style

Style is the man himself, says Buffon, and indeed a writer's style is a very personal matter. I would use only the tenderest of terms in criticizing a student's style, for when you criticize someone's style you are criticizing the person. Nevertheless, a writer should not consider that his prose style cannot be improved upon.

It was Flaubert's rule that there was always *le mot juste*, the correct word:

> Whatever one wishes to say, there is one noun only by which to express it, one verb only to give it life, one adjective only which will describe it. One must search until one has discovered them, this noun, this verb, this adjective, and never rest content with approximations, never resort to trickery, however happy, or to vulgarisms, in order to dodge the difficulty. Preface to *Pierre et Jean*, de Maupassant quoting Flaubert.

On the other hand, William Faulkner said that a writer who has a lot to say—"a great deal pushing to get out"—hasn't time to worry about style; this from an American master with one of the most gnarled, idiosyncratic, and beguiling styles of the era. Saul Bellow contends that a writer's style should enable him to express himself easily, naturally, and copiously, in a form that frees his mind and energies.

Evelyn Waugh, however, has this to say:

> Properly understood, style is not a seductive decoration added to a functional structure; it is of the essence of the work of art. The necessary elements of style are lucidity, elegance, and individuality. . . .

Simplicity vs. Elegance

American writers of the twentieth century would flinch at Waugh's requirement of "elegance." Hemingway said that "Prose is architecture, not interior decoration." He had been taught by Ezra Pound to "distrust adjectives as I would later learn to distrust certain people in certain situations. . . ." Since Hemingway, the short, declarative sentence, whose elegance is that of simplicity, has been the model. Melville's "Call me Ishmael" and, from the Bible, "Jesus wept" are held to the exemplary.

Perhaps an overly simplistic style gets in the reader's way by making her overly aware of the author in his limitations and thus of the fact that she is reading a work of the imagination instead of experiencing it; so, too, an overly elegant style may also block the reader's voluntary suspension of disbelief. The argument can be made that the best style is one that appears to be no style at all, and perhaps the writer's true style begins to emerge when he makes no deliberate effort to produce one.

At the beginning of their careers many writers have a need to overwrite. They choose carefully turned-out phrases; they want to impress their readers with their large vocabularies. By the excesses of their language, these young men and women try to hide their sense of inexperience. With maturity the writer becomes more secure in his ideas. He finds his real tone and develops a simple and effective style.

—Jorge Luis Borges

The Elements of Style

A writer's style is more than his diction—word choice—or his rhetoric—his intention to persuade; it is his use of sentence rhythms, short, long, simple, complex, or of compound sentences connected by *ands* that suggest the diction of the King James Bible. Style is reflected in the use and originality of metaphors, the form of the conditional, or the use of the present tense instead of the more conventional past; in differences of punctuation, the use of dashes, parentheses, and exclamation marks; in the use of dashes rather than quotation marks to set off dialog; in the use of italics, the upper case, even semicolons; in fact, style emerges from all the author's quirks and mannerisms, weaknesses and strengths.

Hemingway's simple declarative sentences are a matter of style. So are Henry James's long, intricate, finely balanced ones with the stinger in the tail, and Proust's even longer ones, pages long, each a miracle of structure and balance. So are Faulkner's untidy but powerful sentences with their negative dependent qualifying clauses set in parallel construction:

> "It was not because of the ratted dreadlocks of her ginger-colored hair, nor because of her pig-like eyes, one brown, one blue, both red-rimmed, nor yet because of the fetor of her

sweat, acrid and pervasive as industrial strength borax, but because of her feet, stained black from treading the ink out of octopus carcasses, that he felt a mild repugnance."

Richard Ford's cramming elaborate stage directions into his dialogs, as seen on page 104 is an element of his style, as is P. D. James's quirk of devoting a paragraph to a speech-tag, which lends a portentousness to her characters' lines, especially those of her detective:

> Dalgliesh said:
> "I see you've got what looks like a complete set of *Notable British Trials*. That must be comparatively rare."

Specification and Style

> An attractive decorator white on the walls set off several fine old pieces of furniture. An inviting fire burned in a small fireplace. In that cozy, very comfortable place the fire was throwing many-colored reflections off the leaded glass windows and sending pleasant odors of pine smoke into the small dining room. Colorful flowers showed in an attached greenhouse contrasting against the snow outside.

The writer here is making some effort to engage the reader's senses. Odor is brought in, and the reflection of the fire on the window glass is an effective detail. The passage fails on its specifics, however. "Attractive decorator white," "cosy, very comfortable space," "pleasant odors," "colorful flowers"—these are what is termed adjectival, the writer urging the reader to feel something rather than causing him to feel it by the precision of the language, the specificity of the detail, and the implications. In Noam Chomsky's *Transformational Grammar*, a "hairy" word is one that is rich in implications—evocative, specific, but with larger connotations. Thus "Ferrari" is a hairier word than a "car," and a "villa" than a "house." Not many hairs are showing here.

Moreover, who is having all these pleasant reactions to this apartment? The passage would have much more impact if someone were entering the place, admiring the eggshell tone of the walls, running a hand over the top of the walnut sideboard, with its frieze of carved fruits and cherubs, and recognizing the greenhouse flowers as azaleas, jonquils, and African violets.

Prose that presents these things so that we see and smell them, rather than just being vaguely informed, depends upon the use of concrete rather than abstract words, and the particular over the general.

1. It was raining.
2. He drew his hand inside and licked rain from his fingers.

1. The day was warm.
2. He squinted in the sun's glare and brushed the back of his hand over his damp forehead.

1. He was a big man.
2. He filled the doorway, ducking his head and shouldering through.

When to Use (and Not to Use) Modifiers

> ... he swung down onto Terrace Road and dropped quite fast through the eucalyptus and cedar, really as fast as he could go, through repetitive turns, the smells by-passing his nose to go directly into his lungs, the greenery overhead sifting and scattering shadows, the dips in the road cupping the sunlight, the banked turns unfolding his shadow, the whole road flattening out. . . .

In the above passage by Thomas McGuane, the reader's senses are roused by the device of the smells of eucalyptus and cedar by-passing the nose to go directly to the lungs, which also renders the speed, in conjunction with the understated "really as fast as he could go." There are few adverbs and adjectives, and the verbs are strong ones—*drop, by-pass, sift, scatter, cup, unfold, flatten*—used as participles that function as both verb and modifier, and carry us swooping downhill through the shifting patterns of light and shadow.

Light and shadow are also dramatically effective in this passage from D. H. Lawrence's *The Rainbow*.

> And she lifted her hands and danced again, to annul him, the light glanced on her knees as she made her slow, fine movements down the far side of the room, across the firelight. He stood away near the door in blackness of shadow, watching transfixed. And with slow, heavy movements she swayed backwards and forwards, like a full ear of corn, pale in the dusky

afternoon, threading before the firelight, dancing his non-existence, dancing herself to the Lord, to exultation.

What an evocative verb here is *threading*—"threading before the firelight," the light glancing off her knees. Again strong verbs have been used, and adverbs are unnecessary. Here are strong words also, in an action sequence from Norman Mailer's *The Naked and the Dead*.

> A machine gun lashed at him from across the river, and he ducked into his hole. In the darkness, it spat a vindictive white light like an acetylene torch, and its sound was terrifying. Croft was holding himself together by the force of his will. He pressed the trigger of his gun and it leaped and bucked under his hand. The tracers spewed wildly into the jungle on the other side of the river.

Lashed. Ducked. Spat. Leaped and bucked. Spewed. The verbs are violent because the scene is violent. The adverb *wildly*, modifying *spewed* may be unnecessary, as spewing implies wildness, but *vindictive* is effective. That is the way the white light seems to Croft, the point of view in this scene.

The following is ruined by adverbs:

> Rapidly shutting his eyes, grappling with the facts, he knew he had been hit at a city intersection. Cautiously opening one eye, the wide field remained as tangible as before. Without thinking, he sat up. Pain slid up from his left leg to his head. "Oh, God!" he whispered after he tore the black pant leg up to his knee and saw the mass of blood coating his leg in a slick glistening layer. Instinctively clutching his hands to the long wound, he futilely pressed the skin together to stop the bleeding. "Oh, God!" he repeated, glancing frantically about him. . . .

"Cautiously opening one eye" is superfluous—opening one eye implies caution—as is "instinctively clutching"—instinct is implied in the act of clutching. The initial *rapidly* is ineffective, and *frantically* would be unnecessary if a stronger verb had been employed.

Which is not to say that adverbs should be deleted from a writer's vocabulary. The judicious use of words ending in *ly* adds color and nuance to the stark action of verbs. In this passage from "The

Horse-dealer's Daughter," D. H. Lawrence makes effective use of the adverbs *floutingly* and *sumptuously*. The passage would lose much if they were deleted:

> The great draught horses swung past. They were tied head to tail, four of them, and they heaved along to where a lane branched off from the main road, planting their great hoofs floutingly in the fine black mud, swinging their great rounded haunches sumptuously, and trotting a few sudden steps as they were led into the lane, round the corner.

Lawrence uses fine adverbs and many adjectives, but each of them tells us something, intensifying the picture rather than blurring it; defining, and qualifying.

Often, however, modifiers preceding a noun will weaken it rather than make it more specific, and writers do well to remember Voltaire's admonition: "The adjective is the enemy of the noun."

In the following passage, each noun and verb has its modifier, which detract rather than add:

> Stretching her slim arms over her head and twisting her short torso, Julie turned away from her disorganized desk and made a quick spin on the heel of her worn leather shoe. Her tailored skirt obediently relinquished its caress of the short, well-formed legs, and the long-sleeved shirt once again settled comfortably around her shoulders and back.

Patterns of modifiers, usually a doubling, will create an unfortunate and sometimes ridiculous rhythm:

> Bright and early in the morning he set out for the big, new school, carrying his brown leather satchel and his heavy tin lunchbox, which he left in the dim, smelly cloakroom, and went to his stiff, little desk, where he greeted Miss Tomkins, the young, pretty teacher.

Many adjectives joined to particular nouns form the bonded pairs of cliches: *friendly smiles, stately oaks, graceful porticoes, hard-bitten cops, frisky kittens. . . .*

Or are redundant: *doleful mourners, tall skyscrapers, innocent maidens. . . .*

The easiest words to dispense with are the little qualifiers, since they don't mean anything anyway: *a little, a bit, rather, sort of, kind of, quite, very, pretty* (as in *much*)—moving along to *slightly, mostly*, etc.

Sort of tired = tired, pretty expensive = expensive, a bit hard = hard, not too happy = unhappy.

Very may give emphasis, but more often it merely clutters. *Majestic* is just as good as *very majestic, gorgeous* is better than *very gorgeous*, and *very fantastic* is, of course, ridiculous.

Positive words are usually more effective than negatives: "He was always late" is better than "He was never on time." And yet how effective Faulkner makes the negative-dependent qualifying clauses he loves to employ, which evoke as they seem to disclaim. "Not because . . . nor because . . . but because. . . ."

Caveats

Theres

Beware the word *there*, deadener of prose.

> There was something that smelled bad. Something smelled bad.
>
> Somewhere there was a shutter groaning. Somewhere a shutter groaned.
>
> There was a speech by Henry. Henry spoke.
>
> Suddenly there was a sound of bells. Suddenly bells rang out.

Passive Voice

Beware the passive voice, another great deadener.

A verb is *active* when its subject is performing whatever action the verb is describing. The verb is *passive* if its subject is being acted upon by something or someone else. The passive voice is always composed of *is, was, were,* or *has been*, plus a past participle.

> The party was interrupted by the appearance of a great white shark. An attempt was made to form a barricade of tables and chairs. Guests were told to remain calm. The SWAT team was called. . . .
>
> Horns were blown, bells were rung, ticker tape was thrown from office windows, embraces were exchanged.

Verbs
As soon as you select the subject of the sentence you should supply it with a verb that makes it *do* something. If you have chosen a passive verb, see if you can't change it to an active one. If you can't change the sentence to active, consider deleting it entirely. You should use passive verbs only when you gain something from them.

Woulds
Beware of extended use of the habitual case.

> In the morning he would leap out of bed early, he would don his boots and slosh down a cup of hot coffee. Usually he would fight with his wife, then he would go outside with his shotgun.

All those *woulds* are essentially undramatic and deadening. Nothing is actually taking place before us, we are of necessity being *told*, not shown; the habitual case is indefinite, unparticular, and not specific. Usually, unless a passage is to be very brief, it is more effective to show a particular case and imply that it is habitual.

Sentence Modifiers
Writing is a process of addition, and it is what is added to qualify the noun or verb that powers the sentence. A sentence is linear, moving from left to right, and it is the modification on the right of the noun or verb, not on the left—after, not before the word—that counts.

"Evenly, slowly, meditatively, she—"did what? The reader has no clue, and certainly no picture, until the verb finally shows up, and we see her stroking her pet bat, spooning up chocolate ice cream, or skating across the frozen pond.

"The huge, black, poisonous—"what? Again, no picture. "The nasty, muttering, pale, little—"could be a banker, a Pekinese, a platoon of soldiers. Again the reader is in the dark until the noun or verb is finally produced.

As the particular is more vivid than the general, the specific than the abstract, the fiction writer strives to present the particular and the specific. It is the *sentence modifier*, which comes after the word, that is more effective in establishing the particular and specific, than the *word modifier*, which comes before the word:

"Animal" is abstract, "cat" general, "Siamese" particular.

"A Siamese cat," however, is not vivid.

"A big Siamese cat" is little better.

"A big Siamese bluepoint with crossed blue eyes, a crook in her tail, and a yowl when hungry that rattled the cans of Kitty-tuna on the shelf" starts to be vivid. The modification comes after "Siamese," and particularizes.

This kind of sentence modification can turn flat statement into rendering:

"The cook stood beside the table waiting for their order."

An adverb does not help much: "The cook stood stiffly beside the table, waiting for their order."

Sentence modifiers help more: "The cook stood beside the table, quivering at attention, his tall white cap pointed like a rocket."

Let's look at McGuane's sentence modifiers again:

> . . . he swung down onto Terrace Road and dropped quite fast through the eucalyptus and cedar, really as fast as he could go, through repetitive turns, the smells by-passing his nose to go directly to his lungs, the greenery overhead sifting and scattering shadows, the dips in the road cupping the sunlight, the banked turns unfolding his shadow, the whole road flattening out, gliding. . . .

And Hemingway:

> George was coming down in telemark position, kneeling, one leg forward and bent, the other trailing, his sticks hanging like some insect's thin legs, kicking up puffs of snow, and finally, the whole kneeling, trailing figure coming around in a beautiful right curve, crouching, the legs shot forward and back, the body leaning out against the swing, the sticks accenting the curve like points of light, all in a wild cloud of snow.

In both these passages, the power of the description has come in the form of sentence modification, and in Hemingway's ski run entirely so.

Repetition

In Shakespeare's *King Richard II*, Richard has been captured by Bolingbroke and has sent for a looking-glass, which is used as a focus by Richard in his soliloquy. These lines are set up in what is called *parallel construction*, dependent upon the repetition of the word *face*:

Was this face the face
That every day under his household roof
Did keep ten thousand men? Was this the face
That, like the sun, did make beholders wink?
Is this the face which fac'd so many follies,
That was at last outfaced by Bolingbroke?

Accidental and careless word repetitions are always poisonous to good prose, but thoughtful repetitions, like those above, can be very effective. Gertrude Stein was a great employer of repetitions (A rose is a rose is a rose), and Hemingway, who learned more at her knee (according to her) or less (according to him), in any case learned somewhere to make effective use of repetition, as in the famous opening paragraph of *A Farewell to Arms*, with its repetition of troops marching and leaves falling, and its premonition of early death.

Types of Sentences

Steinbeck makes use of repetitions in this passage from *The Grapes of Wrath*, and also uses compound sentences, which are no more than simple sentences linked with *and*. Steinbeck also used *and* to begin paragraphs in order to give a Biblical roll to his novel of the great trek of the Okies in the 1930s.

> And a homeless hungry man, driving the roads with his wife beside him and his thin children in the back seat, could look at the fallow fields which might produce food but not profit, and that man could know how a fallow field is a sin and the unused land a crime against the thin children. And such a man drove along the roads and knew temptation at every field, and knew the lust to take these fields and make them grow strength for his children and a little comfort for his wife. The temptation was before him always. The fields goaded him, and the company ditches with good water flowing were a goad to him.
>
> And in the south he saw the golden oranges hanging on the trees, the little golden oranges on the dark green trees; and guards with shotguns patrolling the lines so a man might not pick an orange for a thin child, oranges to be dumped if the price was low.

Mark Twain also uses *and* linkage; for example, it effectively begins this scene from *Huckleberry Finn*. Huck is making his escape from the hut where Pap has locked him up, and the passage moves on with a sense of breathless haste in simple and incomplete sentences:

> I took the sack of cornmeal and took it to where the canoe was hid and shoved the vines and branches apart and put it in; then I done the same with the side of bacon; then the whiskey jug; I took all the coffee and sugar there was and the ammunition; I took the wadding; I took the bucket and gourd; took a tin dipper and cup; and the skillet and the coffee-pot. I took fish lines and matches and other things. I cleaned out the place.

This is fine, breathless narration, the short sentences taking the reader step-by-step through the action. Simple sentences may be best for describing action, but run-on sentences can be effective also. Here are contrasting examples from my novel *The Adelita*:

> Suddenly he was on the ground, groaning, every bone in his body seemingly broken. His mare lay kicking and writhing with the hair of her chest on fire. He could smell the stink of burning hair and flesh. There was no light overhead. Horses screamed, men shouted, another shell struck with the awful shriek of exploding shrapnel. He crawled away before he managed to get to his feet and run dodging between the trees, past Ignacio's shattered body, and into a thorn thicket, where he lay on his back panting, gazing upward through drifting dust and smoke. More shells fell. There was a monotonous whining that he discovered came from his own throat. Riderless horses galloped past. The sky reappeared through the smoke. Not far off he could see the train, and now in the silence there was a calm chirruping of birds, the clicking of crickets. He could not stop panting.

> Before Luis had finished, he was out of the thicket in a stumbling run just as a riderless grey trotted by, halting whickering as he seized the reins, but pivoting away as he planted a boot in the stirrup, so that he had to hold his other leg up and the saddle under him, heading among the trees in a circle, calling out to three or four of the escaudrilla dismounted holding their horses, and in a sweep of increasing radius, call-

> ing to more men, seeing the torn and bloody dead, and dead horses, but not so many as he had first thought when it had seemed all must be dead of the shelling.

The second passage is one long sentence, which follows the circuitous form of the action itself, as MacBean first crawls, then mounts the circling horse, then rides in a circle trying to assemble his men. Both passages, the first for the most part made up of simple sentences, and the second, of one complicated sentence, with a great deal of modifying clauses, are effective.

In the Hemingway and Steinbeck passages quoted above, the simple sentence construction does not become monotonous because the paragraphs are relatively short, and they alternate with passages of action or dialog; neither writer allows narration to run on for very long. But monotony of predicates following subjects, like horses wagons in a wagon train, is preferable to this kind of backward writing:

> Rubbing his fingers in circles about his temples, he felt the blood prodding through his arteries to reach his head. Idly scanning the green lands, he saw a column of smoke rising above the ground. Issuing forth with uneven bursts of shoving gray masses, it quickly blemished the purity of the sky. Drawing encouragement from it, he crossed over more knolls. Deceived by the clarity of the air, the smoke, like an illusive rainbow, he retreated behind each raising of the ground, always hiding its origin.

Here is one of Robert Louis Stevenson's journal entries that was to be revised into *The Silverado Squatters*:

> Signs of the greatness of Silverado are not wanting. . . . and quite far down, buried in foliage deep out of sight of Silverado was the last outpost of the old mining operation, a great tail of gravel and some remains of wooden pipe.

Here is the finished product:

> Signs were not wanting of the ancient greatness of Silverado . . . and far down, buried in foliage, deep out of sight of Silverado, I came on a last outpost of the mine—a mound of gravel, some wreck of wooden aqueduct, and the mouth of a tunnel, like a treasure grotto in a fairy story.

Old has been changed to *ancient*, *pipe* to *aqueduct*, and the technical mining term *tail* to the more descriptive *mound*. The prosaic diction of the journal has been upgraded, made more "elegant," with an alliteration in "wreck of wooden aqueduct." The passage is dramatized by the addition of the "I" observer, with his telling simile "treasure grotto in a fairy story," which transfers a sense of the observer's excitement to the reader.

Alliteration and Assonance

From Walter van Tilburg Clark's story "The Rapids," this passage: ". . . the heavy water gushed all on the farther side, and narrowed until, from the lowest ledge, it jetted forth in a single head, making a big, back-bellying bubble. . . ." The forced labial explosives of the *B*s of the last three words express very dramatically the obstruction to the jetting forth of the water that forms the "back-bellying bubble."

> A few light taps upon the pane made him turn to the window. It had begun to snow again. He watched sleepily the flakes, silver and dark, falling obliquely against the lamplight. The time had come for him to set out on his journey westward. Yes, the newspapers were right; snow was general all over Ireland. It was falling on every part of the dark central plain, falling softly upon the Bog of Allen and, further westward, softly falling into the dark mutinous Shannon waves. It was falling, too, upon every part of the lonely churchyard where Michael Furey lay buried. It lay thickly drifted on the crooked crosses and headstones, on the spears of the little gate, on the barren thorns. His soul swooned slowly as he heard the snow falling faintly through the universe, and, faintly falling, like the descent to their last end, upon the living and the dead.

In this passage at the end of James Joyce's "The Dead," the *S*s accumulate like the snowflakes themselves, with the sound concentrated especially at the beginning of the last sentence—"His soul swooned slowly. . . ." This is lulling, as are the repetition of "softly falling," "faintly falling," "thickly drifted," "falling faintly," etc.; the long vowel sounds increase the somber effect. Gabriel's sleepy mood of epiphany, of the relation of the living to the dead, is rendered in sounds.

Rudyard Kipling's son died in the great Somme offensive in World War I, serving with the Irish Guards, and here Kipling, in his heartfelt work, *The Irish Guards in the Great War*, describes

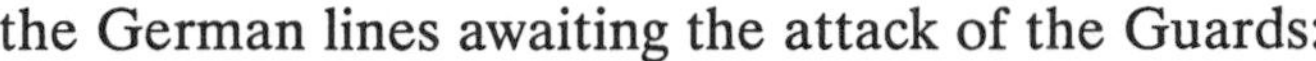

the German lines awaiting the attack of the Guards:

> . . . these were studded with close woods, deadlier even than the fortified villages between them; some cut with narrowing valleys that drew machine-gun fire as chimneys draw draughts; some opening into broad, seemingly smooth slopes, whose every haunch and hollow covered sunk forts, carefully-placed mine-fields, machine-gun pits, gigantic quarries, enlarged in the chalk, connecting with systems of catacomb-like dugouts and subterranean works at all depths, in which brigades could lie till the fitting moment. Belt upon belt of fifty-yard-deep wire protected these points, either directly or at such angles as should herd and hold up attacking infantry to the fire of veiled guns. Nothing in the entire system had been neglected or unforeseen, except knowledge of the nature of the men, who, in due time, should wear their red way through every yard of it.

This passage is a masterpiece of sober, somber, descriptive prose, moving slowly to its powerful climax. How apparently simple is the phrase "wear their red way," but how much writer's art and sweat is there.

T W O

Dialog

Suit the action to the word,
the word to the action.
—The Tragedy of Hamlet,
Prince of Denmark,
Shakespeare

Dialog is action. It is an integral part of scene and an important means of revealing character. It crystallizes relationships, conveys information, forwards the plot, and precipitates revelations, crises, and climaxes. Its characterization and expository functions are important, but dialog bent too much to uses that are not those of action can become static. Dialog must keep moving forward. Notice that in Shakespeare's soliloquies there is always a progression to a change of heart or a resolution to action.

Dialog takes pains to appear totally realistic without being so at all, for it is very much the product of conscious craft. It should express character, advance the action, and record pertinent information, and it should do all of these at once. It must be pointed, be relevant, and move swiftly, while giving the impression that it is a transcription of live speech. Taking a newspaper as an analogy, dialog should give just the headlines but make the reader believe he is receiving the whole text.

Use Profanity Judiciously

Beginning writers determined to breach a censorship that no longer exists by recording every obscenity in the speech of youth, soldiers, or prison inmates, will succeed only in boring the reader by their literal fidelity. Here is an editor's advice to the author of a novel called *Lullaby*:

> The younger generation: delete every other profanity. As ye ken, words on the page ring louder than words in the ether, which is why in speech it is more emphatic to say '*Lullaby* is really excellent,' and in print, '*Lullaby* is excellent.' You do want the diction of the young to be more profane than that of their elders, but by too accurately replicating speech you've managed to overdo it.

Here is Hemingway on the same subject:

> . . . Try and write straight English; never using slang except in dialogue and then only when unavoidable. Because all

slang goes sour in a short time. I only use swear words, for example, that have lasted at least a thousand years for fear of getting stuff that will be simply timely and then go sour. *Selected Letters*, Hemingway to Carol Hemingway

Conciseness Is the Key

A good rule in dialog is: One thought at a time, and keep the lines short. In the following passage from Philip Roth's *Portnoy's Complaint*, see how swiftly each line moves, and how the whole progresses so that at the end much has been revealed, and the situation is very different from what it was at the beginning:

They come to visit: "Where did you get a rug like this?" my father says, making a face. "Did you get this thing in a junk shop or did somebody give it to you?"

"I like this rug!"

"What are you talking," my father says. "It's a worn out rug."

Light-hearted. "It's worn, but not out. Okay? Enough?"

"Alex, please," my mother says, "it is a very worn rug."

"You'll trip on that thing," my father says, "and throw your knee out of whack, and then you'll be really in trouble."

"And with your knee," says my mother meaningfully, "that wouldn't be a picnic."

At this rate they are going to roll the thing up any minute now, the two of them, and push it out the window. *And take me home*!

"The rug is fine. My *knee* is fine."

"It wasn't so fine," my mother is quick to remind me, "when you had the cast on, darling, up to your hip. How he *shlepped* that thing around! How miserable he was!"

"I was fourteen years old then, Mother."

"Yeah, and you came out of that thing," my father says, "you couldn't bend your leg, I thought you were going to be a cripple for the rest of your life. I told him, 'bend it! Bend it!' I practically begged him morning, noon, and night, 'Do you want to be a cripple forever? Bend the leg!' "

"You scared the *daylights* out of us with that knee."

"But that was nineteen hundred and forty-seven. And this is nineteen sixty-six. The cast has been off for nearly twenty years!"

My mother's cogent reply? "You'll see, someday you'll be a parent, and you'll know what it's like. And then maybe you won't sneer at your family any more."

In the following scene, from James M. Cain's *The Postman Always Rings Twice*, the lovers, Frank and Cora, have just tried to murder Cora's husband. They have failed, and have almost been caught in the process. See how the passage moves from their fear, swearing "never again," to returning confidence, boasting, and the implication that they will indeed try again.

"Never again, Frank."

"That's right, never again."

"Just our dumb luck that pulled us through."

"It was my fault."

"Mine too."

"No, it was my fault. Next time I'll listen to you, Frank. You're smart. You're not dumb like I am."

"Except there won't be any next time."

"That's right. Never again."

"Even if we had gone through with it they would have guessed it. They *always* guess it. They guess it anyway, just from habit. Because look how quick that cop knew something was wrong. That's what makes my blood run cold. Soon as he saw me standing there he knew it. If he could tumble that easy, how much chance would we have had if the Greek had died?"

"I guess I'm really not a hell-cat, Frank."

"I'm telling you."

"If I was, I wouldn't have got scared so easy. I was *so* scared, Frank."

"I was plenty scared myself."

"You know what I wanted when the lights went out? Just you, Frank. I wasn't any hell-cat at all, then. I was just a little girl, afraid of the dark."

"I was there, wasn't I?"

"I loved you for it. If it hadn't been for you, I don't know what would have happened to us."

"Pretty good, wasn't it? About how he slipped?"

"And he believed it."

"Give me half a chance, I got it on the cops, every time. You got to have something to tell, that's it. You got to fill in all those places, and yet have it as near the truth as you can get it. I know them. I've tangled with them, plenty."

"You fixed it. You're always going to fix it for me, aren't you, Frank?"

Much is also swiftly accomplished in this telephone dialog from Lionel Davidson's *The Rose of Tibet*. Houston is initiating an affair with a married woman he has met. The dialog is minimal, but the reader is given enough hints to be able to fill out ensuing scenes from his own imagination:

. . . after debating with himself for a couple of days, Houston telephoned her.

It was an afternoon in July, a high blue day of reeling heat. Houston told her he was going to Roehampton.

"Lucky you."

"Why don't you come?"

A pause. "Oh, I think not."

"Can't you swim."

"Yes, I can swim."

"I'll pick you up, then."

That was how it started. Years later the whole of that curious and aimless summer seemed to crystallize for him in the single moment; the moment of replacing the receiver in the hot, empty flat and of feeling the first lurch: of excitement, disgust, apprehension.

In the following passage, see how the lines of dialog can be tightened and moved more swiftly by pruning inessentials:

Ben was reading the news article, brows knit over his nose. He handed it back. "What's your point, Jan?"

"They ~~killed him,~~ murdered him!"

"Possession of cocaine is a felony. ~~It's legal to shoot a felon trying to escape."~~

Another thought clutched at her mind: "Ben! Where did you get that stuff in there? ~~Who'd you buy it from?"~~

She could see from his eyes that the same thought had occurred to him. "The Brotherhood," he said.

"Then ~~we're next! They've probably been watching that house for a long time,~~ they must know we've bought ~~some~~ from them. Oh, Ben, let's get rid of it, ~~let's take it out of the house right now, take it anywhere!"~~

~~"I don't think we need to worry just yet, Jan.~~ They wouldn't ~~want to~~ come here unless they were sure of finding something, and ~~they wouldn't come~~ just for the two of us, ~~either, they'd want a lot of people."~~

"But we ~~have people here all the time.~~ We haven't been careful ~~at all~~ and you know they watch everything we do, the neighbors watch, everyone's watching. ~~They've probably known for a long time that we've had it here. Please,~~ please, let's take it away right now, ~~if we don't we're just asking for it, we're just playing right into their hands, don't you see?"~~

"Look, we ~~can't let them run our lives. We~~ play their game ~~only~~ if we let them ~~scare us, if we let them~~ ruin every line we cut. ~~That way they get us going and coming; we don't enjoy what we're doing anymore, and they can arrest us for it too."~~

The easy legerdemain of the editorial pencil has speeded up the dialog of the preceding passage:

Ben was reading the news article, brows knit over his nose. He handed it back. "What's your point, Jan?"

"They murdered him!"

"Possession of cocaine is a felony. It's legal to shoot a felon trying to escape."

Another thought clutched at her mind: "Ben! Where did you get that stuff in there?"

She could see from his eyes that the same thought had occurred to him. "The Brotherhood," he said.

"Then they must know we've bought from them. Oh, Ben, let's get rid of it!"

"They wouldn't come here unless they were sure of finding something, and just for the two of us."

"But we haven't been careful, and you know they watch everything we do, the neighbors watch, everyone's watching. Please, let's take it away right now!"

"Look, we play their game if we let them ruin every line we cut."

Here is another passage that can be enhanced by judicious pruning:

1) "Oh, look," said the girl, "there's a seal on the beach."
"Where?" asked the man.
"Just there, near the cliffs. See, he's waddling, dragging himself."
"That's strange," the man said. "They usually don't come in like that."
"He looks like a tiny one, a baby, from here," she said.
"Yes, they get much larger."
"Shall we walk over?"

2) "Oh, look," said the girl, "there's a seal on the beach. Look how he's waddling, dragging himself. He's a tiny one, a baby."
"They usually don't come in like that," the man said. "Shall we walk over?"

Nothing important has been lost in the compression. In lines two and three of (1), and even line five, she is telling the man things he can see for himself; and the location of the seal could believably be accomplished by pointing, which can be implied and need not even be mentioned. The compression shakes a lot of junk out of the original, and moves it much more swiftly to what needs to be accomplished here, which is to get the man and the girl over to examine the baby seal.

Exposition Through Dialog

Here is information presented in dialog much more dramatically and effectively than it could have been done in exposition. This is from the Salinger story "For Esme—With Love and Squalor." We have been told that the protagonist, here referred to as "X," has not come through the last days of war "with all his faculties intact." The fact is effectively proven by Clay's comments that X's hands shake, he looks bad, and he has lost weight:

Clay watched X trying to get a cigarette lit. "Jesus," he said, with spectator's enthusiasm. "You outta see your goddam hands. Boy, have you got the shakes. Ya know that?"
X got his cigarette lit, nodded, and said Clay had a real eye for detail.
"No kidding, hey. I goddam near fainted when I saw you at the hospital. You looked like a goddam *corpse*. How much weight ya lose? How many pounds? Ya know?"

Dialog can convey information more dramatically than straight exposition, but dialog devised purely for that purpose will seldom sound natural, characters telling each other things they already know too obviously for the reader's benefit.

"Where the hell is Jack?"
"Your son is at the piano in the drawing room, where he practices eight hours a day."
"Where's Marcia, then?"
"Your daughter is reading to her grandmother, your mother, as she does every afternoon at this time."

The above passage might be believable if the interlocutor is senile or recovering from a bout of amnesia. The next one is merely ridiculous, although all of us have heard a real estate agent saying, "This is the fireplace. And here's the tiny kitchen."

"And this is your room, Fred, with its divan-bed and colorful paintings on the walls, and its window looking out on the ocean."
"Er—what ocean is that?"
"You can tell from the fact that the sun is setting in it that it is the Pacific Ocean."

The real purpose of dialog is not exposition, but the presentation of experience, and too many facts can turn a scene static and dull, as well as unbelievable.

In the following passage, each character is telling the other what the other already knows, and for the reader's benefit, but the exchange seems believable in the heat of argument:

"Ralph, you have proved on that quarter section," Blaine said in his high, short-of-breath voice. "It is good land. You have worked hard."
"Well, you can just write a letter to the *Cheyenne Sun* how they have run off another homesteader. And how it is a crime four or five big outfits can hold the Sweetwater for seventy miles. I can't bring Jessie out here, Jim."

In this monolog the reader is being conveyed information about the narrator, a private detective, which of course he knows himself, through the device of his client's dossier on him:

"... you've built up quite a reputation for finding missing persons. It seems to be your specialty, right?" He gestured toward my folder. "And we wanted someone who has experience in Europe. My office ran quite a thorough check on you. Five years Paris correspondent for UPI, two years London. Two years with Interpol. Then you returned to LA and set up your own agency...."

She traced the long scar on his upper hip with a finger.
"Tell me again what happened," she asked.
"I've told you before."
"Did it hurt?"
"Sure it did. But I can't remember much."
"That's why you got the medal, isn't it?"
"They made a mistake."
"I thought they gave the medal to anyone who got hurt."
"No, that was the Purple Heart."
"Why won't you ever talk about it?"

We are learning of these characters in this dialog, by implication. The man has both a Purple Heart and a medal for bravery, but he is modest and doesn't like to brag. The girl is inquisitive and a bit stupid. The reader may be suspicious that this exchange is aimed at him, but it is natural enough for lovers or old friends to bring up matters of the past and recount them to each other—thus providing necessary information. This dialog might better have been initiated, for instance, by a movement of the young man which revealed the scar to the girl.

Speech Tags

Duffer dialog tends to begin lines of speech with junk words, which have no purpose other than establishing a vague sense of authenticity, but which set up an irritating rhythm to the speeches:

"Oh, Jimmy, would you get this spider out of my wig?"
"Well, Francie, I'd rather not. You do it, Pete."
"Uh, I'd rather not."
"Say, isn't anybody going to help me?"

"Hi, Sugar, Merry Christmas!"
"Hi. Are you ready to tell the Christmas story tonight?"
"Sure. I practiced real hard."
"Wonderful. I can't wait to hear it."

On the principle that in dialog not all that is really said is recorded, some inessentials can be omitted in the above exchange. For instance, the speaker in the second line may well respond with, "Hi!," but the word can be left out as implied, in order to speed the flow of the dialog. In the third line, "I practiced real hard" implies the "Sure," which is also unnecessary. "Wonderful" is implied in "I can't wait to hear it."

"Hi, Sugar, Merry Christmas."
"Are you ready to tell the Christmas story tonight?"
"I practiced real hard!"
"I can't wait to hear it."

"Hi, there, honey, what's your name?"
"Catherine."
"That's pretentious. Listen, Kate, can I get you a drink?"
"No. Catherine."
"Waitress, get Kate here a drink. What did you say you wanted?"
"Nothing, thank you. It's Catherine."
"Scotch and water for Kate here. Hey, did you meet my friend Charley? Charley, Kate."
"Hey, where'd this little number come from, Floyd?"

The above is *stripped dialog*. There are no speech tags, but the author has distinguished the voices well enough so that we are not confused as to who is speaking each line. Stripped dialog, however, is not the ultimate good thing in recording speech, for the word *said* is as innocuous as a bit of punctuation. See how a sprinkling of speech tags—Frank said, Mary said, Mom said—would have alleviated the following confusion without dampening the emotion of the speeches:

"That's right, I said she deserved it! She was turning into one of them. She was one of them!"
"Frank, oh please don't say—"
"Shut up, Mary! I said it and I meant it!"
"You Goddamn stupid son of a bitch. I hate your stupid guts!"
"You shut up too, you're as bad as your sister. I wish to God you'd stayed at school with her that weekend."
"Oh, Frank, you don't mean any of it. He doesn't mean it,

Chuck. Say you don't, please, Frank!"
"He means it all right, Mom."

The reader, with considerable effort, can figure out who is speaking here, but resents being put to the trouble.

"I hope you'll decide to come," Frank said.
"Oh, I really can't decide," Mrs. Montgomery said. "It would be the first time, you know."
"Isn't that being sentimental and morbid?" Mary said. "We'd really want you to come, you know."
"Oh, I just can't decide. I can't make up my mind."
Jack moved impatiently in his chair. "I think you've got to come."
"Well—" Mrs. Montgomery gazed at him with misty eyes. "Well, all right then! I will!"

The speakers above are made perfectly clear by the speech tags, which are integrated gracefully enough into the passage; nor does the word *said* seem repetitious. It can be left out, as in Mrs. Montgomery's second speech, where it is clear who is speaking, and again in Jack's line, where the action points to the speaker. If this conversation were to continue for several pages, other occasions could be found where the speaker could be identified by action, stage business, or thought, without a speech tag, but clarity is more important than finding other means of identification.

He and *she*, when sufficient to identify the speaker, are less obtrusive than proper names, which tend to take on a repetitive quality that may become irritating. It is well to remember that two speakers do not usually refer to each other by name, unless some emphasis is intended. When this occurs, the proper name at the end of the speech tends to have a plaintive or indecisive quality. Coming at the beginning, it is apt to seem forceful or imperative.

"Come with me, John!"
"Mary, you know you have to do it yourself!"
"You promised to help me, Johnny!"
"Mary, I just don't know what to think about this!"

Richard Ford, in *A Piece of My Heart*, is not concerned with filtering out any unnecessary *said*s, but in packing in as much information, description, and action as possible into the stage directions accompanying the speech tag. Thus he carries the action along simultaneously with the speaking, not stopping one to advance the other:

> A few yards above the beaver house, he could make out a number of white plastic jugs of the character used to contain antifreeze, floating bottom-up in a more or less circular pattern around another jug, which appeared to be impaled on a stob a foot and a half out of the water, the whole arrangement situated fifteen yards from the marshy beginnings of the woods.
>
> "Right there," the old man whispered, pointing at the impaled jug and the four others circling it. "Row me to that boy there."
>
> Mr. Lamb raised the box and resituated it on the well between his feet and smiled at him over his shoulder.
>
> "What is that?" he said, jiving the paddle until he could feel the bottom seize on the blade.
>
> "Huh?" the old man said, not hearing him right and directing his good ear around into better line with the sound.
>
> "What is all that?" he said.
>
> "That's Landroo's fish feeder," the old man said, snorting as if the idea of a fish feeder were perfectly ludicrous.
>
> "What does it do?" he said, worrying some of the cold marl off the blade with his fingers and getting a potent smell of the bottom, which was foul and smoking and made his stomach heave. He pushed the paddle back quickly and splashed his fingers in the eddies.
>
> "You see," Mr. Lamb whispered, "Landroo's a cane-pole fisherman, like any upstanding nigger would be. And back up behind his little house, he's got him what appears to be a toolbox built, with a hinged door over the top of it. Except it ain't a toolbox at all." He stopped and studied the white jugs as they slid toward him, as though he felt he'd explained the feeder as much as it needed explaining.
>
> "But what the hell is it?" he said, hauling up another annoying bolus of blue smoking gunk and slapping it back in the water stoutly.
>
> "What?" the old man said, frowning, having forgotten the conversation entirely and become reengrossed in stealthing up on the jugs.

In *The Friends of Eddie Coyle*, George V. Higgins tacks an identifying *said* onto each line of dialog:

"You get the license number on the bus?" Waters said.
"Yeah," Foley said.
"Sooner or later that's going to tell us who was in it, right?" Waters said.
"Likely," Foley said, "unless it was stolen."
"Assume it's not," Waters said, "what have we got."
"The names," Foley said.

The reader accepts the convention and is not bothered by the repetition, but any of these systems of dialog—stripped, dedicated 'he saids' like George V. Higgins's, or decorated with stage directions like Richard Ford's—will become monotonous in time, just because dialog will lose its dramatic quality if used to excess. Writing too-long passages of dialog with little descriptive detail or action sacrifices the visual sense to the aural, and the eye is more effectively appealed to than the ear.

Varying speech tags is *not* a way to insure against monotony in long exchanges of dialog, and many a writer has made a fool of himself by being discontented with *said*.

"If you're wondering what's good, the chili's our specialty," she grinned.
"That sounds good," I agreed. "But I've been longing for a good cup of homemade soup."
"Oh, I wouldn't have the soup if I were you," she counseled. "The chili's better."
"Okay, chili," I conceded.

The speech verbs in the last three speeches are all redundant. "That sounds good" is already an agreement. Obviously she is giving counsel in the matter of the soup. The fact that he concedes is clear enough without the speech verb.

Duffer dialog also leans heavily upon adverbs to qualify *said* or other neutral speech tags. An adverb almost always weakens a verb in the description of action, where it tends to replace a stronger or more accurate verb; however, in dialog, where stronger verbs than *said* are rarely necessary, they lessen the neutral quality of the universal and useful speech verb, and make it seem that *how* a line of dialog is said is more important than *what* is said.

"Do you know what a gambit is?" asked Emily unexpectedly. "It's a sacrifice."
"That's in chess, isn't it? An exchange?" Joyce said disinterestedly, glancing out over the bay.
"No," Emily corrected, "it happens in life, too."
Joyce made her face appear pained.
"I'm an alcoholic." Emily announced her condition as if it were somehow equivalent to being a chemist. "I was drunk every day until I found Jesus," she added happily.

To every verb its adverb. Are any of them but the last necessary?

Dialect

Phonetic spelling may be the easiest way to indicate dialect peculiarities, but it is a crude device. Misspelled words tend to jump off the page and assume undue importance, and the apostrophes indicating missing letters take on the appearance of barbed-wire entanglements. The following passage, from Stephen Crane's *The Red Badge of Courage*, is almost unreadable:

"Th' general, he sees he is goin' t' take th' hull command of the 304th when we go inteh action, an' then he ses we'll do sech fightin' as never another regiment done."
"They say we're catchin' it over on th' left. They say th' enemy driv' our line inteh a devil of swamp an' took Hannieses battery."

In *Call It Sleep*, Henry Roth is clearly proud of his ear for the Jewish and Irish dialects of his New York City ghetto, and no doubt the dialog is accurate aurally; but visually, which is the way the reader must absorb it, the page becomes a torture garden:

"Whose skates are dey?" She took a step toward the wooden stairs. "Yaw's?"
"Sure dey're mine. Ball-bearin's' n' ev'yting. Go like lightnin'. Yuh wanna loin?"

How much cleaner the following soliloquy *looks*, with no apostrophes, *g*'s and *d*'s merely left off, and a modicum of peculiar spelling. This is Jones, from John Kennedy Toole's *A Confederacy of Dunces*:

"Hey! You soun just like the Lee mother. Too bad you two

ain met. She love you. She say, 'Hey, boy, you the kinda fool oldtimey nigger I been lookin for all my life.' She say, 'Hey, you so sweet, how's about waxin my floor and paintin my wall? You so darlin, how's about scrubbin my tawlet and polishin my shoe?' And you be sayin, 'Yes, ma'm, yes, ma'm. I'm well behave.' And you be bustin your ass fallin off a chandelier you been dustin and some other whore frien of her comin in so they can compare they price, and Lee star throwin some nickel at your feet and say, 'Hey boy, that sure a lousy show you puttin on. Han us back them nickel before we call a police.' Ooo-wee."

Archaic Language

Similar problems are faced by a writer trying to reproduce speech in a historical novel. How far should he go? A suggestion merely? A heavy flavor? A neutral flavor, but employing an archaic or classical rhythm so as to let the reader do the work? Of the two passages that follow, the first is from *The Black Rose*, by Thomas B. Costain, a historical writer of the old school, who tends toward *prithee* and *forsooth*, with some restraint; the other is from Thomas Keneally's *Blood Red, Sister Rose,* a Joan of Arc retelling, with dialog in a blatant modern idiom. Both methods seem workable:

> "The whelp of Gurnie!" he said. Then he threw back his head and indulged in a loud roar of laughter. "Well met! You may take a message to your grandfather. Tell the old nip-cheese he has been wasting his time." Then he turned to his daughter. "How often, child, must I tell you not to demean yourself in this way. This baseborn fellow is beneath your notice."
>
> Walter's pride got the better of his discretion. He walked down the steps to the street level. "The Gurnie strain is a nobler one than Tressling, my lord," he said. "We have held our land for more than five centuries."
>
> The lord of Tressling laughed again. "You crow loudly, my young cockerel. . . ."

> At two o'clock, while he was resting, the count of Navailles came in. . . . He was large in his armour beside the thin duke who lay in a shirt and drawers, bare-legged, bare-footed, on the bed.
>
> Navailles: How are the bowels, Jean?

Duke: No problem.

Navailles: We had a carrier pigeon from our man over in the town. He says houses by the river haven't any soldiers in them. They're occupied by the people who ought to occupy them. Meals are cooking. Kids getting put on the breast. All that.

Duke: Good.

Navailles: If they'd let you talk to the little prick. Alone, just the two of you.

Duke: It's not a perfect world.

Foreign Speech

Problems similar to establishing dialect or archaic speech occur also when foreign phrases are employed or when foreign speech is given in apparent translation. How are foreign words to be gracefully interpreted? Clarity can be gained by context and ensuing locutions, but most simply by repeating the phrase a second time, in translation. This was Hemingway's practice in *For Whom the Bell Tolls*:

"Back to the palace of Pablo," Robert Jordan said to Anselmo. It sounded wonderful in Spanish.

"El Palacio del Miedo," Anselmo said. "The Palace of Fear."

"La cueva de los huevos perdidos," Robert Jordan capped the other happily. "The cave of the lost eggs."

Focusing of Dialog

In this passage from Carlos Baker's biography, *Ernest Hemingway: A Life Story*, Hemingway is recuperating from his wounds in an Italian hospital:

Agnes returned from Florence in mid-November, bringing with her an ARC nurse named Elsie Jessup, who had been granted a period of sick leave. Miss Jessup was blond, somewhat English in manner, and carried a swagger stick. Ernest listened and watched with his customary care. Like the little priest from the Abruzzi, to say nothing of Elsie Macdonald, Captain Serena, and Count Greppi, Miss Jessup might some day serve as a character in one of his stories.

Hemingway made effective use of this remembered little stick of Elsie Jessup's as the focusing point in a dialog that establishes the themes of love and death in *A Farewell to Arms*:

"How do you do?" Miss Barkley said. "You're not an Italian, are you?"

"Oh, no."

Rinaldi was talking with the other nurse. They were laughing.

"What an odd thing—to be in the Italian army."

"It's not really the army. It's only the ambulance."

"It's very odd though. Why did you do it?"

"I don't know," I said. "There isn't always an explanation for everything."

"Oh, isn't there? I was brought up to think there was."

"That's awfully nice."

"*Do* we have to go on and talk this way?"

"No," I said.

"That's a relief. Isn't it?"

"What's the stick?" I asked. Miss Barkley was quite tall. She wore what seemed to me to be a nurse's uniform, was blonde and had a tawny skin and gray eyes. I thought she was very beautiful. She was carrying a thin rattan stick like a toy riding crop, bound in leather.

"It belonged to a boy who was killed last year."

"I'm awfully sorry."

"He was a very nice boy. He was going to marry me and he was killed in the Somme."

"It was a ghastly show."

"Were you there?"

"No."

"I've heard about it," she said. "There's not really any war of that sort down here. They sent me the little stick. His mother sent it to me. They returned it with his things."

"Had you been engaged long?"

"Eight years. We grew up together."

"And why didn't you marry?"

"I don't know," she said. "I was a fool not to. I should have given him that anyway. But I thought it would be bad for him."

"I see."

"Have you ever loved anyone?"

"No," I said.

We sat down on a bench and I looked at her.

"You have beautiful hair," I said.

"Do you like it?"
"Very much."
"I was going to cut it off when he died."
"No."
"I wanted to do something for him. You see I didn't care about the other thing and he could have had it all. He could have had anything he wanted if I would have known. I would have married him or anything. I know all about it now. But then he wanted to go to war and I didn't know."
I did not say anything.
"I didn't know about anything then. I thought it would be worse for him. I thought perhaps he couldn't stand it and then of course he was killed and that was the end of it."

The problem here was to move the conversation of these newly met people as quickly as possible on to the important topics that will press the story forward. Catherine tells Frederick that the little stick belonged to a boy who was killed last year, and the conversation turns to that boy. Frederick changes the subject to Catherine's hair, but she relates that, too, to her dead lover, and almost hysterically goes on to say that she would have given him anything if she had only known, would have married him or anything. So Hemingway has brought us, in a few short lines, not only to the main thread of the novel, but has foreshadowed its development like the warning tolling of a bell.

Dialog is often framed around some such conversational *object*, such as the stick or the hair, above. Another device is shown in the following scene from *The Portrait of a Lady*. Here James has constructed this passage with Isabel Archer and Lord Warburton by batting a word back and forth from line to line, like a Ping-Pong ball:

"That reason that I wouldn't tell you—I'll tell it to you after all. It's that I can't escape my fate."
"Your fate?"
"I should try to escape it if I were to marry you."
"I don't understand. Why should not that be your fate as well as anything else?"
"Because it's not," said Isabel femininely. "I know it's not. It's not my fate to give up—I know it can't be."
Poor Lord Warburton stared, an interrogative point in either eye. "Do you call marrying *me* giving up?"
"Not in the usual sense. It's getting—getting—getting a

great deal. But it's giving up other chances."
"Other chances for what?"
"I don't mean chances to marry," said Isabel, her colour quickly coming back to her. And then she stopped, looking down with a deep frown, as if it were hopeless to attempt to make her meaning clear.
"I don't think it presumptuous in me to suggest that you'll gain more than you'll lose," her companion observed.
"I can't escape unhappiness," said Isabel. "In marrying you I shall be trying to."

Here is another example of a passage of dialog constructed out of linked repetitions, from Robert Penn Warren's *World Enough and Time*:

"Mr. Beaumont," she said, "you are a very foolish and fanciful young man, who reads too many books and knows nothing of the world."
"I am old enough to know one thing."
"I am older than you, Mr. Beaumont, in years, and a thousand years older in suffering, and I tell you that you are foolish."
"Not so foolish as you, begging your pardon."
"So you are rude as well as foolish," she said, and bit her lip.
"I am rude enough to speak the truth, and tell you that there can be no impediment between us except your heart."

Repetition may also be used to enclose a scene, returning to a line that initiated the scene, to round off the whole:

I said he must come with us, but he shook his head.
"But you must have faith. I think it will not be long before he comes."
"He had better hurry."
"And so must you hurry. There will be many in pursuit."
"You can have faith in me," I said, and clasped his hand.

Sustaining Reader Interest
Readers will tend to skip through large blocks of dialog as they will through solid blocks of print of any kind, looking for the open field and action ahead. A useful device, if a speech is to run more than, say, three or four sentences, is to show by some means that it is to be important.

"Let me tell you what they did to Bob Fletcher," Jack said. His knuckles were white where he gripped the rail.

As soon as dialog begins, the writer should follow the reactions of each character to the other, or others. More than one ball needs to be kept in the air. Much other than speech in the exchange will be of little or no significance, and there is no need to record it, but the significant, the suggestive, the telling implication, the revealing gesture, the meaningful slip-of-the-tongue or involuntary start, should be hunted down and captured. On many occasions the gesture is more dramatic than the spoken word, oblique reference more telling than flat-out statement. Dialog should be short and to the point, but the accompanying stage directions can enlarge upon the meanings and implications.

Also useful in creating variety is what can be called *camera distance*, moving close up with a slowing of time, or pulling back with a consequent swifter passage.

In the following scene from my novel *The Adelita*, the setting is the Mexican Revolution, the year 1916. Robert MacBean has served with Obregón's revolutionary army. His father, who has been terribly worried about his safety, has found him in Veracruz. The dialog moves from indirect discourse to direct in quotes, to thoughts, speculations as to his father's mental processes, and to gesture, facial expression, and action, in order to move the passage swiftly and effectively:

> I asked what "preparedness" meant.
>
> "It means our being ready to fight the hun," my father said in a voice shaky with emotion. It was ignominy that we had not yet entered the war to aid our friends the French, Belgians, and English against the hun: he, who had never been to war, was contemptuous of President Wilson, who had kept America out of it.
>
> "If I was your age—" he started. He was then fifty-two, I calculated. "It is the greatest war in the history of mankind," he said.
>
> I said I had had enough of war to last me at least that long, thank you. He stared at me with his jaw bunched. I had a disturbing sense of having become something to him that I had never been before.
>
> "Of course you'd feel that way!" he said, fiercely, fondly. "They killed poor Frank, did they?"
>
> I nodded and squeezed lime into my beer.

"And you were with Obregón's fellows. Sonorans."

"With Obregón." I listened to what he was resisting saying to me: *I knew you should never I was crazy with worry when you Couldn't you have Why didn't*

"Well, you are safe now, Bobby. And you quit them."

I felt my lips stretching into the shape of a grin.

"They are a hellish bunch," he said, raising his whiskey glass. I didn't know whether he meant Obregón's fellows, or all Mexicans.

"Well, I was one of them," I said.

"I just meant they are not like us, Bobby." I saw him frown with embarrassment to remember that I was half Mexican. "You know what I mean," he said. "Hard for people like us to understand why they act the way they do, like animals sometimes. The huns the same."

"I understood well enough," I said.

The band was playing "Dixie" now, and he turned to watch them, in profile to me. He wore an expression of self-conscious severity, as though ignoring bad manners.

Later we walked along the quays. . . .

Here are novelist Elizabeth Bowen's Rules of Dialog:

1. Dialog should be brief.
2. It should add to the reader's present knowledge.
3. It should eliminate the routine exchanges of ordinary conversation.
4. It should convey a sense of spontaneity but eliminate the repetitiveness of real talk.
5. It should keep the story moving forward.
6. It should be revelatory to the speaker's character, both directly and indirectly.
7. It should show the relationships among people.

Other suggestions may be added:

1. One thought at a time.
2. Over three sentences per speech runs into danger.
3. If dialog does run into a speech, break it up with interruptions by other speakers, by action, or thoughts, or convince the reader the speech is to be important.
4. Dialog should allow the reader to read as much as possible between the lines, in what is left out, and in the stage direc-

tions, actions, and gestures that accompany the dialog.

5. Always read dialog aloud to see how it sounds:
   1) "Damn you!" he hissed.
   2) Yells We Doubt Ever Got Yelled (from the *Kentucky Enquirer*) via *The New Yorker*. "Comrade Berlinguer," students yelled in Communist-run Bologna, "now more than ever, you are either with the Christian Democrats or with workers . . . the Communist Party or the bosses. . . ."

THREE

Indirection

A scene of execution opens Frederick Forsyth's thriller *The Day of the Jackal*. The passage progresses in terms of "things," to which the reader's attention is directed instead of the imperative of the horror to come: the cold, the stake, the scuffing foot, the blindfold, etc. At the climactic moment, attention is directed away from the fatal courtyard to the blaring of the Berliet's horn, and the pigeons fluttering skyward proves the fusillade and the death much more effectively than if the writer had tried to describe the impact of the bullets and the body flung backwards. The reader's imagination has been primed to perform this function:

> It is cold at 6:40 in the morning of a March day in Paris, and seems even colder when a man is about to be executed by firing squad. At that hour on March 11, 1963, in the main courtyard of the Fort d'Ivry a French Air Force colonel stood before a stake driven into the chilly gravel as his hands were bound behind the post, and stared with slowly diminishing disbelief at the squad of soldiers facing him twenty metres away.
>
> A foot scuffed the grit, a tiny release from tension, as the blindfold was wrapped around the eyes of Lieutenant-Colonel Jean-Marie Bastien-Thiry, age thirty-five, blotting out the light for the last time. The mumbling of the priest was a helpless counterpoint to the crackling of twenty rifle bolts as the soldiers charged and cocked their carbines.
>
> Beyond the walls a Berliet truck blared for a passage as some smaller vehicle crossed its path towards the centre of the city; the sound died away, masking the "Take your aim" order from the officer in charge of the squad. The crash of rifle fire, when it came, caused no ripple on the surface of the waking city, other than to send a flutter of pigeons skywards for a few moments. The single "whack" seconds later of the coup-de-grace was lost in the rising din of traffic from beyond the walls.

Note Forsyth's insistence on specifics, always the foundation of any novel of suspense. The time is precise: 6:40 a.m. on March 11, 1963. The place is the main courtyard of the Fort d'Ivry. Twenty soldiers of the firing squad face the condemned man from twenty meters away. The man's name is given in full: Lieutenant-Colonel Jean-Marie Bastien-Thiry. His age is thirty-five. The truck that honks is a Berliet. This specificity continues throughout the novel. When the Jackal makes love to the Baronne he experiences three orgasms, she five. When he is finally killed, it is with half a magazine of nine-millimeter bullets from an MAT 49 in the chest.

Implication

Modern fiction can leave out more than the fiction of a century ago. More economy is necessary because the reader's threshold of irrelevancy is lower. Part of the irrelevant is what is obvious, or what the reader can supply out of his own imagination, experience, or past reading. Indeed, what the reader's imagination can furnish may be more vivid and dramatic than the author's offering of words on the page. The writer's accomplishment between the lines becomes as important as the lines themselves.

The Reader as Participant

The modern reader is heir to a long tradition of the written word, and he is quick to catch on to fiction that leaves out more and more. Fiction strives by various devices to entice the imagination of the reader into active cooperation. The writer wants the reader to both interpolate (fill in the gaps) and extrapolate (complete the hints). The reader wishes to cooperate. Perfect cooperation between the writer's art and the reader's imagination leads to the reader's delight and the writer's fulfillment.

The writer's bag of tricks includes the selection, exaggeration, and simplification of those elements she has chosen to show as significant: implication, symbols, images, metaphors, allegories, parallels, and contrasts.

The reader can be expected to infer that a man with his elbows coming out of the sleeves of his coat, who is unshaven and shuffles along with his shoulders bent, is down on his luck. Moreover, he enjoys the chance to make the deduction. So in this passage from Joyce Carol Oates's short story "Ceremonies," the reader deduces that the father is jealous of Rockland's barns:

> For most of us, a Saturday evening's ride usually consisted of a drive along the creek past Rockland's place, in automobiles that were now beginning to displace carriages, filled with mother and father and children and usually someone's grandfather or grandmother, or both. Everyone would stare at the house and the barns, especially the great main barn with its metal roof and no Mail Pouch ad on the side, and someone—either grandparents or children—would cry out, "No lightning rods! No lightning rods!" In those days a building without lightning rods was considered an affront, even a challenge, to fate. These rides, begun jubilantly, would usually end with the father turning snappish for the rest of the evening, sometimes going out to stand by the barns and stare off his land with a look the children interpreted well enough.

We are not told what the children's interpretation is, but we can deduce it, inferring the father's attitude as well as his children's from the evidence given. The fine bit of detail of the lack of the Mail Pouch ad on the side of the barn implies that Rockland is wealthy enough that he does not need to supplement his income from Mail Pouch's advertising budget.

The following scene, with its implications, is from the John O'Hara story "Fatimas and Kisses." Lintzie and Lonnie, his wife, run a little store on the ground floor of their house.

> One day when I went to buy cigarettes, which he was not supposed to sell me, I waited for Lintzie or Lonnie to appear and wait on me, but neither came. I went back and reopened and closed the door so that the bell would ring again, and she came running downstairs.
>
> "Oh, it's you," she said.
>
> "Will you give me a pack of Camels and a pack of Fatimas," I said.
>
> "Charge or pay?"
>
> "Pay," I said.
>
> "Who are the Fatimas for? Some girl?"
>
> "For my uncle," I said.

"Yeah, your uncle standing out there with the bicycle. You better watch out, Malloy. Her old lady catches her smoking cigarettes, they'll tell your old man and you'll get hail-Columbia. Give me thirty-five cents."

"Where's Lintzie?" I said.

"To Reading. Why?"

"Just wondered," I said. I looked out toward the sidewalk and at the half-ton panel truck parked at the curb, driverless. She put two packs of Camels and two packs of Fatimas on the counter.

"I'll treat you to the butts," she said. "Okay?"

"Thanks," I said.

"The next time her old lady comes in, I won't say anything about you buying her kid Fatimas. Okay?"

"All right," I said.

Malloy has discovered Lonnie's infidelity, and his casual blackmailing is handled by implication, much more effectively than if it had been made explicit. Many jokes take their effect in this same way, and when Renata, in *Humboldt's Gift*, accuses Charley Citrine of always reading a menu from right to left, we know she is implying that he is a cheapskate. Or when Lear, confronted by Cordelia dead, says, "Pray you, undo this button," the implication that his emotion is so great that his collar has become tight is stronger than any ranting would be.

Here is a passage from the Gospels, Jesus encountering Doubting Thomas after the Resurrection:

Now Thomas, one of the twelve, called the Twin, was not with them when Jesus came. So the other disciples told him, "We have seen the Lord." But he said to them, "Unless I see in his hands the print of the nails, and place my finger on the mark of the nails, and place my hand in his side, I will not believe."

Eight days later, his disciples were again in the house, and Thomas was with them. The doors were shut, but Jesus came and stood among them, and said, "Peace be with you." Then he said to Thomas, "Put your finger here, and see my hands; and put out your hand, and place it in my side; do not be faithless, but believing."

Thomas answered him, "My Lord and my God!"

That Thomas now believes is implicit in his words, "My Lord

and my God!" and what he has seen is more strongly realized in his emotion and capitulation than if the hand, and the wound, had been explicitly described.

In *Play It as It Lays*, Joan Didion uses the desert where the film crew is on location as a landscape of futility. It is very clear, without explanation, why Maria begins to cry, and the passage is more powerful because the author lets us figure it out for ourselves:

> In place of a lawn, there was a neat expanse of concrete, bordered by a split-rail fence, and beyond the fence lay a hundred miles of drifting sand. . . . The sand was blowing through the rail fence onto the concrete, drifting around the posts, coating a straight-backed chair with pale film. Maria began to cry. "Honey," the woman said. "You pregnant or something?" Maria shook her head and looked in her pocket for a Kleenex. The woman picked up the broom and began sweeping the sand into small piles, and edging the piles back to the fence. New sand blew as she swept.

Symbol and Metaphor

We are told by his biographer, Leon Howard, that it was Herman Melville's practice to let his mind play with concrete details until they became "luminous with suggestive implications." Until they turned into symbols, in fact, which then formed a conduit between the concrete and the abstract, the particular and the generalization.

Examples in literature abound where an author has filled some particular with this luminosity: the riven rock in *Under the Volcano*, Vronsky riding the mare to death in *Anna Karenina*, the Marabar Caves in *A Passage to India*, Dr. T. J. Eckleburg's eyes on the signboard lowering over the blasted landscape in *The Great Gatsby*.

In Malcolm Lowry's *Under the Volcano*, the symbols of death, decay, and parting crash like kettle drums on the day Yvonne returns to Cuernavaca and the Consul. As they move from the bar to his house, they encounter the old woman with a stick with an animal claw handle, and the little chicken she carries inside her dress, "over her heart," and in a printing shop window a photograph of the great rock in the Sierra Madre split by forest fires, and called *La Despedida* — the cloven. They encounter the funeral with the child's coffin, and the band playing "*La Cucaracha*," and when they reach the house at last, "a hideous pariah dog followed them in."

All the above may strike the reader as a bit much, but it is the style of that difficult but rewarding novel.

Flannery O'Connor writes in *Mysteries and Manners*:

> To take an example from my own book, *Wise Blood*, the hero's rat-colored automobile is his pulpit and his coffin as well as something he thinks of as a means to escape. He is mistaken in thinking that it is a means to escape, of course, and does not really escape his predicament until the car is destroyed by the patrolman. The car is a kind of death-in-life symbol, as his blindness is a life-in-death symbol. The fact that these meanings are there makes the book significant. The reader may not see them but they have their effect upon him nonetheless.

In his *Journal of a Novel*, John Steinbeck has this to say on the subject in *East of Eden*:

> About the nature of the Trasks and about their symbol meanings I leave you to find out for yourself. There is a key and there are many leads. I think you will discover the story rather quickly for all its innocent sound on these pages. Now the innocent sound and the slight concealment are not done as tricks but simply so that a man can take from this book as much as he can bring to it. It would not be well to confuse the illiterate man with the statement of a rather profound philosophy. On the other hand, such a man might take pleasure in the surface story and even understand the other things in his unconscious. On the third hand . . . your literate and understanding man will take joy of finding the secrets hidden in this book almost as though he searched for treasure, but we must never tell anyone they are there. Let them be found by accident. I have made the mistake of telling my readers before and I will never make that mistake again.

Continuing Metaphors

Many of Ross MacDonald's later novels have the same theme, the destruction that parents wreak upon their children. In *The Underground Man*, he uses pelicans to symbolize this:

> She was silent and then she said as if at random: "Did you see the pelicans at Dunes Bay? They can't have any more young ones, did you know that? Their bodies are poisoned

with DDT, and it makes the eggs all break."

And later:

> . . . he was too old to need a mother, really. He had to live out his time of trouble, as she had. He belonged to a generation whose elders had been poisoned, like the pelicans, with a kind of moral DDT that damaged the lives of their young.

Continuing metaphors such as this one of the poisoned pelicans can act as the armatures that serve the structure of fiction, theme lines instead of plot lines. In *The Portrait of a Lady*, one of these lines concerns doors. Henrietta Stackpole is an American journalist, and Ralph Touchett says of her that she "walks in without knocking at doors. . . . She thinks one's door should stand ajar."

Ralph says of himself to his cousin Isabel: "I keep a band of music in my anteroom. It has orders to play without stopping. It renders me two excellent services. It keeps the sounds of the world from reaching my private apartments, and it makes the world think that dancing is going on within."

His metaphoric statement is pathetic because of his illness. Isabel thinks that she would have liked to pass through the anteroom and enter his private apartments.

Later in the novel a door enters thematically into a scene between Isabel and her husband, Gilbert Osmond. She has come into his room without knocking:

> "Excuse me for disturbing you," she said.
>
> "When I come to your room I always knock," he answered, going on with his work.
>
> "I forgot. I had something else to think of. My cousin is dying."
>
> "Ah, I don't believe that," said Osmond, looking at his drawing through a magnifying glass. "He was dying when we married; he'll outlive us all."

Osmond insists upon the petty privacies in the face of great human needs. His soul is about the size of his drawing, which he must study through a magnifying glass.

Earlier a passage was quoted from Arthur Hailey's *Hotel*, in which a Victorian clock was symbolic of its owner's Victorian morals. In Thackeray's *Vanity Fair* a clock is put to a different symbolic usage. The clock is in the house in which old Mr. Osborne and his daughters live, "a chronometer surmounted by a cheerful brass group of the sacrifice of Iphigenia."

As the Greek fleet lay ready to sail for Troy, the north wind blew continually so that the fleet could not beat its way out of the harbor; until, to appease the gods, Agamemnon sacrificed his daughter Iphigenia. Following the description of the clock comes this passage:

> The obedient bell in the lower regions began ringing the announcement of the meal. The tolling over, the head of the family thrust his hands into the great tail-pockets of his great blue coat with its brass buttons, and without waiting a further announcement, strode downstairs alone, scowling over his shoulder at the four females.
>
> "What's the matter now, my dear?" asked one of the other, as they rose and tripped gingerly behind their sire.
>
> "I suppose the funds are falling," whispered Miss Wirt; and so, trembling and in silence, this hushed female company followed their dark leader.

The tolling of the clock has signified another sacrifice of Iphigenia. Mr. Osborne is described in military terms, as a dark leader, with his great blue coat with its brass buttons. The funds are falling, and one of the daughters will be sacrificed to appease the gods.

Objective Correlatives

This is T. S. Eliot's term, from the essay "Hamlet and his Problems," in *The Sacred Wood: Essays on Poetry and Criticism*:

> The only way of expressing emotion in the form of art is by finding an "objective correlative"; in other words, a set of objects, a situation, a chain of events which shall be the formula for that *particular* emotion; such that when the external facts, which must terminate in sensory experience, are given, the emotion is immediately evoked. . . .

In the text of this book, the term is used in a more restricted sense, as of something actual, concrete, or particular, which is the correlative of a subjective state that, otherwise, could be described only in abstractions. For instance, Gatsby standing on his pier gazing out at the green light across the water objectifies his pathetic conviction that the past with Daisy can be recaptured.

In Nabokov's *Lolita*, Humbert Humbert's glimpse of the aging Lolita's hands and arms objectify for him his loss, by time, of the nymphet of his obsession:

> . . . there she was with her ruined looks and her adult, rope-vein hands and her gooseflesh white arms. . . . and her unkempt armpits, there she was (my Lolita!), hopelessly worn at seventeen. . . .

In Chekhov's story "The Peasants," a man defeated by life in Moscow decides to move with his children back to the home in the country where he was brought up. His childhood memories of peasant life have deceived him. Here he is looking into a filthy hut, in which a ragged girl is sitting by the stove:

> A white cat rubbed against the fire irons on the floor. Sasha (the protagonist's child) beckoned to it.
> "Puss, puss. Come here, pussy."
> "She can't hear," said the little girl. "Deaf."
> "Why?"
> "Somebody hit her."

The final line illuminates the squalor, rancor, drunken fighting, and despair of peasant life.

In the children's novel *The Magic City*, by the British writer E. Nesbit, the villain of the piece is revealed as the nursemaid of the eight-year-old protagonist. As she stands waiting for the sentence for her crimes, the nursemaid says:

> "I'll speak my mind if I die of it. You don't understand. You've never been a servant, to see other people get all the fat and you get the bones. What do you think it's like to know if you'd just been born in a gentleman's mansion instead of a model workingman's dwelling you'd have been brought up a young lady and had the openwork silk stockings."

The *openwork silk stockings* are the objective correlative here not merely for the indignities and deprivations of a nanny's position in Victorian England, but for the whole British class system.

In the passage that follows, from Patrick White's *The Tree of Man*, Mrs. Parker, a farm woman, has come into town where she sees some of the local gentry. Notice how the author bears down on *things*, especially the bits of silver paper, which are shown in action. They affect Mrs. Parker's thinking about herself and the gentry, but these thoughts are extrapolated so that the author does not have to describe them. The *things* in the scene are the objective correlative for Mrs. Parker's thoughts:

> There was a gig too, outside the store, that did not belong by rights to that scene. No dust lay on the splendid varnish of the bright gig. The horse, hardly in a lather, shook the flies from his dark face, and with them a shower of clinking brass, that slashed, and flashed, and dared. Altogether there was an air of great daring about the horse and gig that made Mrs. Parker shy. So that she approached determined not to look, with her awkward, wooden movements exposed, she felt, in the open wastes of dust.
>
> It was Armstrong's turnout, she began to realize, that young Armstrong sometimes drove. At that moment he was not present. Inside the store, perhaps, buying something unimportant, for anything of importance was brought from Sydney to the brick house. And now the horse waited, striking at the ground with his shapely hoofs, shifting the gig gratingly, in which sat the two young women.
>
> Amy Parker did not so much see this as know, in shame beside the tamarisk. That the women rocked with the gig, laughing and eating caramels and tossing the silver paper onto the road. No other pastime could have been theirs, because none would have been careless enough. They belonged to that gig, under the parasol that one of them held, and that shifted indolently and mottled their skins.
>
> Any words let fall were not interpreted by the woman on foot as she passed in the shadow of the tamarisk; nor could she have looked at the faces, she was too displeased with her own. This was now brick-coloured, with a little down of hairs. She wore a hat that once she had thought pretty, with a bunch of shiny cherries, but now she held her head away, to hide the silliness of cherries on her cheap, crushed hat.
>
> And all the time the harness of the gig jingled cruelly, like the words of a distant conversation that would seem to have a personal bearing, even though unintelligible. As the young ladies laughed, and twirled their parasol for occupation, and tossed the silver paper onto the road.

Epiphanies

Epiphany in the lower case refers to a divine or profane manifestation, of "showing forth." The term has been appropriated into the discussion of literature by its use by James Joyce in *Stephen Hero*, the early draft of *Portrait of the Artist as a Young Man*:

> By an epiphany he meant a sudden spiritual manifestation, whether in the vulgarity of speech or of gesture or memorable phrase of the mind itself. He believed it was for the man of letters to record these epiphanies with extreme care (saving them for later use, that is), seeing that they themselves are the most delicate and evanescent of moments.

In the 1950s, the necessity for an epiphanic ending to a short story became a formulaic necessity. The story was stacked toward an ending in which the protagonist had some kind of revelation, of something luminous made manifest. "When she stripped off her watch he saw, on the inside of her wrist, the small purple bar of her Dachau serial number," after which it is implied "we will never again be as we were."

Or consider the Somerset Maugham story of two men, far out in the east, who over drinks are discussing leprosy and the deadening of sensation in the extremities that is the first symptom. One of the two holds up his lighted match, with which he will light his pipe as soon as he has finished speaking, while the other observes with horror that the flame is touching his finger.

In Joycean terms, *epiphany* refers to a more "delicate and evanescent" moment, such as the conclusion to his short story "Araby," from *Dubliners*:

> I lingered before her stall, though I knew my stay was useless, to make my interest in her wares seem the more real. Then I turned away slowly and walked down the middle of the bazaar. I allowed the two pennies to fall against the sixpence in my pocket. I heard a voice call from one end of the gallery that the light was out. The upper part of the hall was now completely dark.
>
> Gazing up into the darkness I saw myself as a creature driven and derided by vanity; and my eyes burned with anguish and anger.

The Necessity of Subtleties

What's the point, after all? Why not be straightforward and out-front, and not resort to these tricky hints and evasions? Because the hint is stronger than the flat statement; the hint, the implication, the equation that the reader must complete out of his own imagination and experience, is our old friend dramatization. Heard melodies are sweet but those unheard are sweeter. If the reader is overinformed, her imagination goes to sleep and her comprehension suffers. If her imagination can be engaged, the fiction, and the reader also, will gain. The fiction will be intensified if the reader is engaged enough to collaborate with the author in fleshing out character, plot, and incident out of her own creative imagination.

FOUR

Information and Sex

Novels are not merely plot and character; they consist of information—they are about something. The grand masters of the bestseller lists are, almost all of them, primarily masters of dramatizing information and research: Arthur Hailey of hotels, banks, power companies, and airplanes; James Michener of a whole host of subjects, including geographical all-abouts of such places as Hawaii, Colorado, and Poland; Paul Erdman of the world of international finance, which he knows so well.

The Novel as Instructor

The 18th Century novel was in general an attempt to replace the aristocratic romance by a literature more in keeping with the reality and morality of the middle class, or, at least, the society in which the middle class played an increasingly important part.
—Encyclopaedia Britannica

The novel as we know it grew up with the middle class, and a good part of its popularity has lain in its function of informing the middle class about the world and society, showing what was new, or "novel," purveying information. The middle class did not wish merely to be entertained, it insisted upon instruction and education as well, and the popular novel has always combined these roles. Part of this instruction has been in sexual mores. After World War II, novelists wore out their Krafft-Ebbings trying to find revelations for the reading public.

Bestsellers are usually warehouses of information, often inside stuff—government, Hollywood, the fashion world, espionage, war. Mystery novels also are often built around some arcane field of knowledge. Dick Francis's thrillers contain inside information on horse racing. Dorothy L. Sayers's masterpiece *The Nine Tailors* is both a crime novel and an education in campanology. John D. MacDonald's *The Scarlet Ruse* is packed with the inside on big-money philately.

Technical information and expertise of process, unless overdone, can be fascinating. See from *The Iliad* (Lattimore translation) this detailed process of a Greek animal sacrifice:

> . . . first they drew back the victims' heads and slaughtered them and skinned them,
> And cut away the meat from the thighs and wrapped them in fat, making a double fold, and laid shreds of flesh upon them.

The old men burned these on a cleft stick and poured the gleaming wine over, while the young men with forks in their hands stood about them.

Even so homely a subject as the electrical system of Travis McGee's houseboat, *Busted Flush*, can be technically fascinating. The following is from John D. MacDonald's *Bright Orange for a Shroud*:

. . . With alterations from time to time I've tried to make the old barge-type houseboat ever more independent of shoreside services. Except when home at Bahia Mar, I like to avoid the boat basin togetherness. Under one hatch I have the whole area paved with husky batteries, enough of them so I can stay at anchor and draw on them for four days before they begin to get a little feeble. When they're down, I can use them to start up an electric trickle-feed generator which can bring them back up in six hours. If I ever get careless enough to run them all the way down, I can break out the big 10 kw gasoline generator and use it to get the electric one started. . . .

Notice the specifics. This attention to electrical process also tells us a good deal about the character of Travis McGee.

The process of stringing barbed-wire, which tamed or ruined the west, depending upon the point of view, is described in this passage from my novel *The Bad Lands*:

The next day when Andrew rode down to Palisades Ranch he found a crew fencing the pasture closest to the riverbank. He halted to observe the process. Posts had already been set and three rolls of wire were mounted on the wagon bed. The three strands were stapled to a post, and the wire unrolled as the wagon was pulled along by the team. After two hundred feet the wagon was halted and one rear wheel jacked up. The wire was then fastened to the hub and the wheel turned like a capstan to take up the slack of each strand in turn. The taut wire was then stapled to the intervening posts.

In John D. MacDonald's *The Scarlet Ruse*, the informational subject is stamp collecting. The lore of stamps is fascinating in itself, but MacDonald has also dramatized the scene of the reader's education by showing us Travis McGee being informed on the subject. There is a projector, black light, a pistol grip light switch, and the stamps themselves dramatically enlarged upon the screen to the accompaniment of the clicking of the projector. No sensory impressions or specifics are skimped: the author includes dates, places, catalog numbers, sums of money, etc. In a very few pages the reader has had a short but intensive course in philately, and not only within a dramatic scene, but with implications surrounding the scene of life and death, with Travis McGee on the case.

Informing the Reader Dramatically

Even when the information is inherently interesting, the fictional trick is to present it dramatically. In *Shogun*, by James Clavell, both the author and his editor are proud of "the Tea-house Scene." Throughout the novel, Clavell is ingenious in educating the reader, in presenting information on Medieval Japan without making the reader feel the recipient of lectures. In the Tea-house scene, Clavell is obliquely presenting matters outside Japan in the sixteenth century: the Portuguese voyagers, Mercator's map, the power of the Pope, the Jesuits, and Christianity in Japan. A number of characters have been assembled in the Tea-house for this purpose. Blackthorne, the British pilot and the protagonist, is being cross-examined in the presence of the Lord Toronaga, presumably for the benefit of the Imperial heir, Yaemon—but actually for the benefit of the reader. Interpreting for Blackthorne is the Christianized Lady Mariko, who is in the service of Toronaga. She is attracted to Blackthorne, and friendly to him in this scene, but Jesuit priests who are also present are hostile, because Blackthorne is a Protestant. Blackthorne is in hazard not merely from the Jesuits but the Japanese themselves, and Toronaga also is in a struggle for power with other Japanese elements. The author maintains all these tensions in Blackthorne's questioning, stage-managing the scene expertly, and, when Blackthorne's point of view has accustomed us to scene and actors, floating to the point of view of Mariko to reveal a Japanese attitude toward what is being told this assembly, as well as her personal attitude toward the Englishman. Only a little information, such as the current situation of the Jesuits, is given as direct, authorial information.

Authors such as Zola, aware of the value of presenting description in dramatic mode, developed formulas for the necessary transfer of information, with characters designated to do the job. An inquisitive or knowledgeable person would be produced to point out something complex, such as a locomotive or a garden, to someone who knew nothing about it, in a conversation created expressly to convey the information to the reader by way of a character rather than by the author directly.

In *The Grapes of Wrath*, Steinbeck's purpose was to present a fictional history of the Joads' flight from the dust bowl to California in the 1930s. Every other chapter focuses upon the Joads, and every other abandons fiction to draw the camera back for a more comprehensive view of the plight of the Okies, moving from the specific to the general, and employing a studiedly Biblical prose for the purpose. *The Grapes of Wrath* is a novel of social protest, and these alternate reportorial chapters allowed the author a great deal of freedom in preaching the plight of unfortunates like the Joads, thereby indicting an uncaring society. The fictional chapters dramatized Steinbeck's preachings in specific terms.

Steinbeck's method in *East of Eden* is considerably more sophisticated. He is well aware of the value of information, of "putting it all in," as he calls it in his account of the writing of the novel. He has a store of information about early days in the Salinas Valley, and he inserts into the novel essays on a variety of subjects, such as lettuce picking, the Model-T Ford and its effect upon the courting methods of a generation, old-time parlor-houses, etc. He manages all this with an "I" narrator within the novel, a modern borrowing from Thackeray's Olympian "I". This "I" however, is fictional, his family, the Hamiltons, contrasted with that of the Trasks and the Cain-and-Abel story that is the fictional plot.

Flashbacks and Tunnelling

The *flashback* is simply a method of conveying information from the past by employing a dramatic scene rather than a summary. The past events are usually brought in by a character's memory at the moment in the present to which the information from the past specifically applies. It should be pointed out that, although the flashback is a useful tool in the writer's wardrobe, it can easily be overused, and the same effect successfully produced by implication, reading-between-the-lines, or a progression of small bits of revealed information.

While writing *Mrs. Dalloway*, Virginia Woolf devised a method for dealing with these background needs:

> It took me a year's groping to discover what I call my tunnelling process, by which I tell the past by installments, as I have need of it. This is my prime discovery so far; and the fact that I've been so long finding it proves, I think, how false Percy Lubbock's doctrine is—that you can do this sort of thing consciously. One feels in a state of misery—indeed I made up my mind one night to abandon the book—and then one touches the hidden spring. *A Writer's Diary*, Virginia Woolf

In the following excerpt from *Mrs. Dalloway*, Virginia Woolf tunnels a good deal of information impressionistically, implicatively, leading to a miniflashback. It is interesting to see Woolf cutting from tunneling thoughts to present action: ("She had done things too!"), and ("In those days he was to write.").

> "But where is Clarissa?" said Peter. He was sitting on the sofa with Sally. (After all these years he really could not call her "Lady Rosseter.") "Where's the woman gone to?" he asked. "Where's Clarissa?"
>
> Sally supposed, and so did Peter for the matter of that, that there were people of importance, politicians, whom neither of them knew unless by sight in the picture papers, whom Clarissa had to be nice to, had to talk to. She was with them. Yet there was Richard Dalloway not in the Cabinet. He hadn't been a success, Sally supposed? For herself, she scarcely ever read the papers. She sometimes saw his name mentioned. But then—well, she lived a very solitary life, in the wilds, Clarissa would say, among great merchants, great manufacturers, men, after all, who did things. She had done things too!
>
> "I have five sons!" she told him.
>
> Lord, Lord, what a change had come over her! the softness of motherhood; its egotism too. Last time they met, Peter remembered, had been among the cauliflowers in the moonlight, the leaves "like rough bronze" she had said, with her literary turn; and she had picked a rose. She had marched

him up and down that awful night, after the scene by the fountain; he was to catch the midnight train. Heavens, he had wept!

That was his old trick, opening a pocket-knife, thought Sally, always opening and shutting a knife when he got excited. They had been very, very intimate, she and Peter Walsh, when he was in love with Clarissa, and there was that dreadful, ridiculous scene over Richard Dalloway at lunch. She had called Richard "Wickham." Why not call Richard "Wickham"? Clarissa had flared up! and indeed they had never seen each other since, she and Clarissa, not more than half a dozen times perhaps in the last ten years. And Peter Walsh had gone off to India, and she had heard vaguely that he had made an unhappy marriage, and she didn't know whether he had any children, and she couldn't ask him, for he had changed. He was rather shrivelled-looking, but kinder, she felt, and she had a real affection for him, for he was connected with her youth, and she still had a little Emily Brontë he had given her, and he was to write, surely? In those days he was to write.

"Have you written?" she asked him, spreading her hand, her firm and shapely hand, on her knee in a way he recalled.

"Not a word!" said Peter Walsh, and she laughed.

The Role of Sex in the Novel

Sex also comes under the rubric of information, the reading public informed of what they were supposed to be up to in the bedroom. In addition it has become almost one of the components of the novel, like plot, character, and setting; indeed sex is inextricable from both plot and character. Plot turns on sexual tensions, and sex is a useful method of presenting character.

After World War II, young writers began pushing hard against publishing timidity. An editor at Random House wrote me a letter demanding the deletion of certain words from a manuscript of mine—scribbling the words in the margin since they could not be dictated to his secretary. In *The Naked and the Dead*, Norman Mailer was forced to spell the soldier's utility expletive "Fugg," although even that constituted a victory.

This battle has long been won, and sex has moved from the shocking to the perfunctory, as in this writer's instruction to himself:

> They fumbled at zippers as they stumbled toward the pillows from the couch which he had flung on the floor.

"Get on top," he directed. . . . (continue explicitly for 100 to 200 words)

Here is a love scene from Edna O'Brien's *August Is a Wicked Month*. The woman's sexuality is rendered by the detail of her arms "singing":

> . . . his hand came around her waist and the rug began to slip because they put their remaining hands—her two and his one—to love uses, tracing each other's faces, touching, lingering, drawing away, feeling a lip's thickness, finding out. She was glad now that her arms were bare, because his touch brought them to life with one sort of move, and another.
>
> "They're singing," she said. "My arms are." Rusted from disuse, they began to come to life. Ripples of pleasure running down the lengths of those bare, white arms.

How much more effective are the implications here, and the reader's imagination engaged, than by those explicit "100 to 200 words."

Implicit vs. Explicit

In his love letter to Emma Bovary, *The Perpetual Orgy*, Mario Vargas Llosa writes:

> The erotic climax of the novel is an inspired hiatus, a sleight-of-hand trick of genius that contrives to give the material hidden from the reader the maximum possible charge. I am referring to the interminable journey through the streets of Rouen in the fiacre, inside which Emma is giving herself to Leon for the first time. It is remarkable that the most imaginative erotic episode in French literature does not contain a single allusion to the female body or a single word of love, that it is simply an enumeration of the names of streets and places, the description of the aimless wandering back and forth through the town of an old coach for hire:
>
> A lad was playing about the close.
>
> "Go and get me a cab!"
>
> The child bounded off like a ball by the Rue Quatre-Vents; then they were alone a few minutes, face to face, and a little embarrassed.
>
> "Ah, Léon! Really—I don't know—if I ought," she whis-

pered. Then with a more serious air, "Do you know, it is very improper?"

"How so?" replied the clerk. "It is done at Paris."

And that, as an irresistible argument, decided her.

Still the cab did not come. Léon was afraid she might go back into the church. At last the cab appeared.

"Where to, sir?" asked the coachman.

"Where you like," said Léon, forcing Emma into the cab.

And the lumbering machine set out. It went down the Rue Grand-Pont, crossed the Place des Arts, the Quai Napoléon, the Pont Neuf, and stopped short before the statue of Pierre Corneille.

"Go on," cried a voice that came from within.

The cab went on again, and as soon as it reached the Carrefour Lafayette, set off down hill, and entered the station at a gallop.

"No, straight on!" cried the same voice.

The cab came out by the gate, and soon having reached the Cours, trotted quietly beneath the elm trees. The coachman wiped his brow, put his leather hat between his knees, and drove his carriage beyond the side alley by the meadow to the margin of the waters.

It went along by the river, along the towing-path paved with sharp pebbles, and for a long while in the direction of Oyssel, beyond the isles.

But suddenly it turned with a dash across Quatremares, Sotteville, La Grande-Chaussée, the Rue d'Elbeuf, and made its third halt in front of the Jardin des Plantes.

"Get on, will you?" cried the voice more furiously.

And at once resuming its course, it passed by Saint-Sever, by the Quai des Curandiers, the Quai aux Meules, once more over the bridge, by the Place du Champ de Mars, and behind the hospital gardens, where old men in black coats were walking in the sun along the terrace all green with ivy. It went up the Boulevard Bouvreuil, along the Boulevard Cauchoise, then the whole of Mont-Riboudet to the Deville hills.

It came back; and then, without any fixed plan or direction, wandered about at hazard. The cab was seen at Saint-Pol, at Lescure, at Mont Gargan, at La Rougue-Marc and Place du Gaillardbois; in the Rue Maladrerie, Rue Dinanderie, before Saint-Romain, Saint-Vivien, Saint-Maclou, Saint-Nicaise—in front of the Customs, at the "Vieille Tour," the "Trois Pipes," and the Monumental Cemetery. From time to time the coachman on his box cast despairing eyes at the public houses. He could not understand what furious desire for locomotion urged these individuals never to wish to stop. He tried to now and then, and at once exclamations of anger burst forth behind him. Then he lashed his perspiring jades afresh, but indifferent to their jolting, running up against things here and there, not caring if he did, demoralized, and almost weeping with thirst, fatigue, and depression.

And on the harbor, in the midst of the drays and casks, and in the streets, at the corners, the good folk opened large wonder-stricken eyes at this sight, so extraordinary in the provinces, a cab with blinds drawn and which appeared thus constantly shut more closely than a tomb, and tossing about like a vessel. . . .

At about six o'clock the carriage stopped in a back street of the Beauvoisine Quarter, and a woman got out, who walked with her veil down, and without turning her head.

The following passage is from my novel *The Bad Lands*. Lord Machray, the Scottish cattleman, and Cora Benbow, the hard-boiled madam of the Pyramid Flat whorehouse, are both outsize people. Here is their meeting and lovemaking, whose qualities are implied rather than stated:

But one day Daisy had called her to the window, where the other girls were looking out and giggling, and there, passing in the street, was the biggest man she had ever seen, bigger than Bill. . . . He was riding a black horse, and he wore a fawn-colored suit, a cravat with a diamond stickpin that looked as big as a muffin, and a black slouch hat that swept down on one side and up on the other. He rode by on the prancing horse waving a hand at them where they watched from the windows, and at the cowboys and the loungers along the street gaping at him with their mouths hanging open like flycatchers. Behind him rode a clean-shaven, soldierly fellow, very straight-backed in a short jacket, with a queer-looking thing tucked under his arm with sticks poking out of it. The big man swung around to shoot a finger at the other, who lipped one of the sticks and high squealing music began. The two of them went on down the street with the dust drifting behind them, the big man waving this way and that even when he had run out of anyone to wave to, and the soldier one behind playing that music that seemed to penetrate to somewhere behind her eyes. All the girls were clamoring—who is it, what could it be, they had never seen the likes of it—and that afternoon they learned it was a Scotch lord named Machray. And perhaps all of them knew from that first glimpse that Pyramid Flat, and the Bad Lands, were never going to be the same again.

That night he came to the house alone. She didn't know what to make of him, although the girls all hung on him, with his lovely way of talking, as though he was the all-time nonesuch. He drank more whiskey than was good for him, and bawled out filthy poetry in a queer, Scotch way of talking, like glue in his mouth. She was considering calling Wax to put him out for the filthy talk when he got up, shook off the girls that had been clustering about him, and came over to her where she stood on the bottom stair.

"I crave a big woman, madam," he said, looking at her as though he had been sober all the time and only humbugging the drunkenness.

She said it was not her practice to go upstairs with the clients.

He bowed his head politely. "I am a big man, as you see, madam, and cannot be satisfied without a partner of large frame and expansive spirit."

She said that Annie was good-sized girl, if that was his preference.

He kept looking at her, in that way he had, as though when he was speaking to a person he was thinking of nothing else in the world but her. "Madam," he said, "that is avoirdupois, not amplitude."

So she had taken him to her room. He had a terrible scar on his shoulder that made the backs of her legs crawl to look at. He had got it at Tel-el-Kebir, he said; in Egypt with Wolseley, fighting the pasha Arabi. She had never heard of any of those except Egypt.

He made love to her as though it was her pleasure that mattered and his own was of no importance. It was something she had never encountered before. Later he told her it made his ballocks churn in a most delightful manner to hear her groaning and squealing. It was not that he had such a length on him, for she had known men hung like stallions that all they knew to do was poke and brag. But because of the way he had made love to her she had opened in a way she had never opened before, and deep in her he had touched some

> springs she had not even known were there. That first night she had realized that Lord Machray owned her if he wanted to take possession, and after he had gone, she knew she was mooning for him worse than the most foolish young whore believing her own lies of lost loves. And Machray had claimed her, and had owned her for two years now.

In this love scene from Henry James's *The Golden Bowl* the reader's imagination is powerfully engaged, at whatever level of sexual sophistication he finds appropriate:

> And so for a minute they stood thus together, as strongly held and as closely confronted as any hour of their easier past ever had seen them. They were silent at first, only facing and faced, only grasping and grasped, only meeting and met. "It's sacred," he said at last.
>
> "It's sacred," she breathed back at him. They vowed it, gave it out and took it in, drawn by their intensity more closely together. Then of a sudden, through this tightened circle, as at the issue of a narrow strait into the sea, everything broke up, broke down, gave way, melted and mingled. Their lips sought their lips, their pressure their response and their response their pressure; with a violence that had sighed itself the next moment to the longest and deepest of stillnesses they passionately sealed their pledge.

As Vietnamese girls in their ao dais know well, the suggestion is more potent than the naked statement, the implication more powerful than the vaguely embarrassing and voyeuristic mingling of limbs and organs, the reader's imagination more vivid than the image in the author's magnifying glass.

PART THREE

The Process

O N E

The Germ

. . . anybody who has survived childhood has enough information about life to last him the rest of his days. If you can't make something out of a little experience, you probably won't be able to make much out of a lot. The writer's business is to contemplate experience, not to be merged into it.
—Mysteries and Manners, *Flannery O'Connor*

The writer's first idea for his novel, the "germ," may be an event or series of events, contemporary or historical, an interesting setting or situation, a theme, mood, or character. In his introduction to the interviews with writers in the first volume of *The Paris Review Interviews*, Malcolm Cowley says of the germ: "Almost always it is a new and simple element introduced into an existing situation or mood. . . ." Henry James described it as "the precious particle."

For James, as for many others, it was an image; for Faulkner it was one that haunted him, with questions formulating themselves around the image, and the answers giving shape to the novel. The germ image of *The Sound and the Fury* was a girl with muddy drawers up in a tree, peering in a window at some family gathering inside the house. What was it?

Henry James's germs were often a character entreating him to tell her story. William Styron was similarly engaged by a woman named Sophie:

> "About five years ago, in the early spring, I woke up with the remembrance of a girl I'd known once, Sophie. It was a very vivid half-dream, half-revelation, and all of a sudden I realized that hers was a story I had to tell." That morning he began to write *Sophie's Choice*. *Newsweek*, May 28, 1979

The novel I am writing at the moment (provisionally entitled The French Lieutenant's Woman*) . . . started four or five months ago with a visual image. A woman stands at the end of a deserted quay and stares out to sea. That was all. This image rose in my mind one morning when I was still half-asleep. . . .*

These mythopoeic "stills" (they seem always to be static) float into my mind very often. I ignore them, since that is the

Of course most novels are germinated from remembrance, from personal experience. Willa Cather said that she never wrote anything that did not come from direct and rather shattering experience.

James Joyce first met Nora Barnacle on June 16, 1904, which he was later to celebrate as "Bloomsday," the eighteen hours of his novel *Ulysses*. Six days later, before his affair with his future wife had established itself, he made a pass at another young lady, whose escort bloodied his nose. Passing by was Alfred Hunter, a Dublin Jew and cuckold, who helped Joyce stanch his wounds. From this germ stemmed the relationship of Stephen Daedalus and Leopold Bloom, mythologized into Telemachus and Ulysses in Joyce's masterpiece.

Henry Miller wrote: "I am seized by the idea of planning the book of my life and I stayed up all night doing it. I planned everything that I had written to-date in about forty or fifty typewritten pages. I wrote it down in telegraphic style."

Virginia Woolf "wrote it down in telegraphic style" also, with the image that was her germ:

> This is going to be fairly short; to have father's character done complete in it; and mother's; and St. Ives'; and childhood and all the things I try to put in—life, death, etc. But the center is my father's character, sitting in the boat, reciting "We perished each alone."

Dostoyevsky's first journal entry for *A Raw Youth* is similarly telegraphic and subjective:

> A school teacher, a novel (a description of the effect Gogol's *Taras Bulba* had on him).
>
> Enemies, the village clerk (as correspondence leads to his approval).
>
> A Christian Hamlet.
>
> A tale about a humble Russian peasant, Ivan Matveevich Prohomidov.
>
> An apocryphal gospel (N. B. Temptation by the devil, a clay bird before those poor in spirit. Socialists and nationalists in Jerusalem. Women, Children.) Etc.

The first entry for *The Possessed* is even more cryptic:

1) Lizabeta [illegible word] Schurov.
2) Kartouzov . . . An attempt of an idea.
3) Three people. Etc.

best way of finding whether they really are the door into a new world.

So I ignored the image; but it recurred. Imperceptibly it stopped coming. I began deliberately to recall it and to try to analyze and hypothesize it. It was obviously mysterious. It was vaguely romantic. It also seemed, perhaps because of the latter quality, not to belong to us today. The woman obstinately refused to stare out the window of an airport lounge; it had to be this ancient quay—as I happen to live near one, so near I can see it from the bottom of my garden, it soon became a specific ancient quay. The woman had no face, no particular degree of sexuality. But she was Victorian; and since I always saw her in the same static long shot, with her back turned, she represented a reproach to the Victorian age. An outcast. I didn't know her crime, but I wished to protect her. That is, I began to fall in love with her.

—"Notes on an Unfinished Novel," John Fowles

It is time I started another novel — there is one waiting in the far recesses of my mind, like an octopus beneath a coral reef, occasionally putting out a feeler or two, prodding quite painfully into my conscious mind. I will have to respond, I can see; dive down and haul it out, and up into shallower, brighter waters, where I can get a good look at it. . . .
— Fay Weldon

Later in his notebook Dostoyevsky develops the character of Kartouzov: "Kartouzov is a poor conversationalist; he never finishes his sentences. He is never embarrassed, apparently he does not suspect that he is funny. He can be quite businesslike when necessary. He conducts himself well, strictly according to etiquette. But only to a certain point, so long as he can remain silent and is not obliged to do anything." And later still: "Begin by drawing a picture of how Kartouzov becomes interested (in the Amazon, E. W.) and intrigue the reader by a description of his early moves; he is critical of the Amazon, he dresses himself up; he is with his friends, the jeweler, the governess; he gets to the point of hating; he raises his finger to the peak of his cap. And suddenly he is in love — everything becomes clear."

Developing the Germ

What is the proper stance of the novelist with the vivid, insistent image entreating her, the feelers prodding into her conscious mind? That of the Zen archer, probably; receptive, right-brain dominant, not goal-oriented (not designing the book jacket or casting the film).

Note-making begins.

Here are my own first notes for a new novel, based on memories from my youth, and to be set in San Diego in the first six months of 1942, at the beginning of WW II:

1. How fast your friends who enlisted after Pearl Harbor got dead in that first year of the war.
2. The young whore who had jumped out the window of the hotel across from the street from the garage where I parked cars — gray-blanket-covered body, pathetic, frilly bedroom slipper lying close by.
3. The famous dirigible (Akron?) coming into the Mesa, sailors handling the mooring ropes. It sailed aloft in a gust of wind, carrying one of the sailors still clinging to his rope. He falls endlessly.
4. The young black in the freight elevator where I was delivering packages, who wanted to make a boxer of me. Pimp for the young whore above?
5. Errol Flynn at the Hotel del Coronado, in off his yacht the *Sirocco*; watching the senior prom, handsome, tall, totally arrogant. The sexual menace to your girl. Later he turned out a Nazi-sympathizer, maybe spying.
6. Tijuana just across the border as the receptacle for local evil;

Tijuana corruption, San Diego innocence.

7. Same theme with girls, but maybe switched so the young whore is the innocent?

Themes seem to be congealing, sex and death.

Thomas Mann said: "I usually have a heap of preliminary notes close at hand during the writing; scribbled notes, memory props, in part purely objective—external details, colorful odds and ends—or else psychological formulations, fragmentary inspirations, which I use at the proper place."

Anthony Burgess writes: "I chart a little at first, list of names, rough synopses of characters, and so on. But one doesn't overplan; so many things are generated by the sheer act of writing.

Flaubert, on the other hand, pondering the failure of his *Tentation de Saint Antoine*, condemned improvisation. He wrote to Louise Colet, who had read the manuscript of *Tentation* and praised it: "It's a failure. You talk of pearls. But it is not pearls that make a necklace; it's the thread. . . . *Everything depends on the plan.* Saint Antoine *lacks* one. . . ."

Elsewhere he writes to Ernest Feydeau: "Books are not made in the same way babies are, but rather as pyramids are, following a premeditated design, and by hoisting great blocks one atop the other by dint of sheer brute strength, time, and sweat."

Experienced writers may trust the emerging novel as a source of its own development, but beginners are well-advised to outline the work, considering the many novels that have been abandoned because the novelist languished waiting for the repeated prod of those feelers from beneath the reef, instead of putting on snorkel and face-mask.

He should come to an understanding of how his brain operates creatively, and learn to manipulate its functions. The creative process has been diagrammed as follows: FIRST INSIGHT—SATURATION—INCUBATION—ILLUMINATION—VERIFICATION.

These stages are performed by different apparatus in the brain, the conscious mind and the unconscious, as they shall be called here, although the functions are also known as left-brain and right-brain. *Conscious* or *left-brain* functions are linear, literal, analytic, and temporal, while *unconscious* or *right-brain* functions are perceptual, connotative, simultaneous, intuitive, and nontemporal.

The First Insight, the germ, the prod of the feeler, is unconscious, even though it may stem from something as actual as a newspaper headline or the sight of a child's sneaker beside a skid-mark in the street. Something has stirred in the perceptual domain, an image flashing to mind that sets up intriguing questions. The conscious mind now ponders these, making lists, setting up a system of file cards for research, formulating computer entries in its left-brain, with its linear, analytic mode, saturating it with relevant information.

But in this saturation stage, the conscious mind begins to falter. Journal notes of scientists often reveal a point where their investigations seem to come to a dead end. The gathered information refuses to form a meaningful pattern. Often the problem will hang fire for a long period, but the saturation seems to be necessary before the next stage can be initiated. The unconscious is not effectively engaged until it has been besieged with facts, impressions, concepts, and an array of conscious ruminations and attempted solutions.

When the conscious mind is thus stalled, the unconscious incubation stage begins. The poet Amy Lowell spoke of dropping the subject of a poem into her mind "much as one drops a letter into a mailbox," and Norman Mailer said that "In writing you have to be married to your unconscious. You choose a time and say, 'I'll meet you there tomorrow,' and your unconscious prepares something for you."

Jerome Weidman writes, in *Praying for Rain*:

> Planning is necessary, but a lifetime of planning will get you no further than the beautifully printed crossword puzzle in the morning paper. The time has come to forget the plan and pick up the pencil. It is not until I pick up the pencil that, I discovered, the creative process goes to work. Once the writer learns this, he must cling to what he has learned the way Troilus clung to Cressida. By the time he has fashioned the shape of the crossword puzzle, he is ready to turn over to his subconscious the task of coming up with the letters to fill in the blank spaces. If he truly has faith, if he comes to terms with his subconscious and is not afraid to trust it completely, it will never let him down because the subconscious never runs dry. It is like the automobile battery that recharges itself as the car is driven. It is a stream that stocks itself for endless fishing. The subconscious spends its owner's time sucking up the life around him, storing and cross-indexing it for convenient access when needed. That is why so many knotty plot points are solved while the writer thinks he is merely knitting

up the ravelled sleeve of care.

So the discovery comes to Archimedes, or Agatha Christie, in the bath. As a physicist remarked, "We often talk about the three Bs, the Bus, the Bath, and the Bed. That is where the great discoveries are made in science." Einstein had so many illuminations while shaving that he had to handle his straight razor very carefully to avoid cutting himself when seized by a "beautiful" solution.

But for this consummation to be reached by the unconscious, the conscious mind must be persuaded or tricked into getting out of the act. Many writers have called upon alcohol or drugs to rescue their creative mind from the dead hand of the conscious.

Beginning art students may be instructed to copy an upside-down drawing in order to free the perceptual from the conceptual, what they actually see from what they *think* they see.

Ray Bradbury keeps a notice on a board beside his desk: DON'T THINK! Writers are well aware of the value of shoveling snow or polishing the silverware, for the conscious mind can be distracted by simple, repetitive activity, leaving the unconscious free to concentrate.

And the unconscious solves the problem. "Eureka!" the solution looks right, is elegant, "beautiful" in Einstein's term. Now the conscious mind takes over the verification process.

The censor, nearer the surface of the mind, is therefore needed to select, filter, to give form. . . . He is the arbiter of taste, the enemy of chaos; but he is also an interrupter, an inhibiter—conservative, repressive. It may be that one of the several reasons why the Russian novelists have been preeminent is that they have always had to contend with an external censorate, reposed in the state; this may have partially displaced, or paralyzed (with outrage), or discharged, the inner censors and therefore have given those novelists relatively free access to the inner prompter, the rich deep-brain source of primary feelings. In the West, on the other hand, the puritanical and ascetic aspects of the Jewish and Christian cultures have apparently deeply encrusted the psyches of writers, so that the flow upward from the deeper regions is relatively inhibited.

—The Writer's Craft, *John Hersey*

The Ingredients of Beauty

Thomas Aquinas considered three ingredients necessary for "beauty": wholeness, harmony, and radiance. The proposed fiction has wholeness if it possesses unity within the limitless and confused background of time and space. Harmony is present in the relations of the parts to one another and in the symmetry of the whole. Radiance comes from the originality, the inevitability of the unexpected, the uniqueness and clarity of the harmonious whole.

T W O

Planning

Technique is . . . any selection, structure, or distortion, any form or rhythm imposed upon the world of action; by means of which, it should be added, our apprehension of the world of action is enriched or renewed. In this sense, everything is technique which is not the lump of experience itself, and one cannot say that a writer has no technique, for, being a writer, he cannot. We can speak of good technique and bad technique, or adequate or inadequate, of technique which serves the novel's purpose, or disserves.
—"Technique as Discovery,"
Mark Schorer

I'd hate to see such an exquisite talent turn into one of those muscle-bound and useless giants seen in a circus. Athletes have got to learn their games. . . . God, I wish he could discipline himself and really plan a novel.
—Dear Scott/Dear Max,
F. Scott Fitzgerald on Thomas Wolfe

Formal planning usually begins with character. The protagonist is the hero or heroine, and as such requires some attribute of herodom—at least a magnetism, a certain glow, as well as aspects with which the reader can sympathize or identify, or at least take seriously. He should be enough of a mover-shaker to make things happen—one who acts rather than one who reacts. If he is doomed, he should bring it on himself. Probably the reader should not see him as a loser, unless he is a charming, magnetic, heroic loser; and if he is ultimately to lose, it should be in action, not in inaction. As the most valid plots come from the development and revelation of character, so the character himself should have some voice in plot development. What does he hate, fear, need, or passionately desire, and what is he going to do about it? And what does he, and what does the reader, as well as the author, discover about him in the process?

Decisions are made, or make themselves: how point of view is to be handled, what the "closure" is that limits the proliferation of characters and the scope of the action. Time sequences are worked out. Notes have been jotted down and are entered upon file cards or the word processor; ideas have been expanded upon, turning short outlines into longer ones. Names are listed (long vowel sounds for principal characters, shorter for lesser). Maps are drawn of streets, residences, sites of action, and nearby towns.

Fred Allen, the comedian, once had the idea that he would like to write a novel, and asked his friend John Steinbeck for advice. Steinbeck responded:

> Don't start by trying to make the book chronological. Just take a period. Then try to remember it so clearly that you can see things: what colors and how warm or cold and how you got there. Then try to remember people. And then just tell what happened. It is important to tell what people looked like, how they walked, what they wore, what they are.
>
> Put it all in. Don't try to organize it. And put in all the details you can remember. You will find that in a very short time things will begin to come back to you, you thought you

had forgotten. Do it for very short periods at first but kind of think you aren't doing it.

Don't think back over what you have done. Don't think of literary form. Let it get out as it wants to. Overtell it in the matter of detail—cutting comes later. The form will develop in the telling. Don't make the telling follow a form.

Quoted by Charles McCabe in *The San Francisco Chronicle.*

Methods of Planning and Not Planning

Many novelists are constrained to the development of synopses by contractual arrangements with their publishers in which an outline and character sketches are a condition of the advance. Such a road-map is usually informal, detailed in some parts and vague in others, running ten to thirty pages. The plot is laid out in narrative form—the red superhighway leading from beginning to end, with perhaps the blue highways also lined out, and even black byways weaving around the main routes. Often writers feel that too detailed an outline becomes a constriction upon invention, that the first draft is a time for vision, for teasing out everything that seems to connect with character and theme, allowing the imagination to flow freely through the materials that have been collected so far.

Trollope confessed that he plotted his novels as he wrote them, not always knowing in advance what the ending would be. Raymond Chandler, too, admits in a letter that he did not plot in advance:

> As to methods of plotting and plot outline, I am afraid I cannot help you at all, since I have never plotted anything on paper. I do my plotting in my head as I go along, and usually I do it wrong and have to do it all over again. I know there are writers who plot their stories in great detail before they begin to write them, but I am not one of that group. With me, plots are not made, they grow. And if they refuse to grow, you throw the stuff away and start over again.

James Gould Cozzens's *By Love Possessed* was begun in 1948 and the completed manuscript delivered to Harcourt, Brace almost ten years later. Thousands of pages of his working drafts still exist and probably more pages were destroyed than saved. It is impossible to compute how many different drafts were written.

Cozzens's planning problem was that "Whatever happens, happens because a lot of other things have happened already."

His plan began with the law firm of Tuttle, Penrose & Winner taking on a case that will lead to a revelation of corruption within the firm. Cozzens, in his notes, is trying to decide what relationship the defendant, R (for Ralph), will have with the firm, and which of the partners will have been the embezzler. The three partners are Noah Tuttle (NT), Julius Penrose (JP), and Arthur Winner (AW), the protagonist.

The ultimate decision was that R would be the brother of Helen Detweiler, Arthur Winner's secretary, and the peculator Noah Tuttle, whose good-intentioned crime must be covered up by his partners after his death.

Cozzens's notes follow (as quoted in *James Gould Cozzens: A Life Apart* by Matthew J. Bruccoli):

I R's Case

Winner Tuttle & Winner

a) R is Helen D's brother—NT was George D's trustee—he was the one who gave Helen her job—his handling trusts is thus in early—
b) R is the banker's son
c) R is the son of Mrs. X, NT's secretary
d) R is NT's nephew—son of a young sister he hadn't spoken to for years because of her marriage, etc.—'estranged' daughter's son (she insisted on marrying someone he disapproved of—the [man's] not a gentleman, etc.—this continuing trait of character in Noah—It is AW who feels something must be done for the boy (The daughter is dead?)
e) R. is the Rector's son
f) R. Marjorie's son by her first marriage—perhaps inherited a touch of his father's 'mental condition'?
g) R son of a woman, now dead, who used to be NT's secretary for years—frightened, he goes to NT. Neither AW nor JP can tell why they should mess into it—NT protests he isn't strong enough to take the thing to trial, do they want to kill him?

II The Embezzlement
A. By Noah Tuttle
a) The old man, his judgment and faculties ruined, has simply got himself into a stupid jam—but it will cost AW all he has because of his partnership liability—the old fool doesn't even know what he's done with it.
B. By Julius Penrose
a) Marjorie's first husband had advanced Marjorie's father $25,000—at the divorce, her problem was to pay this back—JP 'in order to marry her' makes this possible by some expert embezzlement ['This Ruinous Woman']
a) he keeps shifting it around from account to account.
b) he took it outright from the Orcutt Trust, part of Christ Church's endowment and has simply paid the interest ever since [now the new rector wants to put the fund into the Diocesan thing and he has to find the money [My dear Arthur, I simply haven't got it. I think you'd better persuade the rector to leave matters as they are
C. By Arthur Winner
a) the expenses of his new marriage?—money to Lawrence?—same settlements he had made for Warren?

III The Firm
A. Tuttle, Penrose & Winner
a) NT thinks they have to take R's case—he is not up to it personally, at his age; but JP or AW must—
b) R's case precipitates the discovery of the embezzlement
1 JP says they ought not to mess into it, and so angers NT who says he will take it himself—he has long ago found out about JP's embezzlement—now he'll use the knowledge—
2 R's father (the banker) wants to buy R out of it: because they refuse, he is out to get JP and so digs up the facts
3 R's parents feel they'll have to leave Brocton—this will mean that JP must produce the funds he no longer has
c) NT took the money—JP to AW: do you wish to make it good? It will be mainly up to you. I have almost nothing (he has been paying off that debt of Marjorie's, unknown to AW—I think you better cover for him as long as you can

Dostoyevsky wrote eight successive outlines for *The Idiot*. Unlike *Crime and Punishment*, which he seems to have conceived whole and intact, *The Idiot* was begun, according to Dostoyevsky's notebooks, without an overall conception in the writer's mind. He wrote of the first Myshkin: "The Idiot's passions are violent, he has a burning need of love, a boundless pride, and out of the pride he means to dominate himself, conquer himself. Those who do not know him make fun of him; those who do know him begin to fear him." But by the seventh outline, six months later, the Idiot has become compassionate, forgiving, humble, the "beautiful" Myshkin of the great novel.

Henry James considered himself a failure as a playwright but did not regret the years he spent trying to master the craft, for in the process he discovered the "blessed principle" of the *scenario*. He hammered out very long synopses before he began writing the three great novels of his "major phase," *The Wings of the Dove, The Ambassadors*, and *The Golden Bowl*. The scenario of *The Ambassadors* is 20,000 words and includes almost all the major scenes, with dialog. These synopses must have been a great aid to the actual writing, for these three long novels were published in three successive years.

Agatha Christie's method of plotting was to immerse herself in a hot bath, consume green apples, and force herself to chart her work-in-progress from beginning to end. Such intense, *conscious* labor is very hard work, and a convenient rationalization is that such linear, analytic synopsis-making fetters the imagination. The alternative is the patient, tantalizing, and frustrating route of teasing the novel out of the unconscious in the writing, with its hazards of writer's block and despair, of crumpled beginnings and cigarette packages. But this process can also be the most exciting of a writer's experience, the finding of connections, the happy discoveries, the dialog between the writer and the written word, the interplay between his mind and the developing work.

THREE

Beginning

Beginning a book is unpleasant. I'm entirely uncertain about the character and the predicament, and a character in a predicament is what I have to begin with.
—Reading Myself and Others, *Philip Roth*

Eventually the writer must be confronted by a page blank except for the number *1* at the top, and perhaps *Chapter One* lower down. If she does not know exactly how to attack this terrible blankness, she can follow Steinbeck's advice to just write, and Ray Bradbury's not to think. Often her fingers will know what to put down if the mind that guides them is not overburdened with conscious thought. The first day, and the next, may be hard slogging with many halts, a couple of pages here, maybe three there, with some zip days and attendant guilt.

Here is Henry Miller's work schedule for 1932-1933, from *Henry Miller Miscellanea*:

Commandments

1. Work on one thing at a time until finished.
2. Start no more new books, add no more new material to "Black Spring."
3. Don't be nervous. Work calmly, joyously, recklessly on whatever is in hand.
4. Work according to Program and not according to mood. Stop at the appointed time!
5. When you can't *create* you can *work*.
6. Cement a little every day, rather than add new fertilizers.
7. Keep human! See people, go places, drink if you feel like it.
8. Don't be a draught-horse! Work with pleasure only.
9. Discard the Program when you feel like it—but go back to it next day. *Concentrate. Narrow down. Exclude.*
10. Forget the books you want to write. Think only of the book you *are* writing.
11. Write first and always. Painting, music, friends, cinema, all these come afterwards.

Tolstoy is reported to have finally settled down to work on *Anna Karenina* the day he came across a piece of Pushkin's that began: "The guests arrived at the country house." The line struck him as a revelation that a novel could be begun by plunging into the middle of the action, as though the reader knew what was going on—catching him up as the novel progressed.

The Narrative Hook

Narrative hook is a commercial-sounding but useful term for a speedy beginning that "hooks" the reader into the story. Here's the opening of Louis L'Amour's *Under the Sweetwater Rim*:

> They had ridden twenty miles since daylight, and at the end of their day they had come upon disaster.
>
> Two hundred feet below and half a mile away the wagon train lay scattered on the freshening green of the April grass. Death had come quickly and struck hard, leaving the burned wagons, the stripped and naked bodies, unnaturally white beneath the sun.
>
> The man in the ill-smelling buckskins brought his mount alongside Major Devereaux. "There was fifteen wagons. You can even count 'em from here. The way they're strung out they must've been hit without warning. Looks like a few tried to pull out of line, like to form a circle, but they hadn't no time."
>
> "One wagon missing, then."

The reader wants to know about that missing wagon. If everyone is dead, there's no point worrying, but if the wagon and its occupants have escaped, he wants to know what happened. The same with Nancy Drew, below; the reader is hooked by the glimpse of the burglar creeping into Nancy's house, if indeed he is a burglar and not something even more sinister.

From *The Secret of the Golden Pavilion*, by Carolyn Keene:

> Nancy Drew, her lovely blue eyes sparkling with excitement, stared in fascination from the cabin of the private helicopter. The craft was headed for the River Heights airport, a few miles beyond. Below, the rooftops of the town stood out

clearly in the moonlight.

"We're almost home, Togo," Nancy said to the terrier beside her. Fastened to his collar was the blue ribbon that he had won at a dog show in a city some distance away.

Leaning forward, Nancy asked the pilot, "Could you please go lower? I'd love to see my house from the air."

The young man shook his head. "It's against regulations. Maybe these will help you." He handed her a pair of binoculars. Nancy adjusted them and in a moment her home came into focus.

"I see it!" she exclaimed. But a second later she gasped in alarm. "A man's climbing into a dormer window of our third floor!"

From Thomas Tryon's *Harvest Home*:

I awakened that morning to birdsong. It was only the little yellow bird who lives in the locust tree outside our bedroom window, but I could have wrung his neck, for it was not yet six and I had a hangover. That was in the late summer, before Harvest Home, before the bird left its nest for the winter. Now it is spring again, alas, and as predicted the yellow bird has returned. The Eternal Return, as they call it here. Thinking back from this day to that one nine months ago, I now imagine the bird to have been sounding a warning. But that is nonsense, of course, for who would have thought that it was a bird of ill-omen, that little creature?

The first paragraph above sets the hook. The novel is narrated in the first person; therefore, we know the action is already completed, and from certain hints here—the bird's sounding a warning, and the phrase "bird of ill-omen"—we're convinced that what has happened has been dire. The reader's curiosity has been caught.

It is caught more heavy-handedly in the first paragraph of Arthur Hailey's *The Moneychangers*:

Long afterward, many would remember those two days in the first week of October with vividness and anguish.

The technique used in this sentence is very close to a device known to mystery-story writers as the *had-I-but-known*. "Had I but known of the incest and cannibalism that were to result, I would not have driven out to the old manse that day." Hailey is jamming a foreshadow of mysterious and dire events at the reader. Tryon's beginning, on the other hand, is more subtle, implying horrors-to-come rather than spelling them out in abstract terms. Hailey however, knows the value of specifics, in dates and days of the month.

Both Tryon's and Hailey's beginnings involve two different time periods, a past of the action and a present of the reconsideration of the action. The same device is used in the famous opening sentence of Gabriel Garcia Marquez's *One Hundred Years of Solitude*: "Many years later, as he faced a firing squad, Colonel Aureliano Buendia was to remember the distant afternoon when his father took him to discover ice."

Here there are three time frames, of "many years later," of "the distant afternoon," and the present between, from which both events may be viewed. The firing squad is almost a parody of "narrative hook," while the discovery of ice is a much more subtle and interesting one.

Another form of narrative hook is a foreshadowing scene like that with which Richard Wright's *Native Son* begins: the scene depicts the fear and loathing of the black family as they try to kill the rat that has invaded their house. At the end of the novel, the white society will be feeling the same emotions as it kills Bigger, the son of that household.

F O U R

Continuing

Writing a first draft is like groping one's way into a dark room, or overhearing a faint conversation, or telling a joke whose punchline you've forgotten. As someone said, one writes mainly to rewrite, for rewriting and revising are how one's mind comes to inhabit the material fully."
—*"Writing in the Cold,"* *Ted Solotaroff*

. . . one does not know a thing until one has put it down to see what will happen to it in a new medium and what it will attract to itself; what one knows is what one did not put, but what comes otherwise to be there—what was dragged into being by the agency of the language used and by the symbol made.
—Henry Adams, *R. P. Blackmur*

Hemingway's principle was to "leave water in the well," stopping each day when he knew what he would be writing the next morning. Other devices are useful also. One is to set the problems to be faced in tomorrow's writing in your head just before bed, so that the unconscious mind will work on them through the night—often to produce the solution by morning. Or studying tomorrow's problems in a hot bath at the end of the day. The hot water, the soaking, and the relaxation seem to effect problem-solving. As previously noted, Agatha Christie used a hot bath and green apples as plotting aids. The smell of apples, particularly rotting ones, has been claimed to aid creative processes.

Lower your standards and keep going is William Stafford's advice for dealing with writer's block.

For facing that blank page of paper in the morning without a single thought in your head: (1) Go back three or four pages and start retyping, taking a run at the problem, so to speak; (2) write a letter to yourself, detailing the problem, suggesting solutions, following some of these through, etc.; or (3) Take a novel by one of your favorite writers and copy out a three- or four-page passage, just to get your fingers and thoughts moving.

With luck, magic will begin to magnetize the writing, and out of thin air things will appear at just the right moment to make a connection or carry along a train of thought: something remembered, something observed, an item from the morning paper, a snippet of conversation overheard at the post office.

Thomas Mann celebrated the fact that certain books appeared on his desk at precisely the right moment, and a collection of reading material accumulated as he progressed that he referred to as "the magic circle."

Through-Lines

Characters, as they begin to curve into roundness, will contribute to the progress of the novel. Decisions as to their personalities, relationships, and fates may have to be rethought because of demands of the characters themselves. Each will have his *through-line*—his overall objective, as well as his objective in a particular scene. In that scene will be other characters with their own objectives, and if those characters quarrel, we will get to know their objectives and their natures more rapidly than if they merely chat. In fact, we can learn a great deal from a spirited scene, including the situation. In a book for actors, *Acting One* (Mayfield Publishing Co., 1984), Robert Cohen employs the acronym *VOTE* to help the actor remember these principles, where *V* stands for *Victory*, his objective or intention; *O* for the *Others*, with whom, for whom, or from whom the *Victory* is sought; *T* for the *Tactics* to be used to gain his end; and *E* for the *Expectation, Excitement, Energy,* and *Enthusiasm* with which the scene must be invested.

Scenic Development

> "What is the use of a book without pictures or conversations?" thought Alice just before the White Rabbit ran by, in condemnation of the book her sister was reading, and this childish comment is supported by novel readers of all degrees of intelligence. Long close paragraphs of print are in themselves apt to dismay the less serious readers and their instinct here is a sound one, for an excess of summary and an insufficiency of scene in a novel makes the story seem remote, without bite, secondhand; for in summary the novelist is selecting, so to speak, from his own selection . . . the summary tends to throw the events summarized into the past; we feel that they must have happened long ago. . . .
> *Some Observations on the Art of Narrative,* Phyllis Bentley

However, the novelist, as he tiptoes or blunders into his first draft, may be forced to summarize as a kind of expanded outline, telling what happens in a scene he is not yet prepared to dramatize. Ultimately, of course, he must move the scene out of summary in order to breathe life into it, for the novelist's burden is to find means of scenically presenting summary and situational information. In *The Moneychangers*, the beginning is merely summary; the reader is being *told*, not shown. In the first paragraph

In a given scene I may know nothing more than how it's supposed to end, most of the time not even that. Scenes are improvised. A character does or says something, and with as much spontaneity and schizophrenia as I can muster, another character responds. In this way, everything I write is spontaneous chain reaction and I'm running around playing leapfrog in my brain trying to "be" all my people.
—"Aim for the Throat," in The Village Voice *(April 26, 1976), Richard Price*

of *Harvest Home*, the scenic development involves the yellow bird. The Nancy Drew beginning, which is developed with great economy, is in scenic form. Louis L'Amour's scene of the destroyed wagon train is also economical. The description and action are dramatized, and situational information is cleverly presented in dialog by the speech of the man in ill-smelling buckskins.

A scene's development, then, might proceed from a summary to an overlong dramatization containing too much detail. The revision process would trim the detail, dialog, and action to the essentials.

> It strikes me that you are constantly in a hurry in your narrative . . . *by telling it, in a sort of impetuous breathless way, in your own person, when the people should tell it and act it for themselves*. My notion always is, that when I have made my people to play out their play, it is, as it were, their business to do it, and not mine. Then, unless you have led up to a great situation like Basil's death, you are bound to make more of it. . . . Suppose yourself telling that affecting incident in a letter to a friend. Wouldn't you describe how he went through the life and stir of the streets to the sickroom? Wouldn't you say what kind of room it was, what time of day it was, whether it was sunlight, starlight, or moonlight? Wouldn't you have a strong impression on your mind of how you were received, when you first met the look of the dying man, what strange contrasts were about you and struck you? I don't want you, in a novel, to present *yourself* to tell such things, but I want the things to be there. You make no more of the situation than the index might. . . .
>
> *Charles Dickens to Mrs. Brookfield*

Methods

Novelists' methods vary. Some, like Steinbeck, put in everything that seems to have any possible relevance and trust to the revision process to chip away the excess. Others build by cautious accretion, adding details and tunneling when necessary. Some are comforted by the stack of manuscript growing beside the typewriter, or, in the case of Thomas Wolfe, on top of the refrigerator. Others prefer the pages to be close to finished as they accrue.

Still, novelists who are the most economical in their presentation of details, who possess the confidence to know exactly how many parts are required to create the whole, just what trifles are necessary to galvanize the reader's imagination—even they will have imagined the scene in all its categoricalness and exactitude before they select and present.

I may—and quite frequently do—plan out every scene, sometimes even every conversation, in a novel before I sit down to write it. But unless I know the history back to the remotest times of any place of which I am going to write I cannot begin work. And I must know—from personal observation, not reading, the shapes of windows, the nature of doorknobs, the aspect of kitchens, the material of which dresses are made, the leather used in shoes, the method used in manuring fields, the nature of bus tickets. I shall never use any of these things in the book. But unless I know what sort of doorknob his fingers closed on how shall I—satisfactorily to myself—get my character out of doors?
It Was the Nightingale, Ford Madox Ford

Hemingway has much the same thing to say:

I've seen the marlin mate and I know about that. So I leave that out. I've seen a school (or pod) of more than fifty sperm whales in that same stretch of water and once harpooned one nearly sixty feet in length and lost him. So I left that out. All the stories I know from the fishing village I leave out. But the knowledge is what makes the underwater part of the iceberg.
From *The Paris Review* interview, Ernest Hemingway

It was a very simple story called "Out of Season" and I had omitted the real end of it which was that the old man hanged himself. This was omitted on my new theory that you could omit anything if you knew that you omitted and the omitted part would strengthen the story and make people feel something more than they understood.
A Moveable Feast, Ernest Hemingway

Flannery O'Connor here examines a passage from Flaubert's Madame Bovary (list is a kind of thick wool).

Flaubert has just shown us Emma at the piano with Charles watching her. He says, "She struck the notes with aplomb and ran from top to bottom of the keyboard without a break. Thus shaken up, the old instrument, whose strings buzzed, could be heard at the other end of the village when the window was

Not so long ago in Syracuse, where I live, I was in the middle of writing a story when my telephone rang. I answered it. On the other end of the line was a man who was obviously a black man, someone asking for a party named Nelson. It was a wrong number and I told him so and hung up. I went back to my short story. But pretty soon I found myself writing a black character into my story, a somewhat sinister character whose name was Nelson. At that moment the story took a different turn. But happily it was, I see now, and somehow knew at the time, the right turn for the story. When I began to write the story, I could not have prepared for or predicted the necessity for the presence of Nelson in the story. But now, the story finished and about to appear in a national magazine, I see it is right and appropriate and, I believe, aesthetically correct, that Nelson be there, and be there with a sinister aspect. Also right for me is that this character found his way into my story with a coincidental rightness I had the good sense to trust.
—"Fires," in
In Praise of What Persists,
Raymond Carver

open, and often the bailiff's clerk, passing along the road, bareheaded and in list slippers, stopped to listen, his sheet of paper in his hand."

The more you look at a sentence like that, the more you can learn from it. At one end we are with Emma and this very solid instrument "whose strings buzzed," and at the other end of it we are across the village with this very concrete clerk in his list slippers. With regard to what happens to Emma in the rest of the novel, we may think that it makes no difference that the instrument has buzzing strings and that the clerk wears list slippers and has a piece of paper in his hand, but Flaubert had to create a believable village to put Emma in. It's always necessary to remember that the fiction writer is much less *immediately* concerned with grand ideas and bristling emotions than he is with putting list slippers on clerks.
Mysteries and Manners, Flannery O'Connor

The Evolution of Theme

As the writing progresses, the novelist begins to uncover connections and relationships that she had not realized in her outlines or planning. The themes, major and minor, begin to appear in different forms. The writer must learn to capitalize on these gifts from the Prince of Serendip, for through them she will begin to discover what her novel is really *about*.

This analogical faculty, the eye that sees likenesses, parallels, contrasts, series, antitheses and reversals, is in part a gift—a way of looking at the world. But the results it brings, in a more intense interweaving, coherence and articulation of parts, are more often than not the fruits of concentrated brooding on work in hand, a searching out of all the conscious possibilities.
—Primer of the Novel, *Vincent McHugh*

The ability to discover relationships between elements in a work is, in a sense, the primary faculty of the novelist. For instance, in the second chapter of *A Portrait of the Artist as a Young Man*, Stephen Hero, in the arms of a prostitute, feels her tongue pressing through her kiss, "an unknown and timid pressure." The next chapter takes him through a period of disgust and remorse, and in reaction, into religion. At the end of the chapter, when he receives communion, he feels the Host upon his tongue in much the same manner; so the contrast, and the repetition, make a powerful connection between these two events. These incidents represent a contrast, but a parallel as well.

. . . Scheherazade avoided her fate because she knew how to wield the weapon of suspense—the only literary tool that has any effect upon tyrants and savages. Great novelist though she was—exquisite in her descriptions, tolerant in her judgments, ingenious in her incidents, advanced in her morality, vivid in her delineations of character, expert in her knowledge of three Oriental capitals—it was yet on none of these gifts that she relied when trying to save her life from her

intolerable husband. She only survived because she managed to keep the king wondering what would happen next.
Aspects of the Novel, E. M. Forster

Here is Jack Kerouac's list of the attitudes necessary to writing:

Belief & Technique For Modern Prose

List of Essentials

1. Scribbled secret notebooks, and wild typewritten pages, for yr own joy
2. Submissive to everything, open, listening
3. Try never to get drunk outside yr own house
4. Be in love with your life
5. Something that you feel will find its own form
6. Be crazy dumbsaint of the mind
7. Blow as deep as you want to blow
8. Write what you want bottomless from bottom of the mind
9. The unspeakable visions of the individual
10. No time for poetry but exactly what is
11. Visionary tics shivering in the chest
12. In tranced fixation dreaming upon object before you
13. Remove literary, grammatical and syntactical inhibition
14. Like Proust be an old teahead of time
15. Telling the true story of the world in interior monolog
16. The jewel center of interest is the eye within the eye
17. Write in recollection and amazement for yourself
18. Work from pithy middle eye out, swimming in language sea
19. Accept loss forever
20. Believe in the holy center of life
21. Struggle to sketch the flow that already exists intact in mind
22. Don't think of words when you stop but to see picture better
23. Keep track of every day the date emblazoned in yr morning
24. No fear or shame in the dignity of yr experience, language & knowledge
25. Write for the world to read and see yr exact picture of it
26. Bookmovie is the movie in words, the visual American form
27. In praise of Character in the bleak inhuman Loneliness
28. Composing wild, undisciplined, pure, coming in from under, crazier the better

29. You're a genius all the time
30. Writer-Director of Earthly movies Sponsored & Angeled in Heaven

FIVE

Finishing

. . . time spent peddling an unfinished novel could be better spent finishing it.
—Margaret Reavey

When is a novel finished? Conrad remarked that no work is ever finished, it is only abandoned, and Frank O'Connor was known to continue rewriting his short stories even after they were published. Often there is a reluctance to let the work go out into an uncaring world. Rewriting can become compulsive, the process turning negative and finally destroying the vitality and integrity of the piece instead of enhancing it.

At some point many novelists must get the manuscript physically out of their possession, to an agent, editor, or a trusted friend, since the physical disassociation is important to the revision process. Time must elapse before the novelist can regard his baby with anything like objectivity, see the blemishes and warts, and above all, see what he wrote instead of what he thought he was writing.

First novels are sometimes contracted for with less than the full manuscript considered—three or four chapters and an outline, say. It is better to present the finished manuscript. Unless there are extraordinary circumstances, a partial novel will receive a much smaller advance than a finished one. On the other hand, a contract and an advance constitute a powerful psychological lift and furnish an impetus for finishing the work. They mean that editorial advice is forthcoming, as well as a 90 percent surety of eventual publication.

Submitting the Manuscript

How does the writer go about submitting his novel, finished or unfinished? Most likely he has no connections with the publishing industry. If the author is established, he will have an agent to handle the business of submission and contract, which is the agent's main function. But if he has not been published, he can't get an agent to look at his work, much less take it on: Catch-22. Few publishers today will read unsolicited manuscripts. Most agents are uninterested in handling short stories, because the market is so small, and they are not usually enthusiastic about first novels.

However, agents appear, and are approachable, at writers' conferences. They can also be reached by mail. The Writers Guild will furnish a list of them, with addresses, upon request. A writer should write a letter of inquiry, describing his accomplishments, and offering a brief description of his novel—putting his best foot forward in the effort to engage the agent's interest.

Editors also appear at writers' conferences, as well as in university-extension and summer-school courses in writing, editing, and publishing. Simultaneously they are searching for new talent that may develop into the next generation's Hemingways or Hellers and fending off the vast heaps of junk manuscripts that threaten to ruin their eyesight and even bury them alive. They are most easily approached when a manuscript has the seal of approval of someone they trust—a staff member of a writers' conference, a teacher, a professor, or an established novelist. They can also be approached by mail. A writer might make herself familiar enough with currently published novels to know of one similar to her own. By phone or mail, she can discover the name of that book's editor, and then write him, mentioning a mutual interest, and asking if the editor would be interested in a look at her manuscript.

Many publishers now have a policy against unsolicited manuscripts—what are called *over-the-transom* submissions. Even where the transom is still open, the track is a perilous one, guarded by dyspeptic first readers who can damn a manuscript before it reaches an editor with the power to accept it.

Even if an editor becomes interested, and letters are exchanged and enthusiasm generated, that editor may have to confess that he is unable to muster sufficient editorial support to contract for the novel's publication, thus dashing the writer's hopes.

One of the great advantages of an agent is her knowledge of the tastes and humors of the editors in a publishing house, so that she is able to direct the manuscript to the editor best suited for the work. She will also obtain a faster response regarding acceptance or rejection. If she is enthusiastic about the novel, she will continue sending it out until she feels it has had every possible chance. She remembers that huge bestsellers such as Norman Mailer's *The Naked and the Dead*, and Pearl Buck's *The Good*

Earth were rejected by a dozen publishers, and Frank Herbert's *Dune* by *every* major house, to be eventually issued by a publisher of automotive manuals.

Coping with Rejection

The writer is very apt to become discouraged when his novel receives rejection after rejection, even though he may know that Jack London accumulated 600 rejection slips before he sold a short story, and William Saroyan, more than 6,000. What he should do instead of stowing away his novel and hurt feelings is to reread the manuscript. Rejection letters may have given him a hint of the novel's insufficiencies, and he may have had advice from a writers' conference or a local writers' group; moreover, as the months pass and his distance from his work increases, he can read the manuscript with a clearer critical vision.

Just running the manuscript through the typewriter again will improve it. Sentences will be shaken free of excess verbiage, a telling detail may be inserted here, a fatuity deleted elsewhere, a new insight into a character invented, a foreshadowing introduced, a too-long scene pruned to dramatic effect. With a little tightening and brightening, an unacceptable manuscript may become an acceptable one.

Years can pass in the process of sending out the manuscript, getting it back, touching it up, and sending it out again. It is a time when the only advice can be: Patience! But it takes a will of steel to follow John Galsworthy's practice of throwing away everything he wrote before he was forty, so he would not be considered merely "promising," or Bobbie Ann Mason's advice not to worry about publication for twenty years, since it takes that long to know what you're doing.

The Publishing Process

The function of an editor . . . is to serve as a skilled objective outsider, a critical touchstone by recourse to which a writer is enabled to sense flaws in surface or structure, to grasp and solve the artistic or technical problems involved, and thus to realize completely his own work in his own way.
—Editor to Author, *John Hall Wheelock*

Dramatically there is a contact, sparks, a contract. The advance is usually half on signing, half on final acceptance. Generally the author can expect to deal with the editor's suggestions for revision in an amicable atmosphere. The editor would be in a different line of work if he hadn't learned to get along with writers. Moreover, he is interested in the author's career and not merely this first novel. Often author and editor will strike up enough of a friendship so that when the editor moves along to another house, the author will accompany him as part of his stable.

In fact, in recent years an editor's duties have become so varied he has less and less time for text editing. More and more of his time is spent trying to acquire bestselling authors, as well as attending meetings within the house, with the marketing people, subsidiary rights editors, publicists, etc. Editing tends to be left in the more impersonal hands of the copyeditor. A good text editor will go to great lengths not to make demands, always to put his suggestions in the form of *queries*. Usually these are scribbled or typed on little pink or yellow gummed squares, which are attached to the margins of the typescript pages. This is the *flagged* copy of the manuscript.

Don't ever defer *to my judgment. You won't on any vital point, I know, and I should be ashamed, if it was possible to have made you; for a writer of any account must speak solely for himself.*
—Dear Scott/Dear Max,
Maxwell Perkins to F. Scott Fitzgerald

The revisions completed, copyediting completed, the second half of the advance is delivered; the novel is now *'in press.'* Months pass, and the galleys arrive, long, ungainly proof sheets. The galleys are usually the author's last chance for changes, but he should be aware of the fact that, beyond a certain minimum, he will be charged a sum set forth in the contract for resetting type.

Publicity and Sales

Usually eight to ten months pass between the acceptance of a novel and its publication. Four to six months before pub-date he will receive *bound galleys*, the corrected proofs cut into pages and bound in a no-frills cardboard cover. Copies will be sent to the list of powerful literary friends the author has been asked to supply, and also to Consequential Authors from the editor's own Rolodex. It is hoped that the circulation of these prebooks will elicit *selling quotes* for the back of the novel's jacket. The necessity for, and log-rolling aspects of, these jacket quotes may be embarrassing to the author, but they are a help in convincing salesmen and bookstore buyers of the novel's salability, in that it has impressed someone with a recognizable name.

A few weeks before pub-date come the first reviews, *Publishers Weekly* and *Kirkus Reviews*, both of which are subscribed to by bookstores. One good and one not-so-good is about par here, along with the author's first hint that he may not be headed immediately for the top of the *New York Times* bestseller list. Incidentally, *Publishers Weekly* is usually kinder than *Kirkus*.

In fact, the editorial conference has already taken place in which the fate of the novel was decided, its chances on the market, the amount of its advertising and PR budget. The die has already been cast, but still there comes the moment of pure pleasure and accomplishment, worth it all, when the novelist holds in his hand the first-print-run copy of his novel, express mailed to him by his editor.

A first printing of 5,000 is small—10,000-15,000, average and more than that, good. The budget is established accordingly. Salespeople tend to get behind a book in line with the budget. Where they might recommend to an independent bookstore twenty-five copies of their publisher's big spring book, they would push for ten of the top-of-the-list books and two or three of the mid-list.

You must be prepared to work always without applause. When you are excited about something is when the first draft is done. But no one can see it until you have gone over it again and again until you have communicated the emotion, the sights and sounds to the reader, and by the time you have completed this the words, sometimes, will not make sense to you as you read them, so many times have you re-read them. By the time the book comes out you will have started something else and it is all behind you and you do not want to hear about it.

– By-Line: Ernest Hemingway, *Ernest Hemingway*

The Author's Perspective

The author's expectations are always too high. Just looking at the number of new titles on display in a bookstore will inform her of that. However, even if the first stirrings of her novel in the marketplace have not been auspicious, there is always a hope that positive reviews and word-of-mouth will start a groundswell and cause the novel to take off like *Catch-22* or *Ironweed*. But, of course, most will not take off. A novelist's experience has been likened to the grief syndrome: anxiety, rage, bitterness, self-reproach, and finally, acceptance. The purest moment of pleasure she will experience is holding that first copy of her novel in her hands.

However, still ahead are possibilities of motion-picture options, of mass-market-paperback contracts, and of foreign rights. There will be some fine reviews and probably some stupid misunderstandings of what the novel is even *about*. It is well to remember F. Scott Fitzgerald's advice, that a writer who pays heed to his good reviews must also pay heed to the bad ones.

By the time the dust has settled, the novelist should be well into his second novel. His involvement with the second work will provide a psychological bulwark against his disappointment with the lack of attention, or the poor sales, of his first published work.

Nevertheless, times are good. At present, the first novelist is getting more attention than at any time in the recent past. Publishers are more apt to take him on than continue publishing veterans of many mid-lists. Even short story collections are currently salable.

In fact the money concern is crucial only insofar as the writer is able to continue to support his obsession, and perhaps a family also. If he's the real thing, he's not in it to drive a BMW or live in the big house on the hill; he's writing because he has to.

The Columbus Tree

The beginning of Peter Feibleman's novel *The Columbus Tree* is examined for its dynamics:

A short introductory chapter describes the town of Suelo, in Spain, setting rather symbolically themes of love, death, and disaster, and ending with the sound of an airplane buzzing closer. The next section sets us immediately in Will's point of view. His hearing the sound of the airplane and thinking he knows who is coming creates suspense. Specifics of his location are strong—on the northwest side of the highest hill. The author, establishing both reality and the point of view, engages as many of the reader's senses as possible: the buzzing of the plane, the pearl-white sky that burns Will's eyes and ears; the smell of wild thyme. Will is further established by sensations such as the wave of sleepiness, and the rather sensual way he moves his back to make a place for his body to fit into, and by his contemplation of his twelve-going-on-thirteen-year-old body. "He was a spindly boy of twelve who would be thirteen tomorrow" is authorial description rather than the thought processes of Will, but the author returns the sentence neatly to Will at the end with "and he looked it, he thought."

Will stood at the northwest side of the highest hill and listened to the plane that was circling to land. He squinted. From the sound he knew it was a seaplane, a small two-seater that had been chartered, and he thought he knew who had chartered it. It was going to land soon, he could tell from the noise of the motors. He could not see it. The buzzing of the plane and the pearl-white stillness of the September sky burned into his ears and eyes at the same time and met somewhere under his stomach. The air was singed; it smelled of the surrounding bushes of dark green thyme. With his eyes shut Will could feel the dry dust in the webs between his fingers, and the odor of thyme was as strong in his mouth as a taste. A wave of sleep came over him and he blinked into the air. He stopped trying to see the plane, and looked down at himself, letting his eyes swing in a kind of zagzag path over his own body. He was a spindly boy of twelve who would be thirteen years old tomorrow and he looked it, he thought. He was ashamed of his size—he was small for his age—and he hated the way his ribs stuck out one by one like shelves through his T-shirt. His body embarrassed him. He had left his mother with her preparations for his birthday party that would take place tomorrow in the Hotel Malage. She was using the birthday as an excuse to have one of the society parties that she had taken to giving more and more lately. She had told Will to run along and take a swim. He had come up here instead.

He lay back between two low bushes and moved his backbone like a snake for a place his body would fit into. After a while he found one—except for a rise that stuck into his left shoulder blade. He sat up and took a flat stone and scraped the piece of earth away. He was lying at a seesaw angle with his feet against a rock and he could see easily down into the town. He cast his eyes like beams below him and let them splay softly over the different kinds of hotels. There were a lot of them. Except for the part in back, most of the Spanish fishing village had been destroyed by the long endless wave of visitors that grew each year. People traveled from all over Europe and from America to Suelo—along the beach there were twenty-two hotels of different classes and still others being built. Looking down Will counted five more before his eyes began to water. He could feel the sun on his knees; the heat licked up just under his crotch. It made him hot there and he felt his piece twitch against his bluejeans. He considered about taking it out for a while. For a year he had known how to do it in fast long jerks until the new feeling, the life-feeling, came. It was a way to let something inside him out of a cage; but he needed to keep it caged now and think. He had a bad problem that kept twisting in his mind. It was about his half-sister.

Her name was Alice Littlejohn, only she had always hated the name of Alice. She preferred to be called just Littlejohn. The odd part was that neither one of them was much like their mother, Helen. Littlejohn was nine and a half years older than Will—going on twenty-three. She lived in New York. Her father was a minister who had inherited a lot of money. He preferred to live

Having established Will, the author now uses Will's eyes to describe the town of Suelo below him. As Will casts "his eyes like beams" over the scene below, the author gives us some information on Suelo as a tourist center, but we are kept aware of Will's physical presence by his watering eyes, the sun on his knees, and the sun's heat in his crotch, which causes him to consider masturbation, and brings us to the main subject here, which is his half-sister Alice Littlejohn. The author is going to be expending a great deal of effort proving the beauty, sexiness, and worth of this lady, and he begins with Will's erotic thought. The thought turns into a passage of exposition on Alice, who prefers to be called Littlejohn—which preference for her patronymic over her feminine name would seem to show that she has still to find herself as a woman.

There follows some swift exposition of Will's own situation, with his mother, Helen.

simply and practice his faith; he had given most of the money to Littlejohn. She came to see Will twice a year wherever he was and Will waited for the visits. She had always been the person in the world he was most connected with. He could not explain that.

Littlejohn's father had divorced their mother and Will's father had been her second husband: he had not had time to divorce her—he had been killed in the Second World War. Now, in 1957, he had been dead thirteen years and one month. Since his death Will had lived alone with Helen, but for the last couple of years he had lived in boarding schools and had stayed with her only on vacations. (Helen traveled a lot, visiting friends and going to this or that resort.) This year he had gone to the Lycée Francais in Madrid where classes were taught in French, though many of the students were Spanish; Helen had decided a European upbringing would be good for him. So far Will's Spanish and French were both good and he could understand some Italian too and a little German. Just over three months ago he and Helen had come down to Suelo for the summer; Littlejohn had joined them here in June.

We are returned closely to Will's point of view by the light swimming in his eyes, and his lashes like black thorns. His thoughts turn to Littlejohn again as he watches the plane coming in to land, which is vividly described as a slant of silver slashing like a knife over the sea. He remembers his sister in very specific terms—the six freckles, like little maps. And he remembers her saying, *"I'm going to have one, Will."* The statement is just ambiguous enough to continue the suspense engendered by the arrival that the airplane signifies. Now we also learn that in the immediate past there have been dramatic happenings, including death and birth.

Now on the hill he opened his eyelids enough that the light swam around in two loose pools. He could see two of his eyelashes like black thorns stuck into the flesh. His life had been confused ever since the day last June that Littlejohn came.

Now she was gone—Will didn't know where—and that was the last of the rattling facts of the summer, and the worst; it wasn't possible, but there it was.

He could see the plane now coming in below to land on the water. Through the heat waves it looked like a long slant of silver that flashed like a knife over the sea. Then he remembered what Littlejohn had said to him when she left this last time. It was a blunt fact, a thing that didn't fit inside his train of livingness at all without mashing all the other facts to pieces. She hadn't told it to anybody else. She had turned from the boat that was waiting for her, and walked back to Will and put her head close on the left side where the six freckles were, so close the freckles stood out from her skin like little maps in front of his eyes, and said, "I'm going to have one, Will." Just that—no more. Then she had turned quickly and left, so that when Will watched the motor launch through the spray that rose behind it like a fan opening out of the sea he had seen not the fan but only the six freckles. Six maps. Six words. *I'm going to have one, Will.* That made so much sense they made no sense at all. When the freckles had faded from his eyes she was already gone in the water.

Hunching back in the dust he thought now that in just three months there had been so many new happenings in his life he had had no time to get used to any of them. There was the fact of life and the fact of death. There was even the fact of murder. Besides that, a Spanish child had died: two people had been killed, two were starting to be born, in this one summer. . . .

The seaplane had landed now. He watched it below him cutting channels behind it like white burns in the water. It waddled in the sea toward the Hotel Malage. Then watching the sky he could hear the singing of crickets in the bushes around his head. He belonged in the green smell growing out of the dust. If he could catch up with the last three months, things would be easier, if he could start back at June, he could get used to the new pieces of living. Like that first morning—the day Littlejohn had come to Suelo—June the Fifth. Though not so much had happened to him that day, still he knew it had all started then.

It had begun when they were driving in her convertible under a streaky gray sky darker than this one. It had been just the two of them. Him and Littlejohn.

On the morning of June the Fifth.

We are returned to Will's senses with a fine descriptive passage—the author is meticulous at tapping as many of the senses as possible. At the end, Will remembers that Littlejohn had come to Suelo on June the Fifth—his recollections of his sister are always *very* specific, *six* freckles, June the *Fifth*, which helps prove to the reader his feeling for her.

They drove that day watching the big black shadows wheel in the sky. Will could see them clearly—they were birds of some kind. Looking back from the convertible he could almost make out the separate feathers. He asked what they were but Littlejohn didn't hear him, for thinking, or else because the top was down and the wind was too loud. South of Seville the air from the hot fields of alfalfa was so thick you could feel it, sick-sweet and heavy on the tongue. Will dipped his jaw and took a mouthful of air and pushed it back out. He decided to ask the question again. He could still see the black shapes turning, like shadows on the sky, as if they were caught in the air. "What are they?" he said.

"Vultures," Littlejohn said without looking. "Dirty birds."

"Why dirty?"

"Because they are. They wait up there watching an animal die till it's dead, and the animal dies watching them wait. They're horrible."

Will looked back again to see what it was the birds were circling over, but they were too far away now. They looked like smoke over the low gray hills. Littlejohn turned a curve and they were gone. Ahead was the smudged sky with long ash-clouds running across it and then he saw a gas station and some people standing outside next to a station wagon: sailors from the American naval

Again the author expertly fills out his suite of sense-impressions to establish the reality of the scene. The shadows wheeling, the smell and taste of the South-of-Seville air, the sensation of the speed of the convertible coming from the wind blowing into Will's mouth. There is a discussion of the birds, which are vultures, harbingers of death to the reader, and "dirty birds" to Littlejohn, who connects them with the "Navy ladies." Now we have a description of Littlejohn, and it is to be given through Will's eyes ("He turned his head and looked at her") which has more authority than authorial description.

base farther on at Rota. The two men were in uniform. The women were dressed in bright colors and one of them had high-combed hard hair like painted tin, shiny—the dead color of yellow that comes from hair dye. "Navy ladies," Littlejohn said. "More dirty birds."

Will could tell she was in a bad mood; she was trying to sound too hard. He turned his head and looked at her.

We have a continuation of the idea that she has not found herself as a woman in the fact that she was dressed as a man, boots, bluejeans, no make-up, short hair—though the hair is sunburned so that it looks as though she is burning, which is a simile that the reader sees speaks of her mental state as well as her hair color.

A very effective detail of Littlejohn's appearance is that her eyes become slightly crossed when she is angry. "The defect made Littlejohn look off-balance and strangely vulnerable. . . ." It gives her face "an odd sexual quality." It is often the defect, the beauty mark, that creates beauty, and this operates in the creation of Littlejohn's beauty and sexuality. This, moreover, is continually reinforced by Will's attitude toward her. He can feel the curve of her windblown shirt over her breast almost as though he had reached out and touched it, and the look of it makes him ache.

Littlejohn was dressed like a man, with boots halfway up to the knees over bluejeans and a white shirt and no cap. She never wore any makeup and the sun had burned her hair white and gold on top, different colors—not like the women at the gas station. Littlejohn's hair was short; it looked like long pieces of flame, like she was burning.

Will dropped his gaze to where the hard sunlight gave Littlejohn's light blue eyes a kind of feverish glitter. You couldn't tell from her profile, but from time to time she was just the smallest bit crosseyed—it was nearly unnoticeable, but it was one of the features he loved best about her looks. It didn't happen unless she was angry or something; then her eyes would flash, and then you saw that the right one listed a fraction of a degree toward the center. The defect made Littlejohn look off balance and strangely vulnerable right at the times when she most wanted to look the opposite. Sometimes it gave her whole face—at times almost too stark to be considered pretty—an odd sexual quality. She was pretty, though. Not as beautiful looking as Helen, but then nobody was as beautiful as Helen. Right now the wind was molding Littlejohn's shirt against her right breast, and Will could feel the curve of it more that way than if he had reached out and touched her. The look of her breast made a sort of ache in him. The more she tried dressing like a man the more she looked like a woman, he knew. She wasn't all that much taller than he was, and trim, but everything was there, the full curve of it, and sometimes the little nipple at the end.

Littlejohn saw him looking and put a hand up through her hair and then back on the wheel. "Will, don't stare at me," she said, "I'm driving."

He sat back and looked ahead again. A car was coming in the opposite direction; it wasn't an American car and the man behind the wheel didn't have American eyes. The strange man's face lit up in the half-second when he saw Littlejohn, just as the two cars passed. His eyes glowed out as if they had a light of their own. Will thought they were Spanish eyes, but he wasn't sure. He had this theory all eyes have countries. Except dead eyes; they must be like photographs of eyes, homeless. Only that was a guess—Will had never seen a dead person. He turned around but the strange man in the car had already disappeared down a side road behind them. The road was at a turnoff that was marked "Sanlúcar." Will could still make out the dust from his car. "I didn't like the way he looked at you," he said.

"Who?"

"That man."

". . . What man?"

"He's gone now," Will said. For no reason he added, "I ought to marry you."

"You can't," Littlejohn said.

"We didn't inherit all the same genes. It's a question of genes. A half-brother isn't really a brother."

"Look, Will," Littlejohn said, "shut up for a while. I'm thinking."

"You don't sound like you," Will said. "You're talking like somebody else."

"Like who?"

"Somebody tough. You're not like that."

He put his hands on the seat next to him. For a second he was word-proud, as if the thoughts in his brain were swelling—he could feel them in his head and in his pants. The thoughts were getting bigger and he sat there listening to the swelling of the words.

"It's going to be a hot day," he said. "Where'll we go?"

Littlejohn didn't answer right away. "I'd like to see Jerez, and I'd like to take a look at the coast around Cádiz," she said finally. "We can stop and have lunch somewhere. There's . . . I have a thing I want to talk to you about. We needn't hurry, as long as we make Suelo while it's daylight."

"It doesn't get dark now till nine," Will said.

They drove a while in silence.

"I've never been to Puerto de Santa Maria," he said. "It's a port town between the American base and Cádiz. Mother's never been there either. She talks about a lot of places she's never been to. She just talks a lot."

"That she does," Littlejohn said. "So do you. That you inherited."

Will crossed his arms and looked to the right. They were passing soft rolling fields now, yellow and green and studded with white houses. It wasn't just the way she was talking. He had known all

A theme of "looking" is struck; she doesn't want Will looking at her. Immediately a car approaches from the opposite direction, and a man with burning eyes, Spanish eyes, looks at her. This time it is Will who does not like the other man looking at Littlejohn. This incident of the man in the passing car is dramatic, and we can be sure the incident, and the man, will turn up again.

Will says he ought to marry Littlejohn, which continues the reinforcement of his feeling for her. Then he accuses her of not talking like herself, continuing the idea of her not being herself yet. Will's thoughts of her swell both in his head and in his pants.

morning that Littlejohn had something special to tell him. She had phoned the day before from Madrid to ask Will to take the bus up from Suelo and meet her in Seville; even Helen had found it suspicious. Littlejohn wouldn't have wanted to spend the day driving around in a car unless there was something she needed to say to Will privately without their mother anywhere near. Helen hadn't much liked the idea but there was nothing really wrong with it; Will had taken the first bus, the early one, and got off at the last stop outside Seville just before ten o'clock that morning. He had waited an hour drinking an orangeade at a white wicker table in a dusty outdoor restaurant under a tin canopy on the main highway. Then he had seen her.

Littlejohn had come in a silly way, driving too fast, rising over the gray hills as if the sun were chasing her. She had skidded to a stop at the restaurant where they had arranged to meet, and she hadn't talked. She had just picked Will up in the rented car and looked at him once, long and hard, the way she always did after a six months' separation, and touched his face with the flat of her hand and then started the car up again and they drove together silently on the road south from Seville through the alfalfa fields in the white sunlight with the death-gray hills behind them. Littlejohn was like that—she didn't say a thing until she got good and ready. Even though she had arranged it, she wouldn't tell him what it was that she had come to tell him until the time was right. It was an old habit, her private sense of timing—Helen always claimed it came from Littlejohn's father, the Reverend John Littlejohn. It was unnatural for a girl to be so quiet, Helen had said when Littlejohn was younger. It was unnatural for a girl to be so full of a minister's silences.

Now, having established this present scene, the author can flash back to where Will met her on this day, before they got into the car. The exposition is swift but made vivid by the details the author has chosen to make the reader "see" it—the orangeade, the white wicker table, the tin canopy, etc., including the sensation of her touch on Will's face. Nor are the major themes neglected; the hills are "death-gray." Littlejohn's silence, "a minister's silence" suggests her father, and makes a useful bridge for Will to think of his own father, and again the idea of death comes in. Clearly this novel is to include sex and death.

She braked now behind a hay truck and waited for a chance to pass it and Will put his head on the seat and thought for maybe the millionth time in his life about his own father. He hadn't known his father but he had seen a picture of him. William Charles Locke, a war hero. You couldn't tell much from the picture but he looked perfectly nice. Nobody ever told Will much about it so he sometimes dreamed about it. He didn't miss his father—he never had; but he dreamed of wars and all the ways his father's plane had chewed into the soft earth. He didn't mind thinking about the men killed instantly; he only didn't like the ones left dying slowly and screaming. Maybe it wasn't like that but he thought it was like that. Maybe war wasn't the way he dreamed it was either.

"Here we are," Littlejohn said. He sat up and looked.

It was true whenever he thought about his father he stopped noticing things. They were coming into the city of Jerez. Littlejohn pulled up in front of a small white-fronted bar that had two tables outside. They went in and sat down and she ordered a glass of wine, and Will ordered a *caña*—a small glass of draft beer. "The beer is weak in Spain," he said, "all the kids take a little." Littlejohn nodded and the waiter went to make their drinks. The waiter had almond-shaped Moorish eyes. The little room was dark and tile-cool. It buzzed with flies. The waiter brought their drinks with a plate of sour-smelling olives and set it down between them. His eyes inched over Littlejohn's body as he straightened. Most men looked at her that way. Will raised his glass when Littlejohn raised hers. They touched glasses, and Littlejohn looked at him. Her eyes were sea-colored over the light yellow wine. She didn't look cross-eyed at all today. She watched Will while she tasted it. "It's sherry."

"Sure."

" . . . Why sure?"

"It's what Jerez is," Will said. "The story is that none of the Englishmen who came here to make wine could say Jerez, so they pronounced it sherry."

"Why did they come here to make wine?"

"The Spaniards were making it," Will said. He had learned all this at school.

"Oh," Littlejohn said. She put her glass down on the tin-toppped table and stroked it. Will watched her hand. The ends of her fingers were shaking. "Do you like Spain, Will?"

He lifted his shoulders.

"You're not unhappy?"

"No."

Littlejohn usually asked him the same question. When she came they went places together and talked to each other. Will could explain things that were on his mind to her in a way that he could not talk to anybody else. Only today she looked edgy, he thought. More than edgy.

"What are you scared about?"

Littlejohn kept her eyes on her glass. "What makes you think I'm scared?"

"You looked funny when you came this morning."

"I haven't had much rest," Littlejohn said, "that's all . . . I threw a few things in a bag and flew from New York to Madrid. I rented the car in Madrid . . . I spent last night in Córdoba. I just need some sleep. That's all it is."

Will took a gulp of his beer and swallowed it. He didn't believe her. The beer was salty and not very bubbly but it had a nice bitter flavor.

"You hungry?" Littlejohn asked, "or should we have lunch later?"

"Later."

More effective sensory details: the smells of olive oil, black tobacco and carnations; the burning hot air; the sulky brown fields; the dust like a sheen in the air. And now comes Littlejohn's announcement that she is to be married. Will is tremendously affected by this information, but instead of giving his thoughts, the author presents his physical sensations—the "visceral equivalent"; he feels as though he has a finger in a weak electric plug.

They got back in the car and drove south through the dusty city of Jerez. It smelled of olive oil and black tobacco and in some places there was the odor of carnations. The heat swam up from the streets in hard baking waves and he was glad when they could see the open road again. As they came out of the choked buildings they passed white-walled *bodegas*, wineries where the sherry was aged and bottled, but by then you couldn't smell anything but dust again with the sun in it.

Will swiveled his eyes in the burning-hot air. The fields on either side of the road had turned a sulky brown. There were splotches of some kind of grain that stuck up, low motionless and shining, in the windless heat. The sun poured down over the car and after a while Littlejohn pulled over to the dirt at the side of the road and put the top up. When she started along the highway again she drove more slowly. Then in the silence she said it:

"I'm going to be married, Will."

He had been watching the dust that rose like a sheen in the air ahead of them and he had been thinking about drinking an ice-cold Coke.

"You hear me?"

For a while Will didn't move. He considered the new fact, but it didn't knife into his stomach like it normally would have—it came more in a fuzzy feeling around his skin, as though he had put his finger in a weak electric plug. He knew Littlejohn was expecting him to have a reaction to it but he only sat there.

The new fact didn't sound at all like her, he thought. It was their mother Helen who was always getting engaged. As a rule Helen decided to marry somebody on the average of once a year; a Christmas when she wasn't planning on it wasn't really a celebration. Littlejohn had decided years ago that she herself would never get married. Back when she was fifteen and Will was six she had told him about it. She wasn't going to look at men seriously. It wasn't in her. She was going to become an anthropologist and study bones.

"I have to. It's time," she said now as if he had asked her why, "it's like this, Will . . . the French have the right idea—you don't necessarily get married because you're dying of love. That kind doesn't always last."

The whole thing sounded like she had been practicing it in a tape recorder.

"Why then?"

Littlejohn said, "You just need a reason to stay alive." It was a funny answer, but she meant it, he could tell. It didn't sound rehearsed.

"Mother will want to know if he has money," she added.

"Does he have money?" Will said. It was the game they used to play when they were younger—getting each other ready for Helen's questions.

"No," Littlejohn said. "I have."

Will yawned, hard.

"My getting married won't change us. I'll come to see you just as often."

"It doesn't bother me," Will said. "I'm fine."

". . . You only yawn like that when you're nervous."

"It's you," Will said. "You're nervous. I watched when you came to pick me up. You were driving away from the sun."

Littlejohn stared at the road in front of them without speaking for a minute or so.

"What's he look like?" Will said.

". . . Oh, he's good-looking, I think," she said slowly. She laughed. "I must have thought so, anyway."

"Where did you first meet him?"

There was a pause. "I can't remember," Littlejohn said.

". . . You what?"

"It's a problem I've always had," she said. "Not remembering."

"How can you marry a man if you don't remember what he looks like?"

"I'll remember him when I see him."

"Okay," Will said.

He couldn't explain the feeling that was inside him now. The electricity in his brain was making side roads down through his body—it was like there was a short circuit in his thinking. On any other day, the idea that Littlejohn might belong to some stranger would have made him sick to his stomach. Will's father was dead but his mother was another kind of silence. Littlejohn had always been his lifeline person. His biggest fear every six months was that something might happen to stop her from coming to visit—it hadn't entered his head she might make a private life for herself

Again we have a visceral equivalent, Will's yawn, but the author isn't quite sure the point's across, so Littlejohn mentions that he yawns only when he's nervous—though this also helps establish the fact that they know each other well. Will responds that she is the one who is nervous, that when she picked him up she was "driving away from the sun," a fairly mystical remark for a twelve-year-old boy. It becomes clear in the ensuing dialog, however, that Littlejohn is not marrying for love or money—she has already said she needed a reason for being alive.

that far away. Only now that she had, he felt only this long loose buzzing like a person separated. He couldn't make it out.

The car went over a bump and for an instant Will's brain went weird and floaty. Then he realized what it was. It wasn't the news about Littlejohn that was making him dizzy. It was the beer. A *caña* was only a few swallows; it was safe as long as you'd had something to eat first—but he had forgot to eat breakfast that morning before he took the bus, and the olives in the bar hadn't been enough to stop the effects of the alcohol. I'm drunk, he thought, this is what it feels like to be drunk. You don't care about anything—you just sit there and tingle.

"I'd better get some food into you," Littlejohn said from the driver's seat. She had been eyeing him.

"I'm fine," Will said loud. "I feel fine."

They were within a few kilometers of the port now—you could begin to smell the sea. On their right was a high wicker fence made of steel and beyond it the American naval base. All you saw of the base was mile after mile of wide flat green.

"How far is Suelo from here?"

"Not so far," Will said.

"You can ask me anything else you want."

" . . . About what?"

"You know what."

Will kept his head turned away and let the focus of his eyes swim along the steel wicker evenly without catching on the metal. He didn't want to talk about it any more. Ahead the road curved sharp to the left. After a few kilometers more, they came to the coast town called Puerto de Santa Maria. Littlejohn turned right and drove into it over a dusty road that passed the small bull ring; then she followed the piers along the sea until they came to a square and a little park and what looked like the main street of the town.

She and Will got out and stood looking up and down. The town was so dry in the white summer sun it looked hazy. There was a layer of dust like a dirty pink stocking in the air.

More visceral equivalents; Will protests too much that it is not Littlejohn's news that makes him dizzy. They come into town; the exposition of the arrival is brief, but the author does not neglect his details—the layer of dust like a dirty pink stocking in the air is especially effective. Details of eating and drinking in Spain seem always to sound

Littlejohn led the way and they sat at a table outside a seafood bar overlooking the park. Will ordered a ration of clams *a la plancha* and one of boiled shrimp and two grilled fresh sardines. They sat and watched the townspeople mill through the streets into bars to have wine or beer with a food appetizer of any kind, hot or cold, for in Spain people rarely drink without eating. There were boys on bikes and people walking. When the *tapas* came Will showed Littlejohn how the clams had burst open on a hot griddle and then been sprinkled with lemon juice. She ate the way Will told her but he could tell she was somewhere off in her mind. She still had the driven look as if something was chasing her. After some of the shrimp and one of the sardines the fuzziness in his own brain began to disappear.

like Hemingway, but these are good Hemingway.

"What else will Mother ask?"

Littlejohn shrugged. "Whether I'm pregnant."

". . . Are you?"

"No," she said. She was staring at the cobblestone street in front of her and her face was quiet as stone.

"What else?"

"Nothing else . . . she may not even ask that. She'll probably just clam up. I'd like another glass of wine," Littlejohn said.

Will ordered it and they finished the shrimp, breaking the pink heads off and sucking them and then peeling the slim bodies. Littlejohn wiped her mouth. "Let's walk," she said.

Good Hemingway detail of eating shrimp after some talk of pregnancy, with an ambiguous expression on Littlejohn's face. Again the wonder of Littlejohn is reinforced by the Spanish women staring at her, and now the car full of drunken sailors comes honking through town.

They strolled through the park that was only a wide paved road with benches on either side, where cars couldn't go. There were old women dressed in solid black with heavy black stockings. Their skin was creased and dry and they watched Littlejohn's boots and hair with the look of the very old or the very young who stare as if their eyes could wipe away the mystery of the object and reveal its true nature.

Will walked a little faster, still waiting for the panic-pain that would come from the fact of her marrying some stranger. He expected it to hit him now that the effects of the beer had worn off but the pain didn't come. He decided to test it. "Where will you live after you're married?"

"Long Island," Littlejohn said. "We . . ."

Someone yelled behind her and they stopped and watched. A red Thunderbird convertible was driving too fast along the main street of the town. There were three American sailors in it, two sitting up on top of the backs of the seats. The sailors were drinking beer out of bottles. The huge car looked like an angry whale in the little town. The sailor who was driving had a bottle too, and they were all three laughing in a loud way. The car floated from side to side over the thin street, not slowing or honking for corners. A couple of fishermen yelled and made filthy gestures as it turned up another street. A skirt of dust flared up and flirted behind it in the noon light.

"There's our navy now," Littlejohn said. "Our brave boys overseas. My God, how can we do it?"

"Do what?"

Littlejohn reacts strongly against this violence. Her politics appear to be liberal, sympathetic to suffering mankind. Again Will mentions that she seems frightened. The author never misses a chance to bring in strong smells; at the docks here the sweet reek of tar and rotting fish. The subject of their mother and the hotel come up, and the fact of the bungalows all being done in different colors is mentioned for the first time. The reader suspects that those colors are going to be important to the story.

"We wouldn't support the Republic in the Spanish Civil War. Now we come in and back up the Fascists. Look at the town . . . our sailors don't even know what they're here for. How could they know, when we can't tell them? The plain stupidity of it. The poor bastards . . ."

"Who?"

Littlejohn kept silent for a moment. "Oh, everybody," she said slowly.

Will watched her. "You *are* scared of something."

They walked past an old Spanish woman who had been watching them. The woman pointed in an accusing way with a finger at the dust left by the American Thunderbird. She nodded her head reproachfully at Littlejohn, as if Littlejohn might have been responsible for the behavior of the car.

"She must think every American knows every other American."

"No," Will said. "She doesn't know what an American is. She just thinks all foreigners know each other."

"How can you tell?"

"It wouldn't matter if they were Spanish sailors from Madrid. A foreigner in Spain is just a person who doesn't come from your home town."

They walked out of the park across the square onto the waterlogged docks that reeked sweetly of tar and rotting fish in the sun.

"Tell me about Suelo. What's it like?"

"Mother likes the owner of the hotel. Holtz. He's a German. The Hotel Malage's all done in colors. Everything has to match."

". . . Match how?"

"Everybody has a different color bungalow. If you live in the blue bungalow then your tablecloth in the dining room is blue and your beach umbrella is blue, and all your towels, and your barstool . . ."

"Jesus," Littlejohn said.

" . . . you can even get blue sun glasses at the desk."

"I'm sorry I asked."

"There's a green bungalow and a red one and an orange one. They have forty bungalows—forty different combinations of colors. Everything in the main building is divided up and . . ."

"Will, forget it. Please . . . I'll see it soon enough. Let's plain walk," Littlejohn said.

They turned and went back again to the town square and then back into the park. Will raised his right hand and fingered his body under the ribs around the stomach as if the ache he was waiting for was hiding there. He thought purposely, *Littlejohn is getting married.* He mouthed the words over, but the stubborn pain refused to come. He was completely sober now and he felt only a sort of dreamy disbelief in the news. He tried to think of Littlejohn standing stiff in front of an altar next to a blank-faced groom in a wedding costume but the picture in his mind was not real.

He walked a little behind her, watching her profile against the light. The light had turned a soft blue, endless, the color you think of when they talk about atmosphere. Her face against it was like something torn out of the sky.

Then, watching her, he could tell that something was about to happen. Not from her expression—her nostrils flared for an instant, but otherwise her face didn't change. He could just tell.

He wasn't sure when he first heard the brakes behind them screeching, but right away he could hear the dog. The shouts of the men came later; the first was the noise a dog makes when it's hit hard, a high long yelling with throbs of sound in it. The screams of the men and the dog were like the noise in his dream when the plane chewed into the earth. Turning, Will saw the red Thunderbird again. It had hit a dog and skidded into a building.

Littlejohn said, "Wait . . ." but Will had already started to run; it was four blocks down the street on the other side of the park. There was a crowd gathering and people shouting. A woman had joined the screaming now; you couldn't tell when she had started. She had pitched herself alongside one of the shop owners on the street. There were two bodies, both men and both of them still alive. There was a child who lay in a broken way, and there was a donkey caught and half crushed between the right fender of the car and the building. There was a lot of blood and the donkey was braying very loud. There was nothing for Will to do. People were helping the men on the ground. Somebody was calling for a doctor. Two of the American sailors sitting in the car looked hurt; one held a red hand to his face. The driver had stepped out of the wreck and stood now to one side of it. He was holding onto his empty beer bottle as though it meant something to him, looking at the mess on the street and shaking his head. He couldn't seem to take in what had happened or what he had done. He scanned the crowd and all at once, without any warning, he looked at Will. Their eyes locked and Will found himself looking back at the face of a man he had never seen. Years later he thought there were many things that he could have known if he had only read the real meaning of the dazed hopeless expression on the face of the drunken American sailor who had crashed into the building.

Now we have the crash, which Will's mind instantly connects with the death of his father. Novelists work in terms of parallels, contrasts, and repetitions, so that the author here forces a connection between this crash and the airplane crash that killed Will's father. There is also a realization on the reader's part that the author will not burden him with arbitrary and meaningless violence, and that this incident is going to connect in some way with larger issues in the novel, either as the beginning of some train of plot or as a symbolic foreshadowing. Also that characterization will be realized in terms of it, for character is most effectively and economically shown in incidents of stress. A point-of-view flaw here: there is a slight attempt to keep in Will's consciousness: "There was nothing for Will to do," but in actuality the author has moved the camera back and away from Will, and what is shown, usually in short, simple, declarative sentences, is an omniscient description of the scene without any overlay of Will's emotion or attitudes as witness.

The author returns the point of view to Will when his eyes lock with those of the drunk driver, and with his visceral sensations at the sight of blood. The crowd scene is well handled by the useful device of always placing people in a crowd in conjunction with other people or with things. Then there is the horror of the hurt dog screaming; Littlejohn sweeps up the dog and comforts it, as much perhaps out of sympathy for Will's distress as for the dog. Will however does not fail to notice the establishing detail of the grease on Littlejohn's arm.

A bunch of curious townfolk were pushing from behind, and Will turned from the sailor and walked out of the accident against the tide of people. He couldn't find Littlejohn. His insides had spread at the sight of the blood, and he could feel his stomach fluttering weakly in two parts like broken wings. He passed a bar they hadn't seen from the park; it looked like an imitation American hard-liquor bar, and it had been full of American sailors out of uniform and girls. The sailors were joining the Spanish people at the edge of the accident; the girls stood alone grouped together in the dark entrance of the bar. Will passed it and turned the corner. Then he saw the dog.

It was the size of a terrier, short, with greasy brown hair and the lean look of a stray, and it had flies around it. It was making the throbbing sound Will had heard before. It was sitting in its own blood, and one of its eyes were hanging out. Will stuck his hand out open but there was no place to touch the dog, and it went on yelling. Then Littlejohn found him.

When she saw Will's face she swept past him and bent down and got the dog. She straightened and held it in a certain way. The dog was still making the sound, but after a while it grew softer in her arms. There was a grease mark on Littlejohn's right wrist. She took the dog across the street to a man who had turned away from the accident. The man looked bored.

"Ask him if there's a vet," Littlejohn said.

Will did.

"Veterinario?" The man lifted his shoulders.

"Se muere ya," another man near him said. *"Déjalo ya."*

"No," Will said fast in Spanish, "where is the animal doctor?"

"No hay," the first man said. He watched Littlejohn. *"Señorita . . . sangre."* He pointed to the blood on the dog.

Littlejohn turned and walked to a woman she had seen standing in a curtained doorway on the corner. It was another entrance to the bar they hadn't been able to see from the park. It was dark inside. "Talk to her in Spanish," Littlejohn said to Will over her shoulder.

"She's not Spanish," a voice behind the woman in the bar said. "She's Dutch. There isn't any veterinary. There's a *practicante* lives two streets over . . . he's only a kind of practical nurse, but he might be willing to bandage the dog for you. He might even be sober," the soft-throated voice in the dark said.

Littlejohn asked, "Is there an American hospital at the navy base?"

"Yes," the woman in the dark said. "That's an idea. You never know about that hospital. They might take dogs . . . they won't take people."

"I'll take him to the *practicante*."

"That's what I would do," the woman said. "Were I a dog lover."

Littlejohn crossed the street fast and they walked where the woman had pointed. She stumbled once. The dog started yelling again and she held it closer till it stopped. Will beat on the door, a heavy woman with a mop opened it. She stared at the dog. Then she started to close the door.

"Take some money out of my purse," Littlejohn said. "Tell her I'll pay double."

"I speak English," the *practicante's* woman said. "Double?"

"Five hundred pesetas. It was hurt in the crash. You must have heard the sound of the crash."

The woman didn't move.

"All right," Littlejohn said. "Twice double . . . open the door."

They followed her into a patio and the woman put the mop down. *"Jaime,"* she called loud to the back, *"levántate ya, jo'er."* There wasn't any answer. *"Hijo puta, ya 'stá bien, no?* Sons bitch asleep from wine,"she said. *"Jaime?"*

"I'll go back and find him," Littlejohn said. "I'd like my brother to wait with you. . . . Accidents make him sick." She went across the patio and knocked on the door.

"You no pay to my husband. You pay me."

"Do it," Littlejohn said. She threw her purse across the patio to Will. Then she went into the back room with the dog.

Will reached in the purse and held a thousand peseta note out to the woman. It was a crisp new bill and she took it from him and held it like a live bird. She folded it as if she were breaking its neck.

"Nervioso?"

". . . No."

"Why you get sick to see accident?"

"My father was killed," Will said, "like that." It wasn't that simple, but he couldn't explain that the sick tightness at seeing accidents was like a birthmark on his brain. He was surprised at the way his voice came out—steady and even. He was breathing hard but he hadn't expected he could speak clearly.

"How?"

"A plane."

". . . You want one drink water?"

He nodded and the woman gave him a clay *botijo* from the

Here we are learning something of Littlejohn; her confused sympathies and her use of her money to try to solve things. Littlejohn's misplaced sympathies for the dog instead of the hurt men or dead child, and her wasting of a thousand pesetas, is to be contrasted with Count Guzman's efforts and risks later on. Now we also have further reinforcement of Will's connecting violent death with his father's death, in the conversation with the Spanish woman.

corner. It was heavy and beaded with cold drops on the outside and he lifted it high. He spilled water out of the smaller hole into his mouth and drank, letting it collect first in gulps at the back of his tongue. He let some of it trickle from the *botijo* over his face. The water was musty and cool and he could taste the clay.

"Which was the airplane of your father?"

"La guerra," Will said.

"Which war?"

"The one of the world."

In effective conversation with Littlejohn, we learn what has been less effectively handled so far—that Will has grown up because he has not been sent into a screaming fit by what he has seen. The *practicante's* room is established with smells.

"The second? I speak English," the woman said, "my sister teach me as follows. I am, you are, he is, Seven Up, side car V O, they will be. Every part of grammar. . . . This my sister is very intelligent teach. She? More what I, oh she much more. She no listen this fucky fucky to sailors. All she got, this whole English grammar perfect. . . . You feel better now?"

"Yes."

"You think I speak English very well?"

"Yes."

"You should talk to my sister," the woman said.

After a while Littlejohn came out alone. She had washed her arms and cleaned the blood off the front of her shirt. She took her purse and lit a cigarette, watching Will. "I remember not so long ago a thing like this would have sent you into a screaming fit for hours," she said, slow. "Why didn't you tell me you'd grown up?"

Will didn't answer.

"Oh well," Littlejohn said. "Why don't you get your dog; I'll wait here."

Will's mind connects these smells with his father. There is a nice contrast here between the thin and sickly children, and the dog on whom a thousand pesetas has been spent. Now the reader receives the sensory impressions of the heat and the sudden breeze. Someone has broken the antenna on the car, which Will tries to make light of; but these incidents, the violence of the car accident, and the anger of the broken antenna are effective in terms of mood.

He crossed the patio to the practitioner's room. It smelled of wine but the table looked clean and there was a bottle of alcohol. There were bandages on it and an empty syringe. The *practicante* was sitting on a cot in the corner smoking black tobacco. You could smell it and wine and old sweat and the alcohol. Will wondered if they found his father's body and tried to save his life and if the foreign room had smelled this way. He never wondered how he lived, but he sometimes wondered how he died. He couldn't help that. The dog was bandaged, but it wasn't asleep. It was lying on a bed. Its remaining eye followed Will across the room.

"He lost blood," the *practicante* said drunkenly in Spanish. "He is lucky, this dog. He has an injection. Be careful how you pick him up."

"Thank you."

"Nothing. *Con Dios*," the man said.

"Adiós," Will told him.

The dog rested against him like a rag.

There were three children staring at Littlejohn in the patio when he went back, the oldest about eight. Two of them were standing against the *practicante's* wife and the other one was hiding behind her. When Will came out all three children turned from Littlejohn and watched the dog. They looked thin and sickly, with the confused dreamy eyes that come from hunger, and the *practicante's* wife had to push them away from her body to open the door.

Will and Littlejohn went out into the light and Littlejohn looked up and blinked. "There isn't any sky," she said, ". . . is there? Like any Spanish sky?"

"No," he said.

The blue was wild now. The dog lay still and Will followed Littlejohn back to the car. The day had been breathless in the last blast of heat but now you could feel the first slice of a breeze from the sea; it came between the buildings and the bars.

"Nobody was killed. I tried to help before, but the people wouldn't let me." Littlejohn touched the grease mark on her wrist. "I went back again and asked. They took the ones who were hurt to a hospital. The sailors in the bars just went back to their whores. It's all forgotten now. What an awful thing we've done to this town."

Will didn't answer.

"I asked about the dog too. It doesn't belong to anybody. You can keep it," Littlejohn said.

They walked up behind her rented blue car and Will saw it. There was something off balance. Somebody had taken the radio antenna and bent it double. It was hanging down like a long broken bone. Littlejohn reached out and touched it.

"The Spanish kids sometimes do that," Will said. "In little towns. They do it to foreign cars."

"I don't blame them. It doesn't matter. I don't use the radio."

"It's cooling off . . . you can put the top down if you want."

"No," Littlejohn said. "I wouldn't drive through this town in an open convertible after the way those sailors drove . . . I'd be ashamed. . . ." She got in the car and Will sat next to her and set the dog in his lap. It was drugged enough to let him do what he wanted. Littlejohn put the car into gear and started off. The streets were thin and crowded and she drove slowly. She braked and honked at every corner. Toward the back of town the people were living in the streets after the heat. They sat on wooden chairs

An effective scene driving out of town in their convertible, under the hatred of those watching; Littlejohn is characterized by her shame. Very strong detail of the woman blinded by the sun off the fender, and a positive riot of odors;

sour wine, hot oil, horse manure and donkey dung, and jasmine. The dog's presence is established by its slobber wet on Will's hand. Littlejohn confesses that she is afraid.

outside watching the car pass. You could see the flat hatred in some of their eyes. The car Littlejohn had rented in Madrid wasn't as big as the Thunderbird but it was American-designed and twice as big as most Spanish cars. It was bulky in the narrow streets and they both felt embarrassed in it. A woman dressed in black, toothless, watched them, blinded by the sun on the fender. You could smell the sour wine and hot oil in the white houses. Will kept his eyes on the town as they drove. The air was fresh but the buildings belched out at him, hot and rotten and gorgeous. There were sights and smells, flowers and flies. There was sun into horse manure and donkey dung in jasmine. The whole town was quiet.

Littlejohn drove out of the town to the rutted road that led to the highway. After that she turned and followed a sign that pointed the way to Suelo. She crossed some railroad tracks and started driving out of the sun. The day was ending.

"Did you see her children?" Littlejohn said.

"Yes."

"What must she think? . . . we spent a thousand pesetas on a dog. Did you see her children?"

"The town is already angry."

"Why not?" Littlejohn said, "why wouldn't it be?"

The earth was cooling faster and they drove a while more. The light had changed again. The sun was low and bloated like an orange disk, big and watery over the gray and the green. The yellow Andalusian summer twilight was beginning. Will felt his hand grow wet and he looked down. The dog was slobbering quietly on the insides of his fingers.

"You were right, Will," Littlejohn said, "I am afraid."

Will looked at her. Her eyes were on the rear-view mirror. She was staring straight at the sun. He looked back at the road.

Her fear proves to be mystical—something is waiting out there. Is it love? Is it death? Is it both? Will is deeply affected by her confession and promises to stay with her. The fact that she needs him causes a flood of visceral sensations in terms of heat, and he is delighted by a detailed image of an old man and some goats.

"It's every place I go. It's like something is waiting out there. I don't know what it is."

Will kept still and listened and Littlejohn cleared her throat.

"It's why I'm getting married. I've been scared a long time. I don't know what it is. I hate not knowing what it is."

She stopped talking and Will thought about it. The facts of the day altered in his mind, and he could feel a flush of something extra inside him as if his heart had squeezed one more beat.

Then in the dizzy sun it happened again. The words swelled in his mind and he could feel the sun and the heat all through him. The heat was in his pants and in his brain and at the base of his throat. She had recognized something in him without being told.

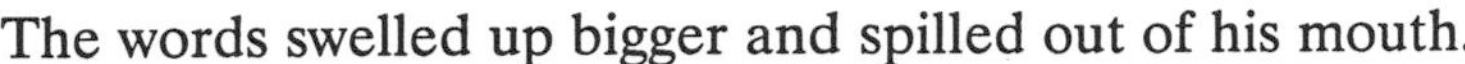

The words swelled up bigger and spilled out of his mouth.

"I'll stay with you," he said. "Till you're married."

Littlejohn watched the sun in the mirror and the road ahead of them.

She blinked a few times.

"I will," he said.

"Fine."

He turned back and they both faced the road. Will sat still with the swelling of himself as if nothing had happened. The dog on his legs was licking his hand again. The road ahead was straight now. There was a herd of smooth brown goats next to the road on the right and an old man tending them, his skin cracked and brown, stung and red from the weather. When the car passed, the man followed it with his sun-broken face and for a crazy second Will wanted to lean out the window and shout to him. He didn't, because it wouldn't have made any sense—but he wanted to. He wished he could have told the old man of this change that had come about in him. He wished he could have touched the goats. He wished he could sing.

Synopsis of a Proposed Novel

Development of the novel *Apaches*, by Oakley Hall, published by Simon & Schuster in the fall of 1986.

I had been planning a novel based on Billy the Kid as part of a trilogy of the West. The first volume, *Warlock*, concerned a frontier marshal very much like Wyatt Earp, and the bringing of law and order to a frontier town. The second, *The Bad Lands*, was based on the Johnson County War (big cattlemen vs. little cattlemen, grangers, etc.) although it was set in the North Dakota badlands. Its principal characters resembled the Marquis de Mores and Theodore Roosevelt. An editor at Simon & Schuster, with whom I'd worked on *The Bad Lands*, asked me if I would write a novel concerned with Apaches.

I replied that I was considering a work based on Billy the Kid, but, with a little research, I discovered that Billy the Kid country (New Mexico) was also Apache country, that Billy the Kid and the Apache chief Victorio had died in the same year, and that the word "Apache" means enemy, and both Billy the Kid and the Apaches were or became enemies of the westering civilization of the 1880s. Connection!

The novel, as I began to conceive it, would be based on the two actual stories, and my main task would be to bring them together meaningfully and dramatically.

Here follows the first, short, outline I wrote for Simon & Schuster. Not much has been fictionalized here; it is more a summation of history-as-I-knew it, before any real research had taken place. I was familiar with Lieutenant Gatewood, whom Paul Horgan had used as his hero in his fine novel *A Distant Trumpet*, and began thinking of him as my protagonist. Later I switched to another actual Indian-fighting officer, Lieutenant Britton Davis, who quit the army after the capture of Geronimo, to manage a cattle ranch in Mexico.

Billy the Kid, and the Apache Chief Victorio perished violently in the same year, 1881. They inhabited the same area, and there were important parallels in their histories and the history of the West. Both have become myths.

Both men operated mainly in New Mexico, specifically in Lincoln County. Both led lives of vendetta and outlawry, and observed an eye-for-an-eye philosophy. Both were sprung into a life of violence (for Victorio an old way of life, for Billy Bonney a new one) by grave wrongs and betrayals. The Apaches' land was stolen from them by false treaties, and they were victimized by corrupt Indian agents. Bonney saw his employers Tunstall and McSween murdered by the county law forces in the pay of their enemies. His own victims subsequently included a sheriff, a jailor, a couple of deputies, possemen, and an Indian agent. The enemy Murphy-Dolan forces were under the protection of the so-called Santa Fe Ring, crooked politicians who ran the Territory for their own profits. The Apaches were systematically cheated by the Indian Ring, which, at the top, consisted of the same individuals.

Bonney was persuaded by Governor Lew Wallace to give evidence in a murder trial on the promise that he would be protected from his enemies. But he was betrayed, and this sent him off into his brutal career in outlawry, culminating in his shooting by Sheriff Pat Garrett. This effectively ended the Lincoln County War. It is interesting to note that Governor Lew Wallace's efforts to end the violence were less than effective; he was much occupied at the time finishing his novel *Ben-Hur*.

Victorio and his band of Warm Spring Apaches had been sent to the San Carlos reservation in Arizona by the terms of a treaty signed with General Crook. San Carlos was simply a concentration camp, where the Apaches were tormented, cheated, and forbidden their tribal rites. Victorio broke out in 1879 and returned to the old hunting grounds in the Black Range of New Mexico. When he was induced to come in again, it was to the Mescalero reservation in Lincoln County at the height of the Lincoln County War. It was while Victorio's band was with the Mescaleros that Bonney was alleged to have killed the reservation agent, Bernstein, who was connected with the Indian Ring and the Murphy-

Dolan faction. Victorio broke out again and began murdering settlers and travelers in lands that had once been Apache fiefdom. He fought at least ten engagements with the U.S. Cavalry, which outnumbered his people (women and children as well as warriors) by as many as four to one, winning every battle but one.

An actual officer who is to be fictionalized here is Lieutenant Davis, who commanded a detachment of Apache scouts. He pursued Victorio the most effectively, following him once into old Mexico, where, from cliffs above by night he heard the old chief singing his medicine song, trying to induce the Apache scouts to desert Davis. In actuality it was not Davis but another who surprised Victorio and beat him so thoroughly that the Apaches were badly crippled when they fled to Mexico for the last time. By pure coincidence an army under the command of the nephew of the governor of Chihuahua happened upon Victorio as his band was making camp at a place called Tres Castillos. The warriors sang their death song as they were slaughtered almost to a man. When the victorious army arrived at Chihuahua, soldiers carried seventy-eight upright poles, each one decorated with an Apache scalp. The Apache women and children were sold into peonage.

Pat Garrett (who became sheriff of Lincoln County after Sheriff Brady had been murdered by Billy the Kid, and his successor removed by the governor) had been a friend fo Billy, and was sympathetic to his motives, but Billy had gone too far. Society had wronged and betrayed him, but society had to be protected from his ruthlessness. On Davis's part, his initial rage at the depredations committed by the Apaches—the wagoneers strapped upside down to their wagon wheels over a slow fire, captured soldiers shot so full of arrows they resembled porcupine quills, with each arrow carefully shot into nonvital flesh, the murders of women, the children made captive, not to speak of the livestock stolen—gave way to sympathy and respect for the Indians in their doomed fight against Manifest Destiny. Coming to love his company of Apache scouts, he felt affection also for the infamous chieftain. Although he remained a tiger on Victorio's trail, he was heartsick when his ambush succeeded and the little band reeled off to old Mexico to meet its fate.

Herman Gollob asked me to provide a longer synopsis, with character sketches, which he could take before the Simon & Schuster editorial board to get me a contract and advance on a novel. The longer synopsis, considerably more fictionalized, follows.

Proposal for a Novel Called *Apaches*, by Oakley Hall

The subject of *Apaches* is outlawry, the conflict of independent men and the old, frontier ways with the drive of civilization. Apache chiefs such as Cochise, Mangas Colorados, Geronimo, and especially Victorio, were driven to the warpath, to outlawry, and ultimately to extinction, by the pressure of the growing white communities as well as by the dishonesty of the Indian agents, the greed of local merchants, and the inflexibilities of the military. This Apache legend will be combined with that of Billy the Kid, which it closely parallels.

The Johnson County (New Mexico) War was in process at the same place and the same time as Victorio's last great breakout. The warring factions in Lincoln County were Tunstall-McSween, the "good guys," and Murphy-Dolan, the "bad." The latter were Lincoln County's Indian Ring, connected with the Sante Fe Ring. They owned the store in Lincoln, bought cheap and sold dear, lent money at usurious rates to the local ranchers, and sold moldy flour and underweight and rustled cattle to the Mescalero Apache reservation. They owned the sheriff, county attorney, justice of the peace, the Indian agent, and Colonel Dudley at Fort Stanton, and had powerful connections in Santa Fe. Tunstall and McSween were murdered, and Billy the Kid became their righteous avenger, murdering in retaliation the crooked sheriff, deputy, Indian agent, and others. Captured, he killed his jailors in his escape. Now he was an outlaw, a hero to the underclass of Mexican-Americans but intolerable to the Anglo-merchant population. So the implacable Pat Garrett was elected sheriff to rid Lincoln County of him.

The Characters

Lieutenant Patrick Crumley is a cavalry officer whose career has not prospered for several reasons. One is that he is not a West Pointer; he received a field commission in the last year of the Civil War as a nineteen-year-old. Moreover he has a propensity for disobeying orders, and for not suffering fools who happen to be his superior officers. He is, however, a favorite of the commanding officer of the department in this time of Apache troubles, General Yeager—Gray Fox to the Apaches—by whom Crumley is often called to act as aide-de-camp and chief of Apache scouts. Crumley is expert in handling the scouts, although like most fellow officers he is an Apache-hater, having seen too much of Apache horrors—tortures, mutilation, and child-killing.

The editor begged me to change Crumley's name, so it became "Cutler." This proved useful in characterization, as his friends called him "Old Cutlery" to express their affection and his hardnose attitude. An addition to the plot is his effort to find out who he is: he may be the illegitimate son of the general and a San Francisco whorehouse madam, or something much more lowly.

Ten years before the story begins, serving as an aide to the general, he attended in Guaymas the festivities opening the Sonora Railroad.

His courtship of and marriage to Maria Palacios takes place within the action of the novel, and so does not need to be treated in flashback or as back-story expository material.

There he has met Maria Palacios, granddaughter of Don Fernando Palacios, owner of the great hacienda Las Llagas del Cristo in Sonora. The hacendado has actively forced his granddaughter and the young lieutenant together; he is old, and someone competent must take over the ancient hacienda at his death. Crumley seems to him much more of the proper man for this than any of the Palacios cousins, with one of whom Maria is enamored. The marriage takes place, and Crumley is to resign his commission to take over affairs at the hacienda.

Just then, however, there is an Apache outbreak. General Yeager is called to deal with the situation and he asks Crumley's help, which Crumley cannot refuse. Maria, then, becomes the wife of a line lieutenant who earns $133 per month at Fort Bowie. She cannot stand the hardships, and, pregnant, pines for her cousin-lover, Pedrito. She communicates with him, and he comes to kidnap her back to Mexico. They flee Fort Bowie but are captured by Apaches. Pedrito is horribly tortured to death, the serving woman is murdered, and Maria only escapes death by pretending insanity. She continues her pretence of insanity even after her rescue, as a means of leaving Crumley and returning to Mexico. Crumley, in the face of his wife's hatred, lives in separation, continuing his unhappy career as a cavalry officer in between Apache wars.

Meanwhile he is stationed at Fort Partman adjoining the town on Placita in Madison County, and the Bosque Alto Apache reservation. His commanding officer would be very pleased to court martial him for disobedience except for Crumley's presently rather distant support by General Yeager; his fellow officers are contemptuous of his lack of West Point background, except for his one friend Captain Bunch. These are the only two effective officers insofar as the Apaches of the reservation are concerned. Crumley has been conducting an affair with Lily Maginnis, wife of a local politico.

Billy Antrim became Johnny Angell. I started out to make him a religious nut, bent upon Old Testament eye-for-an-eye, but he would not come to life until he transformed himself into a frontier jokester and humorist, but with the Old Testament attitude.

Billy Antrim is a cowboy in the service of a young English rancher, Turnbull, who is charming and beloved by all associated with him, and hero-worshipped by Billy. Billy himself is uneducated, a decent person, honest, loyal, very handsome, and successful with women—enjoying particularly the "old gold girls," those Mexican-Indian, half-breeds. He is to become first a righteous avenger of wrongs, gradually a murderer and outlaw. But in the process, maturing and sobering, he comes to find himself a doomed hero, who cannot extricate himself from his role and legend without disappointing the very people of the territory with whom he most loyally identifies—the Mexican-American underclass to the dominant Anglo society.

Officers

General Yeager is crotchety and opinionated, very unregimental. He understands the Apaches and sympathizes with their plight, though he is severe and determined in his pursuit of those who break out of the reservations and commit depredations. He values Lieutenant Crumley from the days when he gave him his battlefield commission and recommended him for the Medal of Honor. He is always called upon when the Apache Wars heat up. Colonel Dougal is in command at Fort Partman. He is not so much a part of the Boland-Enders Indian Ring as he is an ally to it and the local power-politics, without which it seems to him there would be democratic chaos of self-righteous fools like Maginnis.

Major Parks has commanded Crumley in an Apache-pursuit and will never forgive Crumley for disobeying an order which made Parks look cowardly.

Captain Bunch is Crumley's pal; together they have some understanding of the situation on the Apache reservation. Bunch is big, boisterous, obscene, and comical; he is having an affair with Prettyface, a young Apache widow.

Prettyface becomes Prettymouth, and she is not a widow but the wife of Caballito's heir, Joklinney, who returns during the story from incarceration on Alcatraz in San Francisco Bay. It should be noted that unfaithful Apache wives were in danger of having the tip of their noses cut off, or bobbed.

People of Placita

Lily Maginnis is a beautiful and cultivated woman married to an impotent and obsessed husband. She tries to make a decent life in a frontier town with her fine dresses, manners, food and drink, her piano-playing and singing at her soirees, which the young officers at the fort are forbidden to attend because of Colonel Dougal's enmity. She cannot leave handsome young men alone, but she is dignified and tragic in her obsessions. She and Crumley have had an affair of some duration, another example of his refusal to obey unjust orders from his superiors.

Frank Maginnis is a lawyer from an old Philadelphia family, who has fallen under the Englishman, Turnbull's, charm. He is a fighter for Right & Justice who cannot believe that just law will not prevail, and will continue to hammer his head against extant injustice until bloody; his foe and personification of evil is the politically dominant Boland-Enders Ring.

Randall Boland is a top-hatted, frock-coated old man, a member of the California Column that came East during the Civil War to fight Confederates. He has remained to go into trade and grow wealthy, and he has connections in Santa Fe with other old Californians. Recently, however, the house of Boland has been on the decline, and he has taken a new partner, Enders, who is more ruthless than he in dealing with the competition of newcomers like Turnbull. Boland sees nothing illegal or immoral in his operations; he is helping to keep order in a frontier community, necessarily lawless; and he possesses the prevailing and convenient hatred of Apaches and "all their kind."

Governor Gleeson becomes Governor Underwood, not a novelist-general but a historian-general. He finds himself writing "history from the inside" because of his involvement in the local war.

Governor Gleeson was a political general in the Civil War, now assigned to a post he believes to be beneath him as military governor of the Territory. He spends more time working on his historical novel about the days of Christ (with whom he identifies) than he does on political and law considerations. He is cultivated by General Yeager.

Sheriff Jack Grant is an honest lawman, humorless and dedicated, who is called in by the citizens when their regular law systems have proved corrupt and cowardly. He is known to always get his man.

Horace Enders does not skip the country. He is the most double-dyed villain of the novel and is shot by Billy.

Horace Enders is the operative force behind the Boland store. He has a withered arm, is bitter, vindictive, and violent. He skips the country when indicted for the murder of Mrs. Maginnis's lawyer, causing the collapse of the whole Boland enterprise.

The Indians

Caballito is the tragic and savage old chief of the Bosque Alto Apaches, who sees that sooner or later he must be forced off the reservation by the actions of the Indian Ring and the stupid Colonel Dougal. He is no wanton killer, for he has understood that depredations give rise to counter-depredations, and it takes the tribe a generation to replace a warrior, whereas the cavalry merely trains a new recruit. He is intelligent and sad, with a sense of tragic destiny of his race; but he has great dash, courage and style, and military smarts. Crumley cannot keep from coming to respect him, and together they have tricked the Indian agent and Colonel Dougal into better serving the part of the Apaches. General Yeager recognizes him as the best man this doomed race has produced.

Nochte is divided into two characters. As Nochte he is the corporal of Crumley-Cutler's band of scouts,

Nochte is an Apache scout; the most intelligent of the scouts, he is their corporal. He is a Tonto Apache, hereditary enemies of the Bosque Altos, yet he cannot help but be sympathetic with them in their outbreak from intolerable conditions. But his loyalty to Crumley comes first, for Crumley disobeyed orders to save Nochte when Nochte's leg was trapped under his dead horse in battle.

Terzoa-khinney is a medicine-man who preaches a new religion to the reservation Apaches, of return of the dead and regeneration of the race with the white-eyes gotten rid of, that the military authorities see as a danger that must be wiped out.

Prettyface is the young squaw in love with Captain Bunch; she is Bunch's and Crumley's informant on the reservation, and in danger if she is found out.

faithful and honorable. Joklinney, mentioned above, has been brainwashed by the Americans while in captivity to believe there is no way the Apaches can win, but he rebels in the end to become a kind of Apache Kid bronco Apache.

The Mexicans

Colonel Kandinsky is chief of the Sonoran rurales and later the Seguridad Publico, the SP's—the irregular, scalp-hunting army assembled against the Apache incursions. (The Mexicans had long had a scalp-hunting extermination policy against the Apaches, one of the reasons the Apaches were unremittingly vicious against Mexicans.) Kandinsky is an exiled Polish nobleman, tall and courtly, as treacherous and ruthless as any Apache, but a great friend of Don Fernando of Las Llagas. He likes Crumley from the Guaymas festivities, and is on several occasions helpful to him.

Don Fernando is old and ailing, and anxious about the succession at his domain of Las Llagas. He has picked Crumley as competent to run the place, but that has all dissolved in his granddaughter's madness. His great-grandson, Don Pepe, is the absolute apple of his eye.

Maria is a foolish, romantic, upper-class Mexican woman of pure Castilian descent, whose feigned madness has saved her from torture and murder by the Apaches who slaughtered her beloved cousin. She has continued to employ that madness until it has become all but real, working it up to a violent hysteria whenever Crumley appears, as he does every year or so, to see his son.

The Story

Crumley is in Sonora as General Yeager's aide-de-camp and translator. They are seeking a treaty with the Mexican generals, including Colonel Kandinsky of the Sonoran rurales, for hot pursuit of Apache hostiles into Mexico. The ability of renegade bands to slip into Mexico has severely handicapped the American effort to keep the Apaches on the reservations, and their depredations in Mexico are as bad or worse than those north of the border. The Mexicans promise a look-the-other-way policy, for government treaties forbid American incursions.

Crumley-Cutler meets Maria and her father at a dance in Guaymas and Palacios encourages his courtship of Maria, and precipitates the wedding as he detests Maria's Mexican *novio*. After the marriage she returns with her husband to the United States where she is miserable.

While in Sonora, Crumley visits the Hacienda de las Llagas where his insane wife resides with their son and her grandfather, Don Fernando. Their romantic courtship and marriage has turned into a nightmare; and the aged and ailing hacendado is desperate for someone to replace him, for there are no heirs but a three-year-old child. Once he had thought Crumley would be the man, but his granddaughter's insanity and Crumley's crusty devotion to duty has precluded this. Dona Maria is imperious, still beautiful, but absolutely terrified of men. Even in her sanity she can never forgive Crumley for the terrible incident during her pregnancy, nor can he forgive himself.

Having gained the Mexicans' agreement, General Yeager with a detachment of troops and Apache scouts chases the renegade Chiricahua Caballito across the border and to the Apaches' redoubt in the Sierra Madre. In an ambush, Major Burns, Crumley's superior, gives the order to fall back in disorder, leaving one of the scouts behind, badly wounded. Crumley the Apache-hater risks his life and disobeys a direct order to rescue the young scout Nochte. Burns threatens a court martial, but the general intercedes. His affection and respect for Crumley more than once saves the lieutenant from the wrath of superior officers.

Crumley is present when Yeager receives Caballito's surrender and is given the charge of accompanying the Apache band across the border and back to the reservation. En route Caballito's braves steal a large herd of cattle from a Mexican ranch, which Crumley is unable to prevent. He then must help this unwieldy body evade the rurales of Colonel Kandinsky. Across the border he is confronted by a U.S. marshal and a customs agent with warrants for Caballito's arrest—this at a time when it was unclear whether or not military authorities must bow to the civil. Crumley manages to trick these authorities.

This is based on an actual trick played by Bretton Davis on the authorities.

Crumley delivers Caballito and his band to the Bosque Alto Apache reservation and resumes his duties at Fort Blanton under Colonel Dougal, who resents him as insubordinate and a pet of the general of the department. Dougal himself is a member of Boland's Indian Ring and a supporter of Boland in the Madison County War, which is heating up. Crumley and Caballito have achieved a relationship of some trust in their trek north, and Caballito complains of short weights in the Apache rations.

Crumley brings in weights to test the agent's scales, finding them heavy by double, embarrassing the agent and infuriating Colonel Dougal.

He is in further trouble with the colonel because of his continuing affair with Mrs. Maginnis, wife of the lawyer who is violently opposing the Boland Ring. Junior officers at Fort Blanton are forbidden to attend her soirees, and Crumley ignores this petty and illegal order.

Johnny Jingo has murdered the sheriff who murdered Turnbull and there have been other shootings. These troubles among the white men make the Apaches at Bosque Alto nervous and turbulent.

Maginnis, with an armed force including Johnny Jingo, rides into Madison to confront the Boland-Enders gunmen, and the two forces snipe at each other from adobe fortresses. Colonel Dougal sends Crumley into town with a detachment ordered to keep the peace on Boland's terms. Crumley does the best he can in a no-win situation, but he manages to offend the colonel by his lack of enthusiasm for his orders and Maginnis by following them at all. The Maginnis house is fired, Lily Maginnis is protected by Crumley, Johnny Jingo and some others escape; Maginnis is shot dead.

Lily Maginnis leaves town to return with a Santa Fe lawyer. She intends to expose and prosecute those responsible for the death of her husband, including the colonel, who has acted illegally in sending soldiers to serve the civil authorities, and has also maligned her virtue. Crumley's testimony is requested, but he refuses; he must be consistent in failing to bow to civilian authority. Meanwhile Lily's lawyer is murdered by Boland henchmen, with Johnny Jingo as a witness. Johnny is fearful of giving evidence, however, as there are warrants out for his arrest for murder.

A midnight meeting is arranged between the governor and Johnny Jingo. Johnny is promised protection if he will give evidence in court that will help the governor in his move against the Boland-Enders Ring. Jingo keeps his promise but the governor does not. The Ring's power has been broken, which is more important to the governor than a promise of convenience to an outlaw. A new and nonpartisan sheriff is elected. Jingo breaks out of jail.

Meanwhile a messiah has appeared among the Apaches at Bosque Alto. It is reputed that he can bring back to life Indians who have been killed by the white-eyes—if the white man can be got rid of, for their presence interferes with his medicine. (This was a religion preceding and very much like the Ghost-dance cult of the Sioux.) The military correctly view it as a dangerous development.

The actual novel is much stretched out here, with many more incidents. After the fight at the reservation, the soldiers are surrounded. Crumley-Cutler, on his fine horse, a gift from his father-in-law, rides for help, pursued by the cult Indians. Meanwhile, Maria has fled with her Mexican lover, and Crumley-Cutler unwittingly leads the Indians to her trail. The lover and the serving woman are murdered; Maria is saved by pretending insanity. Crumley-Cutler and his scouts rescue Maria, but she continues to pretend insanity until he is forced to send her back to her father in Mexico. Caballito breaks out of the reservation on a final occasion somewhat later in the novel.

Colonel Dougal leads a force including Crumley to arrest the messiah. The arrest is badly mishandled and it is clear that all that was wanted was the death of the messiah. Caballito and his band flee on the warpath again and en route to Mexico once more.

Crumley, with a troop of cavalry and the loyal scouts, sets out in pursuit. Other troops join them. A succession of battles is fought, each time with Caballito coming out on top or slipping away. Only once does he suffer a defeat, when Crumley and the scouts ambush him from a higher peak. Nochte translates for Crumley what the squaws are calling: the white-eyes will never capture Caballito, for if they are trapped the women will eat him so he will never be seen again.

Crumley catches up with Caballito again in Mexico by night under a steep cliff, above which the Apaches have encamped. Caballito sings his medicine song to try to get the scouts to desert to the all-Indian cause, but they remain loyal to Crumley. Other officers and troops are arriving and it is clear that Caballito's band is surrounded.

The next day, however, there is a flurry of shooting from an unexpected quarter; it is a large force of Mexicans. Crumley's best friend, Captain Bunch, is killed, and Crumley in his fury rides down and kills the Mexican captain who has ordered the shooting. The main Mexican force comes up; it is the Seguridad Publico irregular army, under a figurehead general and Colonel Kandinsky. The Americans are summarily ordered out of Mexico; Crumley is placed under arrest for the shooting of the Mexican captain.

Crumley-Cutler does not shoot a Mexican officer, but he is held in danger of a firing squad until Colonel Kandinsky rescues him.

Crumley is thus on hand to see the slaughter of Caballito's band by the Mexican irregulars. Almost all the bucks are slain, running out of ammunition and singing their death songs. Caballito himself is not found among the dead, as though the squaws had carried out their threat. The army marches triumphantly on to the town of Janos, carrying aloft seventy-eight poles supporting as many scalps. In Janos the women and children who have survived are sold into slavery. After a session with Colonel Kandinsky, whom he understands has befriended him as the heir to the Hacienda de las Llagas, Crumley is released and heads north. He crosses the border to encounter the railroad pushing west across New Mexico, following the telegraph line that already exists.

Back at Fort Blanton he finds General Yeager. The general is resigning his command due to the unrelenting pressure from the newspapers, politicians, and even his own superiors, who will not observe the treaties he has made with the Apaches. Yeager recognizes that without his protection, Crumley may be in serious danger from Colonel Dougal and others he has offended, and offers to take him along to the Department of the Platte, where he has been reassigned. But Crumley refuses to go; there are things he must still do in New Mexico.

Johnny Jingo has been arrested by the new sheriff, Jack Grant, and a posse. Johnny escapes again, with the help of a girl who has hidden a revolver in the outhouse. He has killed his jailors in the process, however, and now he has become an outlaw and intolerable to the Anglo, middle-class, urban population of Madison, which has turned violently against lawlessness. Although Johnny remains the hero of the dispossessed, he is doomed and knows it.

Lily Maginnis pleads with Crumley one last time, confessing her pathetic and hopeless love for the young outlaw. Crumley goes to find Johnny to persuade him to flee to Mexico, his only hope. Johnny refuses, newly mature, still humorous but with a deeply tragic vision of the necessary ends of those like himself and the Apaches, whose country this once was. He knows what he means to many people, although he also knows that one of them will betray him. His ultimate death at the hands of Jack Grant is only a postscript.

Crumley is to see Lily Maginnis one last time. She has quickly recovered from her grief at Johnny's death. She has a new lawyer, who is helping her with her legal problems, a handsome young fellow. She is as sane as Crumley has ever known her, full of optimism, sexy, and in charge of her destiny.

All the ending is changed, bringing the Billy the Kid and the Apaches stories to a single denouement. Read the book for further information.

With his court martial hanging over his head, Crumley crosses the border, headed for the Hacienda de las Llagas, his wife, his son, the dying hacendado, and his responsibilities for the new life he must take up there.

Suggested Reading

Novelists no longer read for fun. Reading is one of the means by which they keep the cisterns of their imagination brimming, and they are always searching for the kind of material I have included here, from the brilliant little stroke of description to the larger matters of form and structure. Needless to say, the novelist should have read all the classics he knows he should have read, the Bible for its language, Cervantes, *Tom Jones*, Jane Austen, the Brontës, Dickens and Thackeray, the great Russians, Flaubert and James, *Huckleberry Finn*, Crane, Virgina Woolf, Hemingway, Fitzgerald, and Faulkner. If he thinks he has embarked upon an experimental novel, he had better read *Tristram Shandy*, for probably Sterne got there first.

There follows a list of contemporary novels and short stories that seem to me to advance the techniques of fiction in such a way as to be valuable to the working novelist, as well as a list of books on the art and craft of writing by writers that I have found to be of considerable interest.

On the Writing Process

Virginia Woolf
A Writer's Diary, letters
Anton Chekhov
Notebooks, letters
Thomas Mann
The Story of a Novel
Albert Camus
Notebooks
Franz Kafka
Diaries, *Letters to Milena*, letters
Joseph Conrad
Joseph Conrad on Fiction, prefaces, letters
Rainer Maria Rilke
Letters to a Young Poet
Andre Gide
Journal of the Counterfeiters (with the novel)
Henry James
Notebooks, prefaces, letters
F. Scott Fitzgerald
The Crack-up
Gustave Flaubert
letters
William H. Gass
Fiction and the Figures of Life
Durrell & Miller
A Private Correspondence
Flannery O'Connor
Mysteries and Manners, letters
W. H. Auden
The Dyer's Hand
H. D. Thoreau
Journals
Malcolm Lowry
On *Under the Volcano*
Norman Mailer
On *The Deer Park*
John Fowles
Notes on *The French Lieutenant's Woman*

Dostoyevsky
Notebooks for *The Idiot*, Notebooks for *Crime and Punishment*

Contemporary Fiction: A Personal List

Agee
A Death in the Family
Let Us Now Praise Famous Men
Algren
A Walk on the Wild Side
Atwood
Lady Oracle
Barth
Lost in the Funhouse
The Sotweed Factor
Barthelme
Stories
Bellow
Seize the Day
Henderson the Rain King
Berger
Little Big Man
Borges
Ficciones
Bowen
The Death of the Heart
Burgess
A Clockwork Orange
Burroughs
Naked Lunch
Calvino
Cosmicomix
Capote
In Cold Blood
Carpentier
The Lost Steps
Carver
Stories
Cary
Herself Surprised
To Be a Pilgrim
The Horse's Mouth
Celine
Journey to the End of Night
Chandler
Farewell My Lovely
Cheever
Stories
Clark
The Oxbow Incident
Connell
Mrs. Bridge
Coover
Stories
Cortazar
Hopscotch
Cozzens
Guard of Honor
DeVries
The Tunnel of Love
Didion
Play It As It Lays
Dinesen
Winter's Tales
Donleavy
The Ginger Man
Drabble
The Realms of Gold

Durrell
The Alexandria Quartet
Ellison
Invisible Man
Ford
Stories
Fowles
The French Lieutenant's Woman
Frisch
I'm Not Stiller
Fuentes
The Death of Artemio Cruz
Gaddis
The Recognitions
Gardner
Grendel
Gass
In the Heart of the Heart of the Country
Golding
The Lord of the Flies
Goyen
The House of Breath
Grass
The Tin Drum
Greene
The Heart of the Matter
Hall
Warlock
Corpus of Joe Bailey
Hammett
The Maltese Falcon
Harris
The Balloonist
Harrison
Legends of the Fall
Hawkes
The Lime Twig
Heller
Catch-22
Herr
Dispatches
Howard
Grace Abounding
Huxley
Point Counterpoint
Irving
The World According to Garp
Johnson
Angels
Jones
From Here to Eternity
The Thin Red Line
Keneally
Schindler's List
Kennedy
Legs
Ironweed
Kerouac
On the Road
Kesey
One Flew Over the Cuckoo's Nest
Sometimes a Great Notion
Kingston
The Woman Warrior
Kosinsky
The Painted Bird
Steps
Kundera
The Book of Laughter and Forgetting
The Unbearable Lightness of Being
Lee
To Kill a Mockingbird
Lessing
The Golden Notebooks
Lewis
The Children of Sanchez
Lowry
Under the Volcano
Mailer
The Naked and the Dead
The Executioner's Song
Malamud
The Natural
Stories
Marquez
One Hundred Years of Solitude

Matthiessen
At Play in the Fields of the Lord
McCullers
The Heart Is a Lonely Hunter
The Member of the Wedding
McGuane
92 in the Shade
Michaels
Stories
Moravia
The Conformist
Morris
The Works of Love
One Day
Morrison
The Song of Solomon
Murdoch
The Black Prince
Nabokov
Pale Fire
Lolita
O'Brien
At Swim Two Birds
O'Connor
Wise Blood
Stories
Olsen
Stories
Paley
Stories
Pasternak
Doctor Zhivago
Patchen
The Journal of Albion Moonlight
Percy
The Moviegoer
Pirsig
Zen and the Art of Motorcycle Maintenance
Plath
The Bell Jar
Porter
Stories
Pritchett
Stories
Pynchon
Gravity's Rainbow
Reed
Yellowback Radio Broke Down
Robbe-Grillet
The Voyeur
Roth
Goodbye Columbus
Salinger:
The Catcher in the Rye
Stories
Solzhenitzen
The First Circle
The Cancer Ward
Stegner
The Big Rock Candy Mountain
Angle of Repose
Stein
Edie
Stone
A Hall of Mirrors
Dog Soldiers
Styron
Lie Down in Darkness
Sophie's Choice
Tolkien
The Lord of the Rings
Tyler
The Accidental Tourist
Vonnegut
Cat's Cradle
Slaughterhouse 5
Updike
Stories
Warren
Night Rider
All the King's Men
Waugh
A Handful of Dust
Brideshead Revisited

Welty
  Stories
White
  The Tree of Man
Wiser
  Disappearances

Helpful Organizations

Organizations that Can Be Helpful to the Writer

Associated Writing Programs
Old Dominion University, Norfolk, Virginia 23529-0079. Publishes a newsletter six times a year, with articles of interest for writers, lists of conferences, prizes, and markets for fiction. Its *Guide to Writing Programs* describes college and university writing programs, and writers colonies, in the U.S. and Canada. Its *Job List* lists jobs for writers in English departments and elsewhere.

The Authors Guild
330 W. 42nd Street, New York, New York 10036. Publishes *Authors Guild Bulletin* four times a year, with news articles and columns on professional writers' concerns. Provides individual advice and assistance to members.

The International Women's Writing Guild
P.O. Box 810, Gracie Station, New York, NY 10028. Publishes *Network*, six issues per year, with articles of interest to its members. Provides market placement information. Annual conference and retreat.

National Endowment for the Arts
1100 Pennsylvania Ave. NW, Washington, D.C. 20506. The Literature Program supports published writers with individual fellowships and provides grants for nonprofit, tax-exempt organizations that publish, distribute, or promote literature.

PEN American Center
568 Broadway, 4th Floor, New York, NY 10012. Furnishes grants and loans for professional, published writers in acute financial distress. Annual literary awards. Branches in Boston, Washington D.C., San Francisco, and Houston.

Poets & Writers, Inc.
72 Spring Street, New York, NY 10012. Its Information Center keeps up-to-date files on more than 7,000 poets and fiction writers, with addresses and other pertinent information; keeps addresses also of all state arts councils, as well as those of other sponsors of readings and workshops nationwide.

Teachers & Writers Collaborative
5 Union Square West, New York, NY 10003-3306. Publishes *Teachers & Writers* magazine, five issues per year, with articles on classroom experiences and tips, and writing exercises for writer-teachers. Hires writers to teach community workshops, and is an information source for those interested in teaching.

Accidental Tourist, The, dialog in, 53-54

Action
  dialog as, 94
  internalization of, 62-63
  vs. observation, 48
  rising, 64
  showdown, 64
  vs. static detail, 19
  See also Motion

Action, characterization by, 46-48
  with gestures and mannerisms, 48-49

Active voice, 86

Acts, three, 65-66

Adelita, The, sentence structure in, 90-91

Adjectives
  overuse of, 85-86
  See also Modifiers

Adventures of Huckleberry Finn, The
  point of view in, 29
  sentence types in, 90

Adventures of Tom Sawyer, The, point of view in, 29-30

AGA West, 208

Agent, how to find, 164-165

Alcott, Louisa May, description in work of, 44-45

Allegories, 117

Alliteration, and assonance, 92-93

Ambassadors, The
  hourglass plot in, 73
  tension in, 67, 69-70

Apaches, synopsis for, 190-201

"Araby," epiphany in, 126

Arcadio, narrative voice in, 57

Archaic language, 107-108

Asher, Don, gestures and mannerisms in work of, 49

Aspects of the Novel
  evolution of theme in, 160-161
  flat and round characters in, 43
  plot defined in, 60

Associated Writing Programs, 208

Assonance, and alliteration, 92-93

At Play in the Fields of the Lord, detail in motion in, 14

Audience. *See* Reader

August Is a Wicked Month, sex in, 134

Austen, Jane, 69

Authorial point of view, 30

Author's expectations, keeping realistic, 168

Bad Lands, The, sex in, 136-138

Baker, Carlos, on Ernest Hemingway, 108-110

Bear, The, sensory perception in, 23-24

Beauty, ingredients of, 145

Beginning
  the novel, 152-155
  the plot, 72-73

Bellow, Saul, sensory perception in work of, 23-24

Bentley, Phyllis, on scenic development, 157

Billy Budd, details in, 10

Biography
  of Ernest Hemingway, 108
  of Raymond Chandler, 58

Biography: The Craft and the Calling, 5

Black Rose, The, 107

Blood Red, Sister Rose, archaic language in, 107-108

Bowen, Catherine Drinker, 5

Bright Orange for a Shroud
  exposition in, 44
  technical information in, 129

Busch, Niven, exposition in work of, 44

Cain, James M., dialog in work of, 96-97

Call It Sleep, 106

Camera distance, 112

Campbell, Joseph, on heroes, 76
Camus, Albert, narrative voice in work of, 56-57
Cary, Joyce, point of view in work of , 34
Case, habitual, 87
Caveats, of style, 86-93
Center of consciousness, 31
Central authority, as chief means to believability, 28-30
"Ceremonies," 118
Chandler, Raymond
  narrative voice of, 57-58
  on outlines, 147
  reader preparation and, 25-26
Changing point of view, risks of, 36, 38
Character
  differences between writer and, 43
  flat vs. round, 43
  listening to, 71-78
  planning for, 146
Character, relationship of, to plot, 61-62
Characterization
  by action, 46-48
  by description, 44-46
  by dialog, 53-55
  by exposition, 40-41
  by gestures and mannerisms, 48-49
  by narrative voice, 56-58
  by opinions of others, 52-53
  in popular fiction, 43
  by setting, tastes, interests, 50-53
  by shading, 48
  techniques, 58
  by thoughts, 55-56
Chekhov, Anton
  objectification in work of, 124
  as storyteller, 2
Children of the Sun, The, historical detail in, 8-9
Clavell, James, information in work of, 130-131
Close narrator, 30
Columbus Tree, The, examination of, 170-189
Complication, of plot, 64
Concise dialog, 95-99
  edited samples of, 97-98
Confederacy of Dunces, A, dialect in, 106-107
Conrad, Joseph
  detail in motion in work of, 18
  sensory perception in work of, 19
Constant, Benjamin, historical detail in work of, 10
Construction, parallel, 88-89
Contemporary fiction, recommended, 203-206
Continuing metaphors, 121-123
Contract
  paperback, 168
  planning novel according to, 147
  two-shoe, 68-70
Contrasts, 117
Coordinating Council of Literary Magazines, 208
Copyediting, 166-167
Cortes, treatment of, in historical fiction, 7-9
Costain, Thomas B., 107-108
Coup, The, point of view in, 35
Cowley, Malcolm, 140
Cozzens, James Gould, planning problem of, 148-149
Crane, Stephen
  detail in motion in work of, 17
  dialect in work of, 106
  third-person point of view in work of, 36
Crisis, plot, 64
Criticism
  making use of, 166
  of style, 80

Davidson, Lionel, dialog in work of, 97
Davies, Robertson, 33-34
Day of the Jackal, The, 116-117
"Dead, The," alliteration and assonance in, 92
Deliverance, point of view in, 33

Description
  characterization by, 44-46
  disadvantages of characterization by, 45
Description, visual, vs. other senses, 21-22
Detached narrator, 30, 32
Detail
  concrete, 4-6
  final clincher, 9-12
  and historical research, 6-13
  in motion, 13-19
  overuse of, 5
  specific, 116-117
Diagrams, plot, 64
Dialect, 106
Dialog
  as action, 94
  characterization by, 53-55
  conciseness of, 95-99
  duffer, 101
  edited samples of, 97-98
  exposition through, 99-101
  focused on object, 110-111
  focusing of, 108-111
  Ford Madox Ford on, 53
  foreign speech used in, 108
  monotony in, 105-106
  to present experience, 100
  rules of, 113-114
  stripped, 102
Dickens, Charles
  gestures and mannerisms in work of, 49
  on scenic development, 158
Dickey, James, point of view in work of, 33
Didion, Joan, 120
Distance, camera, 112
Distant narrator, 30
Distant Trumpet, A, detail in motion in, 14
Dog of the South, The, action in, 47
Donleavy, J.P., point of view in work of, 35
Dostoyevsky, Feodor
  on germ of idea, 141
  planning problem of, 150
Double plot, 73
Dramatization
  defined, 2
  historical research and, 7-8
Duel in the Sun, exposition in, 44
Duffer dialog, 101

Eagle and the Serpent, The, sensory perception in, 21-22
East of Eden
  information presented in, 131
  symbolism in, 121
Edited dialog, samples of, 97-98
Editor
  how to find, 165
  role of, 166-167
Editor's advice, on profanity, 94
Electric Cotillion, The, gestures and mannerisms in, 49
Eliot, T.S., on objective correlatives, 123
Emma, 69
Epiphany, defined, 125-126
Episodic plot, 73-74
Ernest Hemingway: A Life Story, 108
Erotica. *See* Sex
Exposition, 44
  characterization by, 40-41
  through dialog, 99-101
External plot, 62-63

Facts, vs. truth, 72
Farewell, My Lovely, sensory perception in, 25-27
Farewell to Arms, A
  focused dialog of, 109-110
  foreshadowing in, 72
  sensory detail in, 20
"Fatimas and Kisses," 118-119
Faulkner, William

description in work of, 46
details in work of, 10-11
narrative voice and, 56
sensory perceptions in work of, 23-24
style of, 81-82

Feibleman, Peter, examination of work of, 170-189

Fiction
central authority in, 28-30
Latin American, 30
rendering of, 2

Fiction, contemporary
characterization in, 43
recommended list of, 203-206
See also Novel

Finney, Jack, 4-5

First-person narrator, 32-35
establishing central authority with, 28
See also Point of view

First-person point of view
vs. third-person point of view, 41
time frames in, 34-35

Fitzgerald, F. Scott
detail in motion in work of, 16-17
five-act structure in work of, 66

Flag for Sunrise, A, detail in motion in, 18

Flashback
defined, 131
and tunnelling, 131-133

Flaubert, Gustav
advice of, 12-13
changing point of view in work of, 38-39
character/plot relationship in work of, 62
on developing germ, 143
Flannery O'Connor on method of, 159-160
floating point of view in work of, 39-41
sensuous work of, 19-20

Floating point of view, 39-41

"For Esme—With Love and Squalor," 99

For Whom the Bell Tolls
foreign speech in, 108
sensory perception in, 22-23

Ford, Ford Madox
on dialog, 53
writing, method of, 159

Ford, Richard
exposition through dialog in work of, 103-104
style of, 82

Foreign speech, 108

Foreshadowing, and suspense, 70-71

Foreshadowing scene, as narrative hook, 155

Form in Literature, 74

Forster, E.M.
defining plot, 60
on evolution of theme, 160-161
on flat and round characters, 43

Forsyth, Frederick, 116-117

Freitag Pyramid, 64

French Leiutenant's Woman, The, double plot in, 73

Friends of Eddie Coyle, The, speech tags in, 104-105

Germ, developing, 142-145

Gestures and mannerisms, characterization by, 48-49

Gig, action in, 48

God's Country and My People, historical detail in, 24

Golden Bowl, The, love scene in, 138

Gospels, 119-120

Goyen, William, narrative voice in work of, 57

Grapes of Wrath, The
information presented in, 131
sentence types in, 89

Great Expectations
gestures and mannerisms in, 49
surprise and suspense in, 71

Great Gatsby, The
action in, 16-17
sensory perceptions in, 19

Green Tree in Gedde, A, point of view in, 36-37

Guzman, Martin Luis, sensory perception in work of, 21-22

Habitual case, 87

Hailey, Arthur
  floating point of view in work of, 39-41
  and narrative hook, 154-155
  setting and taste in work of, 51-52

"Hamlet and His Problems," 123

Hardy, Thomas, description in work of, 45

Harvest Home, narrative hook in, 154

Hemingway, Ernest
  biography of, 108
  on profanity and slang, 94-95
  sensory perception in work of, 20, 22
  sentence modifiers in work of, 88
  style of, 81
  three-act plot structure in work of, 66
  writing method of, 159

Hero, mythological, 74-77

Herself Surprised, point of view in, 34

Higgins, George V., speech tags in work of, 104-105

Historical detail, examples of, 6-13

Historical research, 6-13

Horgan, Paul, detail in motion in work of, 14

"Horse Dealer's Daughter, The," modifiers in, 84-85

Hotel, 51-52

Hotel New Hampshire, The, sensory perception in, 23

Hourglass plot, 73

Houston, James, action in work of, 48

How Green Was My Valley, narrative voice in, 56

Humboldt's Gift, sensory perception in, 24-25

Idiot, The, planning of, 149-150

Iliad, The, technical information in, 128-129

Images, 117

Imagination, reader's, 117-120

Implication, 117-120

Information
  dramatically providing reader with, 130-131
  See also Research

Internal plot, 62-63

International Women's Writing Guild, The, 208

Irish Guards in the Great War, The, alliteration and assonance in, 92-93

Irving, John, sensory perception in work of, 23

James, Henry
  character/plot relationship in work of, 61-62
  detail in motion in work of, 15
  on dramatization, 2
  and innovative point of view, 28, 39
  love scenes in work of, 138

Johnson, William Weber, historical detail in work of, 7

Journal narration, 30

Journal of a Novel, 121

Journals, planning, of writers, 142-145

Joyce, James
  alliteration and assonance in work of, 92
  and epiphany, 126

Keneally, Thomas
  archaic language in work of, 107-108
  two-shoe contract in work of, 69

Kerouac, Jack, list of writing essentials for, 161-162

Kesey, Ken
  on narrative voice, 34
  point of view in work of, 36

Kipling, Rudyard, alliteration and assonance in work of, 92-93

Kirkus Reviews, 167

Kundera, Milan, on characterization, 42-43

"Lady with the Pet Dog, The," 2

L'Amour, Louis, and narrative hook, 153

Language
  archaic, 107-108
  foreign, 108
  See also Dialog

Latin American fiction, use of second-person point of view in, 30

Lawrence, D.H., modifiers in work of, 83-84, 85

Les Misérables, surprise and suspense in, 71

Letter narration, 30

Life of Raymond Chandler, The, 58

Little Women, description in, 44-45

Llewellyn, Richard, narrative voice in work of, 56

Llosa, Mario Vargas, on sex in *Madame Bovary*, 134-136

Lolita, objectification in, 124

Long Goodbye, The, narrative voice in, 57-58

Love scenes. *See* Sex

MacDonald, John D.
  exposition in work of, 44
  technical information in work of, 129

MacDonald, Ross, continuing metaphors in later novels of, 121-122

Madame Bovary
  changing point of view in, 38-39
  character/plot relationship in, 62
  detail in motion in, 13
  sensory perception in, 20
  sex in, 134-136

Magic City, The, 124

Maguffin, 65-66

Mailer, Norman
  characterization by thoughts in work of, 55-56
  modifiers in work of, 84

Malinche and Cortes, historical detail in, 7-8

Mannerisms, and gestures, of character, 48-49

Manticore, The, 33-34

Manuscript, submitting, 164-166

Matthiessen, Peter, detail in motion in work of, 14

McGuane, Thomas, 83, 88

Melville, Herman
  description in work of, 9-10
  and symbols, 120

Metaphors, 117
  continuing, 121-123
  and symbols, 120-123

Methods, of writing, 158-160

Middle class, novels written for and about, 128

Miller, Henry, work schedule of, 152

Mimesis, defined, 2

Modifiers
  sentence, 87-88
  when to use, 83-86

Moneychangers, The
  floating point of view in, 39-41
  narrative hook in, 154-155

Monotony, in dialog, 105-106

Morris, Wright, historical detail in work of, 24

Motion, detail in, 13-19

Motion picture options, 168

Motivation, general and specific, for plot, 72-73

Mrs. Dalloway, tunnelling in, 132-133

Multiple narrators, 30

Mysteries and Manners, 121

Myth, and plot, 74-77

Nabokov, Vladimir, 124

Naked and the Dead, The
  characterization by thoughts in, 55
  modifiers in, 84

Nancy Drew, and narrative hook, 153-154

Narration. *See* Point of view

Narrative hook, 153-155

Narrative voice
  characterization by, 56-58

and point of view, 29-30
used to cover character and plot inadequacies, 33

Narrator
types of, 30
See also Point of view

National Endowment for the Arts, 208

Nesbit, E., 124

New Yorker, The, descriptive profiles in, 51

Nigger of the Narcissus, The, detail in motion in, 18

Novel
finishing, 164
how to begin, 152-155
how to continue with, 156
as instructor, 128-130
role of sex in, 133-134
of suspense, 116-117

Novel, commercial, and floating point of view, 39-41

Novelist
importance of reading others' novels for, 202
See also Writer

Oates, Joyce Carol, 118

Object, dialog focused on, 110-111

Objective correlatives, 123-125
defined, 123

O'Brien, Edna, sex in novel of, 134

Observation
vs. action, 48
and perception, 12-13

O'Connor, Flannery
on Gustav Flaubert's method, 159-160
on symbols, 121

Odyssey, The, dramatization in, 3

Oedipus Rex, tension in, 67

O'Hara, John, 118-119

Olympian omniscient style, Tolstoy and, 37

Olympian point of view, 30

Omniscient point of view, 30

One Flew Over the Cuckoo's Nest, point of view in, 34

"Open Boat, The," detail in motion in, 17

Outline
detailed, 147
importance of, 143

Over-the-transom submissions. *See* Unsolicited manuscripts

Paperback contracts, 168

Parallel construction, 88-89

Parallels, 117

Paris Review Interviews, The, 140

Passive voice, 86

"Peasants, The," objectification in, 124

Pen American Center, 208

Perception
and observation, 12-13
sensory, 19-26

Piece of My Heart, A, speech tags in, 103-104

Planning
formal, 146
methods of, 147-148

Play It as It Lays, 120

Plot
defined, 60
double, 73
episodic, 73-74
hourglass, 73
how to begin, 72-73
internal and external, 62-63
and myth, 74-77
relationship of character to, 61-62
vs. story, 60
three-act structure of, 65-66
which ones work, 77-78

Plot diagrams, 64

Plot progression, 66

Plotting, questions to address in, 78

Poets & Writers, Inc., 208

Point of view
  central authority and, 28-30
  changing, 36, 38
  child's, 31
  choosing, 30-32
  first person, 28, 32-35
  floating, 39-41
  Olympian, 30
  omniscient, 30
  strict, 8
  third person, 35-39
  third person vs. first person, 41
  types of, 28

Popular fiction, characterization in, 43

Portis, Charles, action in work of, 47

Portnoy's Complaint, dialog in, 95-96

Portrait of a Lady, The
  character/plot relationship in, 61-62
  continuing metaphors in, 122
  detail in motion in, 15
  dialog in, 54-55, 110-111
  setting, tastes and interests in, 52

Portrait of the Artist as a Young Man, use of epiphany in, 126

Postman Always Rings Twice, The, dialog in, 96-97

Powell, Anthony
  characterization by tastes in work of, 50
  two-shoe contract in work of, 68

Praying for Rain, 144-145

Printing, first, 167-168

Profanity, use of, 94-95

Pronoun
  to identify speaker, 103
  and point of view, 36

Prose, sensuous, 19-25

Proust, Marcel, 17-18

Publication, publicity and sales after, 167-168

Publicity, and sales, after publication, 167-168

Publisher
  planning novel by agreement with, 147
  working with, 166-167

Publishers Weekly, 167

Publishing process, 166-167

Queries, copyeditor's, 167

Question of Upbringing, A
  tastes and interests in, 50
  two-shoe contract in, 68

Questions, about plotting, 78

Rainbow, The, modifiers in, 83-84

Reader
  how to inform dramatically, 130-131
  imagination of, 45
  making promises to, 67-71
  as participant, 117-120
  sense perceptions of, 25-26
  sustaining interest of, 111-114

Reading, importance of for novelists, 202

Reading list, suggested, 202-206

Red Badge of Courage, The
  dialect in, 106
  point of view in, 36

Rejection, coping with, 166

Reliable narrator, 30

Remembrance of Things Past, 17-18

Rendering
  of fiction, 2
  vs. reporting, 5

Repetition
  linked, 110-111
  and parallel construction, 88-89

Research
  for detail, 5
  historical, 6-13
  providing information through, 128

Resolution, 64

Reviews, 167-168

Revising, 166

Rising action, 64

Rose of Tibet, The, dialog in, 97

Roth, Henry, 106

Roth, Philip, dialog in work of, 95-96

Rules, of dialog, 113-114

Sacred Wood, The: Essays on Poetry and Criticism, 123

Sales, and publicity, after publication, 167-168

Salinger, J.D.
- exposition through dialog in work of, 99
- setting and taste in work of, 50

San Francisco Examiner, description in, 50-51

Sanctuary, description in, 46

Scenic development, 157-158

Schindler's List, tension in, 69

Scott, Justin, action in work of, 47

Second-person point of view, in Latin American fiction, 30

Secret of the Golden Pavilion, The, narrative hook of, 153-154

Sensory perception, 19-26
- and absense of sound, 23-24
- smell as strongest, 22-23

Sensuous. *See* Sensory, Sex

Sentence modifiers, 87-88

Sentences, types of, 89-92

Setting, tastes and interest, characterization by, 50-53

Sex
- implicit vs. explicit, 134-138
- role of, 133-134

Shading, characterization by, 48

Sharp, Alan, point of view in work of, 36-37

Shedd, Margaret, historical detail in work of, 7-8

Ship Killer, The, action in, 47-48

Shogun, information presented in, 130-131

Showdown action, 64

Silverado Squatters, The, sentence structure in, 91-92

"Simple Heart, A," sensuousness in, 19

Slang. *See* Profanity

Smell, as strongest sensory perception, 22-23

Some Observations on the Art of Narrative, 157

Sometimes a Great Notion, point of view in, 36

Sophie's Choice, 140

Sound and the Fury, The, narrative voice in, 56

Specification, and style, 82-83

Speech
- foreign, 108
- *See also* Dialog

Speech tags, 101-106

"Spotted Horses," 10-11

Steinbeck, John
- information in work of, 131
- on planning novel, 146-147
- sentence types in work of, 89
- on symbols, 121

Stevenson, Robert Louis, 90-92

Stone, Robert, detail in motion in work of, 18

Story
- as euphemism for lie, 2
- vs. plot, 60
- *See also* Fiction, Novel

Stranger, The, narrative voice in, 56-57

Stripped dialog, 102

Style
- caveats pertaining to, 85-93
- criticism of, 80
- elements of, 81-82
- simple vs. elegant, 80-81
- and specification, 82-83

Styron, William, 140

Subtleties, necessity of, 126-127

Sun Also Rises, The, 65

Surprise, and suspense, 71

Suspense
and foreshadowing, 70-71
and surprise, 71
and time, 67

Suspense novel, 116-117

Swarthout, Glendon, historical detail in work of, 9

Symbol
and metaphor, 120-123
as one of writer's tricks, 117

Synopsis
example of, 190-201
See also Outline

Teachers and Writers Collaborative, 209

Techniques, for characterization, list of, 58

Tender Is the Night, detail in motion in, 16

Tension, creating, 67-71

Tess of the D'Urbervilles, description in, 45-46

Thackeray, William, continuing metaphors in work of, 122-123

Theme, evolution of, 160-161

They Came to Cordura, historical detail in, 9, 11

Third-person point of view, 35-39
vs. first-person point of view, 41
types of, 30

Thoughts, characterization by, 55-56

Three-act structure, 65-66

Through-line
defined, 63
novel's progression and, 156-157

Time, and suspense, 67

Time and Again, detail in, 4

Time frames, in first-person narration, 34-35

Tolstoy, Leo
Olympian omniscient style of, 37
on shading, 48

Toole, John Kennedy, dialect in work of, 106-107

Tree of Man, The, objectification in, 124-125

Truth, over facts, 72

Tryon, Thomas, and narrative hook, 154

Tunnelling, and flashbacks, 131-133

Twain, Mark
point of view in work of, 29-30
sentence types in work of, 90

Two-shoe contract, 68-70

Tyler, Anne, dialog in work of, 53-54

Unbearable Lightness of Being, The, characterization in, 42-43

"Uncle Wiggly in Connecticut," 50

Under the Sweetwater Rim, narrative hook of, 153

Underground Man, The, continuing metaphors in, 121-122

Unreliable narrator, 30

Unsolicited manuscripts, 164

Updike, John, point of view in work of, 35

Vanity Fair, continuing metaphors in, 122-123

Verb
active vs. passive, 87
speech, 105-106

Verisimilitude, defined, 2

Visual description, vs. other senses, 21-22

Voice, narrative
characterization by, 56-58
and point of view, 29-30

Voice, passive, 86

War and Peace
double plot in, 73
shading in, 48

Warren, Robert Penn, 111

Waugh, Evelyn, on style, 80

Weidman, Jerome, on planning novel, 144-145

Weston, Harold, 74

White, Patrick, objectification in work of, 124-125

Wise Blood, symbolism in, 121

Wizard of Oz, The, internal and external plot in, 63

Woolf, Virginia
  on germ of idea, 141
  and tunnelling, 132-133

World Enough and Time, 111

Writer
  differences between protagonist and, 43
  as observer, 13

Writer's block, getting past, 156

Writer's conferences, meeting agents at, 164-165

Writers Guild, 165

Writers' organizations, 208-209

Writing
  list of essentials for, 161-162
  methods of, 158-160

Writing process, books on, 202-203

Wuthering Heights, double plot in, 73